THE SCHOOL OF DOING

"Isaac Klein's wonderful book, *The School of Doing*, illuminates the remarkable ripple effect Gerald Freedman's teaching has had on so many of us. Page after page is stitched with wisdom and dotted with insight. Reading this book is like sitting in the green room with some of theater and film's most gifted artists and overhearing their secrets of craft. Each offering is its own haiku, its own marvelous meditation. Buy this brilliant book and get your highlighter ready!"

—Ashley Gates Jansen

"What a wonderful book to read, of how actors, designers, directors and all departments create their ART, how they go about telling a story. A fascinating read. I loved it, especially the lessons of Gerald Freedman, who was the first to open my mind to myself."

—Chita Rivera

"I think the world has been waiting for a beautiful book about Gerald Freedman. Because Gerald is a beautiful soul that finds expression in beautiful work and in a person with a beautiful personality. All of this is richly evoked in Isaac Klein's eloquent, absorbing, and necessary book."

—Austin Pendleton

"Gerald Freedman was a lion of the Public, one of the foundational faces behind this amazing theater. This book is a valuable contribution to preserving the legacy of this great man."

—Oskar Eustis

"Gerald Freeman was an inspiration when he directed me in Shakespeare in the Park. Almost a half century later he inspired me again and my son, JD Cullum, when he directed us both in a production of *The Dresser*. His love and enthusiasm for the theater never waned or changed. I truly admire the man. The book by Isaac Klein, *The School of Doing*, is a book I would recommend to any aspiring actor."

— **John Cullum**

"This book is like a letter from an old friend. I've read it and re-read it, trying to absorb its lessons. Some were things I knew, some were things I'd forgotten, some were things I'd never heard, but all were vital. For those who know Jerry, this book is his voice, friendly yet stern, reminding us of the pursuit of excellence. For those who don't, this book will be a light in the wilderness. Not just how to act, but how to approach a life in acting."

— **Neal Bledsoe**

"Gerald Freedman is the gentle, affable giant upon whose shoulders generations of exceptional theatre people stand securely and proudly! He is ever and always worth listening to!"

— **Jack O'Brien**

"If you are seeking the epitome of professional training for the theater, you must pause mightily before the name of Jerry Freedman. This is a man of distinguished credentials with a spectrum of knowledge and unsurpassed experience. Don't miss a rare opportunity to yes, "collaborate" with a youthful, energetic, highly regarded man of the world of theater."

— **Joseph Papp**

(From a letter written in 1991. Reprinted with permission.)

He spelled ⟶
Sei wrong, but
the intention
is true. I fixed
it.

The
SCHOOL
of DOING

LESSONS FROM THEATER MASTER
GERALD FREEDMAN

FEATURING CONTRIBUTIONS FROM
KEVIN KLINE · OLYMPIA DUKAKIS
CHITA RIVERA · PATTI LUPONE
& MANY MORE

ISAAC KLEIN
FOREWORD BY MANDY PATINKIN

FLYING DODO LLC

Interior design by Andy Omel
Front cover photo by Donald Dietz
Back cover photo by Sun Niles
Printed by CreateSpace

ISBN 978-0-692-95367-9 (paperback)
ISBN 978-0-692-98353-9 (e-book)

For Robert Beseda, who made all of this doing possible.

FEATURING

DEBBIE ALLEN
CHRISTINE BARANSKI
BONNIE BARTLETT
RICHARD BENJAMIN
ROBERT BESEDA
GLORIA BIEGLER
NEAL BLEDSOE
JOHN BOWHERS
MATT BULLUCK
VICTORIA BUSSERT
JEANNE BUTTON
ANNA CAMP
TIFFANY LITTLE CANFIELD
LAWRENCE CASEY
NORMAN COATES
JOHN CONKLIN
MATT COWART
JOHN CULLUM
GRACIELA DANIELE
WILLIAM DANIELS
MARY JANE DEGNAN
JOSIE DE GUZMAN
DANE DEHAAN
JOHN DILLON
OLYMPIA DUKAKIS
JOHN EZELL

LOGAN FAHEY
JULES FISHER
TONY FORMAN
JANET FOSTER
ROBERT FOXWORTH
BOB FRANCESCONI
ELIZABETH FRANZ
GENE FRIEDMAN
PENNY FULLER
NICHOLAS GALBRAITH
PAUL GEMIGNANI
BERNARD GERSTEN
ANITA GILLETTE
QUIN GORDON
LEE GRANT
JERZY GWIAZDOWSKI
BARNEY HAMMOND
SHELDON HARNICK
GEORGE HEARN
DESMOND HEELEY
HAL HOLBROOK
JOHN HOUSEMAN
MARY IRWIN
ASHLEY GATES JANSEN
ANNALEE JEFFRIES
HOWARD JONES
REBECCA NAOMI JONES

STACY KEACH	MISSI PYLE
BARBARA KESSLER	CHARLOTTE RAE
KEVIN KLINE	CHITA RIVERA
AL KOHOUT	WILL ROGERS
EDDIE KURTZ	STEVEN ROUTMAN
JAKE LACY	BILL RUDMAN
MARK LAMOS	ROB RUGGIERO
JOHN LANGS	AMY SALTZ
CAROL LAWRENCE	DOUGLAS W. SCHMIDT
MING CHO LEE	GABE SCOGGIN
PEGGY LOFT	JOHN SEIDMAN
PATTI LUPONE	JEREMY SKIDMORE
MARGARET LYNCH	ROBERT STATTEL
JACKLYN MADDUX	BRIAN SUTOW
BILLY MAGNUSSEN	JORDAN THALER
JOHN MAUCERI	JOHN TOIA
KELLY MAXNER	RICHARD TROUSDELL
MOLLYE MAXNER	ALFRED UHRY
TRAVIS McHALE	GAYE TAYLOR UPCHURCH
BRIAN MURRAY	STEVE VINOVICH
JACK O'BRIEN	RAY VIRTA
CIGDEM ONAT	GREG VORE
PJ PAPARELLI	ROBERT WALDMAN
JOSEPH PAPP	SAM WATERSTON
MANDY PATINKIN	JEREMY WEBB
AUSTIN PENDLETON	ANNA WOOD
HARRY POSTER	JOHN WOODSON

CONTENTS

Professional Training • Learning How to Learn • Questions and the Search for Answers

Read the Play, Write Things Down • Vocabulary • Given Circumstances • Story • Slogan • The Spine of the Play • The Spine of the Character • Spotlight: Gerald's Text Work • Objective • Action • Why We Need This Work • What Is Happening? • Backstory • Stage Directions • Preparation, Preparation, Preparation • Bringing Your Homework into Rehearsal • The Work Goes On

Truth • Making Something Happen • When to Make an
Adjustment • Working with Resistant Actors • Cutting Text
and Time • Transitions • The Audience • The Art Pack •
Assistant Directing • Spotlight: Assisting Jerome Robbins •
A Director's Evolution

FOREWORD
BY MANDY PATINKIN

If you're lucky, somebody says something that lands, that makes a light bulb go off in your soul, that connects with you for the rest of your life. And for me that somebody is Gerald Freedman.

I would not have been anything that I've become, in terms of whatever I'm considered as an artist, without Gerald Freedman. When I speak now, it is from the seed germinated by Gerald Freedman. I really feel that he has birthed most of us who are in the game. He is my artistic DNA. He is my artistic father. He's my egg and my sperm all in one. He's one of the only human beings—you can get both from one. You can get the whole package from Jerry Freedman if you want to.

Jerry has a ruthlessness for the truth, a belief in eradicating the cancer of falsehood and lie, a desperate, untiring commitment to a never-ending search for honesty and truth, however it's achieved. He's the real deal.

Jerry is an Olympic gymnast of emotion and intellect. And his gymnasium is the theater.

It was 1972. I was at Juilliard, and this director Gerald Freedman was coming in to direct us in Webster's *The Duchess of Malfi*. And I get cast as Bosola, and my classmate Bill [William Hurt] gets cast as Ferdinand.

For the first three weeks, he had us sit down around a big table.

I'll never forget sitting around that table, which is where my entire life as an artist began, and he taught me everything I know about my craft. I had no craft before that room, that day. I had physical exercises, speech exercises, but I had no craft that I could understand, that I knew what to do with.

I always thought Bill was smarter than me, because he was, and I remember he said to me once, "You need to dig deeper." I knew what he meant, but I didn't know how to do it. How do you dig deeper? How is that helpful? You don't get out a shovel and figure out how to play a part.

Jerry was trying to get us to understand an action. We were around the table for three weeks in total, and at some point in the middle, we get up and do this scene. And I thought, "I fuckin' nailed it." And Jerry said, "What did you do?"

"The scene."

"I understand you did the scene, but what were you doing?"

And then I sort of described the scene: "Well the guy comes in, and does this and that, you know, sort of what the scene is."

"What do you mean *sort of* what the scene is?"

"Well, I was doing what the scene was."

"What *was* that? What were you *doing?*"

"This."

"Can you do it again?"

"I think so."

"You think so? I'm supposed to hire you because you think so? Because you think you can do it again, as opposed to you *know* you can do it again? Eight times a week? What do you mean you *think* so?"

After the table, we got up on our feet, we put it on the stage, and we started to do it at the little theater there. And there we were in our costumes, performing, and I was onstage with Bill, and he went up! Brilliant Bill went up! And my back was to the audience, I was facing him, and I kind of mouthed his line to him. And he said, "I know the words. I don't know how to act." He said that, right in the performance, which Jerry always felt was one of the most courageous things he'd ever seen an actor do in his life. And in hindsight, I do too, because it was Bill's intolerance for falsehood, for inadequate truth, that made him unable to speak, not his inability to know the words, or the blocking, or the fuckin' people who were there watching. He felt he did not know what he was *doing.*

To connect. To be truthful. To be real. To be so deep that you live it, you don't have to search for it. That's how I interpret it all these years later.

"You need to dig deeper." I realize now that young Bill Hurt was really saying, "You need to find more freedom." And how do you find it? You connect. You look for those actions. You ensure you know what you're doing, and you get your job done, eight shows a week, twenty-one takes in a row. Sixteen hour days.

This business of action had to do with spine, with the central nervous system of the being you're trying to portray. The work is the road map of your life's connection to the character.

Every song I sing, every part I play, is all about my action. I've been scared working on a role, but I've never been scared when I know what my actions are, when I'm just making it clear.

Jerry said to me, "That is your creativity: to find in your own existence what it is to make it alive for you, to connect it for you, to be your truth."

All you're trying to do is be truthful, be alive, and not pretend, while you're pretending. To not lie, while you're lying. To play.

Years later, Jerry and I worked on *Enemy of the People*. I never saw anybody sit so quiet for so long, and then when he would say something, it would be, "What are you doing? What are you thinking?"

I remember Gerald said in one scene, "What are you doing?"

"I'm talking to them."

"Well, what are you doing when you're talking to them?"

"I'm trying to get them to pay attention."

"That's not very active…"

And finally, I said, "I'm *rallying* them."

"Well, do that."

And then it was easy. Then I was *rallying* the troops. And I have used that action in almost every single script I've worked on since.

I work with Jerry every day. I never do not do his work.

This work of Jerry's is to the truth, to the spine, to the action, to the word, to paring it down to its simplest connective meaning to you. Your vocabulary, your actions, your bible of words, which are not mine, or hers, or his. They are your markers on your path to your place of destination. It's an individual fingerprint that we all look at, and learn. No two are alike.

We're all relatives, all of us in this business, who choose to do Jerry's work. We're all related, whether you know Jerry or not. And what is that DNA connection? We have a greater sensitivity to the human condition. And we're not better for it. And we're not worse for it. We just are. We all have that same genetic code. And the price is high. And the glory is high too. Not the glory of success, the glory of feeling alive. That's what Jerry's real quest is about to me. Being alive.

In the end, it's how you're present with the other person, how you're alive.

Jerry Freedman is about being alive. Being alive is being truthful. And that's his addiction. His addiction is to the truth, and to life. Life is truth; it's not good or bad, or this or that, it's not a scale of 1 to 10. It is. To be.

His rule is: Do the work. Tell the truth. That's his rule. And never give up. He never gives up. God, let me be like that.

Jerry has stayed so young, because I really believe that teaching is the fountain of youth. And he spends his time with young, gifted, hungry, thrilling humanity. And that's it.

I love this man, and I love this craft that we do. It has given me my life. Jerry gave me my life. And I love it, with all its good and all its rough.

Gerald Freedman gave me my art. He gave me my craft. He took the mystery out of it, and made it doable. And then allowed me to add the mystery after I learned how to walk. He gave me my fuckin' life.

My prayer is that people get to feel Jerry's heartbeat, Jerry's life force.

He is my absolute mentor, and my absolute teacher, and my dear friend.

I got a way to work. I got it. Jerry Freedman gave it to me.

PREFACE

The greatest teacher I've ever had is Gerald Freedman. He stoked the fires of my lifelong passion for theater and, through rigorous training, equipped me with the tools I needed to pursue it. He challenged me. He engaged me. He showed me who I was, and who I could become, if I kept doing the work. Without him, I would not be where I am or who I am today.

There are thousands of others who feel similarly about Gerald—in schools, theaters, and communities around the world. His singular teachings resound in so many hearts and minds, but they've never been written down in full. I've made it my mission to do so.

Gerald Freedman was instrumental in creating some of the most important theater of the last century. As a young man, he went back and forth between directing stars such as Jack Lemmon, Joan Crawford, and Humphrey Bogart for the screen in Hollywood, and working onstage in New York with Jerome Robbins, for whom he assistant directed the original *West Side Story*. He went on to direct many classic and new works for producer Joseph Papp, including the world premiere of the musical *Hair* as the inaugural production of the Public Theater. He served as Artistic Director of the New York Shakespeare Festival (now known as the Public Theater / Shakespeare in the Park), Stratford's American Shakespeare Theater, Cleveland's Great Lakes Theater, and as co-Artistic Director of the Acting Company with John Houseman. He directed celebrated productions of plays, operas, and musicals on and off Broadway, regionally, and around the world. He won an Obie Award, and was the first American to direct at Shakespeare's Globe in London.

Even with these extraordinary achievements, Gerald's greatest work happened in the classroom. He studied with masters like Alvina Krause, Harold Clurman, and Robert Lewis. He went on to teach acting and directing at Northwestern University, Yale University, the Juilliard School, and the University of North Carolina School of the Arts, where he became Dean of the School of Drama in 1991, and proceeded to turn the program into one of the most highly-ranked and well-respected drama conservatories in the United States.

The defining mission of Gerald's life was the training of first-rate theater artists. In pursuit of this objective, he broke down the all-too-often nebulous realm of drama into practical, accessible components, and worked tirelessly to make each element clear to every last one of his students.

I am one such student. In the eleven years since my graduation, Gerald has remained my mentor. I continue to learn from him every day as I apply his lessons in my work.

In February 2011, at the age of 83, Gerald suffered a series of strokes. His life has changed significantly since then. Gerald remains in decent health and good spirits, but his strokes have left him hindered by aphasia; speech is more challenging for him now than it was before. He is now Dean Emeritus at the University of North Carolina School of the Arts, having retired from teaching and directing.

Over the last decade, Gerald and I often discussed the prospect of writing a book together about his teaching. Soon after his strokes, we agreed it was time to get to work. We were reminded of life's fleeting preciousness, and now that he was retired, Gerald needed a new project.

Needless to say, this book is extremely important to Gerald. It is his opportunity to share his knowledge with the global theater community—to offer a training manual for those who never had the good fortune to work with him, and a thorough refresher for all of us who did.

This book is equally important to me. Gerald is more than my teacher. Gerald is more than my mentor. Gerald is the person whose wisdom I hear most often in my head, and hold closest in my heart. Gerald has singular, powerful insights, unavailable in any other theater text. His distillation of the creative process is a vital resource for every theater professional and aspiring student. Many of his lessons are invaluable not only for the performing arts, but for life itself.

When I began my work on this book, my intention was to create a simple, straightforward record of Gerald's teachings. I thought I'd conduct a handful of interviews with Gerald, in which we'd discuss each subject of his curriculum, and then I'd transcribe and edit those interviews, and voilà, a book! That was my theory. In practice, it was not so simple. I found that Gerald's aphasia made it difficult for him to discuss the work, and I realized that his greatest insights had never come from independent oration, but rather from wrestling with each idea, from grappling for the truth with his students in an ever-evolving quest for cognition. To get the really good stuff, I was going to have to dig.

Over the course of four and a half years, I spent countless hours poring over mountains of old notebooks, articles, speeches, transcripts, videos, and audio recordings of Gerald in action in the classroom and rehearsal hall. Meanwhile, I spent months working with Gerald in his North Carolina home, and together we edited and refined my findings to best support the truth of his vision.

In addition, I conducted interviews with 130 of Gerald's colleagues and former students, and orchestrated their voices in the hope of corroborating and clarifying the many tenets of his training. (While it was not possible to include every interviewee in this book, all offered unique insights into Gerald's methodology, and my own understanding of the work was enriched by considering it from each respective perspective.)

This book is a tapestry of myriad pieces, woven together in the order and form I hope most effectively convey Gerald's curriculum.

Over his years as a director, teacher, dean, leader, mentor, colleague, and friend, Gerald Freedman has championed so many of us. It is my supreme honor to champion him, and share his great wisdom with the world.

—Isaac Klein
Fall 2017

NOTES FOR READING
THIS BOOK

Throughout the following chapters, my own words are set in italics.

Quotes from Gerald Freedman are set in regular type.

> Quotes from others are indented, and each speaker's name is
> **CAPITALIZED IN BOLD.**

All quotes from others were obtained via one-on-one interviews I conducted personally, unless otherwise cited.

Gerald's quotes were taken directly from personal conversations, interviews, notes, speeches, articles, transcripts, and class recordings. Working together, Gerald and I occasionally made minor edits to these quotes, and they have been reproduced here with his permission. Some quotes were taken from copyrighted works. Those quotes are cited with endnotes, which appear as superscript numbers in the main text and correspond with the endnotes list in the back of this book.

Some speakers refer to Gerald as "Jerry."

Gerald addressing the School
of Drama, onstage at the
Gerald Freedman Theatre at
the University of North Carolina
School of the Arts in 2010.

CHAPTER ONE

SCHOOL BEGINS

In 1991, at the age of sixty-four, Gerald Freedman was appointed Dean of the School of Drama at the University of North Carolina School of the Arts. Under his leadership over the next twenty-one years, the department grew to become one of the most highly-regarded drama conservatories in the United States.

To build a program of such caliber, Gerald codified a process—a way of working with a basic set of craft tools and principles—and crusaded for the integration of that process throughout the department. He focused the four-year program on the instilling of fundamentals, striving to inspire in his students a lifetime of ongoing growth and discovery.

In setting a tone and program for the School of Drama, I have to create a world for the art to flourish.

Sometimes I wish it weren't called the School of Drama. It should be called the School of Doing.

The business of theater has changed, but the training of an actor is no different than it was four hundred years ago. Nothing about what I have to say is new. Actors have worked this way forever.

Conservatories of acting weren't necessary seventy, eighty years ago. There was a network of stock companies where the young actor could work and learn from watching, from being onstage. That's always the best way. But that system disintegrated, and professional programs came into vogue.[1]

The fact is, you don't have to go to acting school at all. You can learn how to be an actor by being in the theater. You could simply teach people how to act by putting them in shows. But we're not that kind of school.

Often in a traditional school, you open a book, and you accumulate knowledge, and you store it up and spew it out. But in a conservatory, *you* are the book. It's a question of looking in. Discovering the table of contents. Reordering it, sorting it out: "Who am I? What's in me?" We're not trying to change your personality, but we're trying to focus it. It's not about grades; it's a whole reordering of how you learn. It's profoundly different from any other discipline.

We are providing students with tools with which to fulfill any assignment. We are not a vocational school, but the training should make them competitive in acquiring jobs and growing in their work.

JAKE LACY (Actor, Former Student):
I remember on the opening parents' weekend, he said, "I cannot guarantee that your kid will be an actor, a working actor, a movie star, a successful person in this business in any capacity. But I can guarantee you that they will leave here a better person, that they'll leave here with the mind of an artist, and I think that matters."

The emphasis in the School of Drama is on process, not results at the expense of process. Someone might be very adept at intellectualizing the process, and be a bad actor. Someone might be instinctive, and be a terrific actor. But to understand that you've got to have a process, I think is essential. That is what we are about.

It takes you at least four years just to learn fundamentals. It takes four years to learn what questions to ask; it takes a lifetime to find the answers. I think we have so little time, and I'm trying to do so much.

In my opinion, a training program with a four-year outline cannot prepare a student for all eventualities. What I propose is a method of training, eclectic by nature, that will provide a student with principles of behavior, discipline, and skills that will prepare him or her for a professional career.

Continuing my professional directing was an initial condition of my accepting the position as Dean. It also validates my authority in a professional training program. Furthermore, it has enabled me to enhance employment opportunities for our graduates through active connections with casting directors, agents, directors, and producers.

JORDAN THALER (Casting Director):
[UNCSA Assistant Dean] Robert Beseda had a full life as an agent before joining Gerald at the school, so they were incredibly blessed to have all of that information onsite as well. The two of them brought an enormous wealth of experience from the business down there, and then they continued to ask colleagues from the business to come down and work with the kids.

In a school of the arts dedicated to training professionals, the standards of teaching must be obvious: to train a student to meet professional demands. But this vision, almost by definition, is subjective. We are artists, not technicians, not academics. We are not measurable. We are defined by our artistry and creativity and our ability to define and communicate them.

I want to create artists who have a link to the past, who can compete in the present, and pass along something to the future.

If you really work at it, and if you do it assiduously, and if you make a program, you can achieve this result.

JOHN CULLUM (Actor, Singer):
He never stopped. He always had something going, and with such enthusiasm and energy. He was going to work at the top of his bent until he couldn't work anymore.

Professional Training

The faculty led by Gerald Freedman was united in their unwavering commitment. The standards were high from the get-go. Every component was carefully calibrated toward preparing the students for the professional world that awaited them.

I remember how daunted I felt when I arrived for my first year at the School of Drama. That feeling only intensified as I fully fathomed the demands of the training, the immensity of the workload, and the length of each day. Looking back, I am grateful for those rigors, because battling through them made me strong, readied me for my life's work, and shaped me into who I am today.

You must be at all times aware that you are in training as an artist in the skills of the theater. Let it be understood right now and forevermore, the use of the term *theater* includes all media and performance possibilities: film, television, and even cabaret or performance art when called upon.

This requires responsibilities on the part of the student in behavior and discipline, as well as the preparation of skills through drill, repetition, research, and rehearsal.

Remember—during the next four years you will be in training. You will not have arrived.

Hopefully, at the end of the four years, you will have acquired some necessary tools to help you in your career choice and to achieve your goals.

Your professional training begins from your first day of school. The key word is *professional*. The theater is not a place for personal indulgence or egocentric behavior. The theater requires collaborative effort and teamwork. Other people depend on you at all times! It requires you to know who you are. You must find your own center, but it also requires you to know what you are doing—and how to do it—so you can release your creative spirit and individuality at the appropriate time. The training period is a time to expand, a time to try out, to stretch yourself in every way.

If I've set a task for you, work on it. That's what I expect adult artists to do. This is your task, now go work on it. Not, I have to nurse you through the next month. If you take a professional job, they'll give you a fearsome combination, and then they expect you to come back doing it, knowing it. They're not going to take you through it. Or even an art class—you get an assignment, you discover a weakness, you have to go away and drill it, work on it until you accomplish it. That is part of your responsibility.

MARGARET LYNCH (Dramaturg, Colleague):
His dedication and his focus and his standards were such that he made you feel that you were in something very important, life or death, maybe, and that everybody was part of it. He wanted you to share that singleness of purpose, and didn't really tolerate less than that.

The two most important qualities in the business are not talent and looks, much to your surprise. They are punctuality and dependability.

You are expected to be in class and rehearsals on time, ready to go! That means you are alert and prepared to listen, move, react, or perform at the designated starting time, not five or ten or fifteen minutes later. It means you are in the proper clothes for that class or rehearsal, ready to go.

Students think I have favorites. I do. My favorites are those who work hard, who keep trying, who get to rehearsal and class *ahead* of time, who exhibit professional habits. This is the place and time to acquire them—professional habits.

Everyone loves people who behave like professionals, and so they hire them again and again. It is direct job-producing behavior. There's no question about it.

What makes "the best"? The talent for practice itself. If the class requires preparation, do it. Faking through fools no one and it only gets you a bad reputation in the professional world.

Professional isn't about talent. *Professional* is about work. Of course, we understand there's a learning curve. It takes four years to begin to acquire a craft. But being on time and prepared only takes a mindset. Start now!

You cannot miss a single class. You cannot be late for a single class. You miss a class or rehearsal on pain of death! You crawl to class or rehearsal if necessary, or have a damn good excuse. If you miss a class, I expect you to go to each of your teachers and explain your absence.

In the business, nobody cares if you have a cold, or if you're not feeling right on. Nobody cares if you were stuck in the subway. All they know is you weren't there. You have to learn to be on time. Be there. Call up. Let people know. All those things that we're harping on all the time. They're part of the acting craft.

BILLY MAGNUSSEN (Actor, Former Student):
The biggest thing I learned from Gerald was understanding the responsibility of time management and preparation. Organizing your priorities and responsibilities, knowing what to focus on, where the proper work should be directed.

Good health is also a major requirement. It is absolutely essential. Actors need healthy bodies and healthy minds. It means you have to take care of yourself. It means you need to be centered as an individual. You must be in good physical condition and maintain reasonable hours of rest and sleep and good nutrition. This is your responsibility. Make no mistake, this requires the most rigorous discipline of all the arts. It also requires tremendous commitment and dedication in the use of one's time.

If you get a reputation for drugs and alcohol, it's death in the theater, because it lingers so long after the fact. Long after the fact, if you're lucky enough to be able to beat it, because we can't take that risk in a collaborative venture. That's it. By nature, I think we're a family, and a nurturing family, but you don't want to endanger the others in that way. So a whiff of that is a bad thing, and it's very hard to erase in the profession. You have to live such a disciplined, clean life. It's true.

Finally, you have to be dead honest, or there's no point to the training. That's the only way you can move ahead here.

Your instrument is you; from your toes to your hair follicles, the inner and outer of *you* is your instrument, and we are here to help you train it.

I'm after you all the time about where and how you exercise discipline. It is not to be a schoolmaster or a parent, it is to train you for how you must learn to work. You don't always see the connection, but I see the connection, because I've been out there. And you have to trust that. Discipline in one area absolutely transfers into another area. If you're sloppy in one area, you're sloppy in your thinking, and you're sloppy in your concentration. I absolutely guarantee it. Don't fancy that you're getting away with it. You are not.

There are only twenty-four hours in a day. They are not enough. Think about it. We are all guilty of procrastinating. I put off and put off. It's disastrous. That's a matter of becoming self-conscious: "Why am I putting this off?" Well, if I'm thinking about it, I'm putting it off. Do it. Get your pencil and start writing something down. You have to discipline yourself to compartmentalize what you need to do.

PJ PAPARELLI (Director, Guest Teacher):
That discipline is what you need as an artist to survive. Students from Gerald's years there have done so well because they've learned a certain discipline, and a rigor that only they can hold themselves to, and not be affected by everybody around them. That definitely was fostered by Gerald. There were many, many actors over the years that came out of UNCSA that I hired, because I knew that there was a certain amount of discipline,

but they were also not too rigid. They had hearts, and they treated people with respect. That is all fostered, comes from an environment that is obviously driven by the leader.

In spite of my patience, my affection for actors, my sympathy for personal problems, it's the work that counts. As a director, I'm responsible to the playwright and the producer. Are we fulfilling the playwright's intention? Will the work find an audience? That is my first responsibility. I cannot let my feelings get in the way of my judgment. What does that mean for you? You can always depend on me to tell you the truth.

TIFFANY LITTLE CANFIELD (Casting Director, Former Student): I always believed he was speaking from an earnest place, which can be hard, and blunt, but it's where I believe I learned, and I still believe this to this day: it's a process. So, you can take some hard criticism, because it's only going to make you better.

If you can't do it here, you'll never be able to do it. This is where you get the training to help you do it outside of here. This is where I try to hopefully build up your stamina so that you can make a living when you get out of here.

Take this time, these four years, to change negative habits if necessary, reorganize your time, refocus your dreams and ambitions. Don't talk about it with your friends and classmates. Talk about it with yourself. That's where it begins.

JOHN DILLON (Director, Guest Teacher): His work ethic was what drove the program. By that I mean that he created a dizzyingly exhausting schedule. In any normal circumstance, students in that situation might have said, "This is too much work, I can't handle all of this," except that there was Gerald, old enough to be their grandfather, busier than they were. How could you possibly claim you were exhausted, when he was doing twice as much as you were, and showing no sign of fatigue?

GABE SCOGGIN (Program Manager, Former Student): You were constantly busy. There was very little down time. There was a comprehensive level of different types of training. So you're learning different things, you're having to manage different things, as well as do all of the general education stuff on top of that. So it was already an environment where you're expected to be at the top of your game to even get through the day, because you're literally busy all day long.

When I first came here, I got resistance from some of the faculty on loading the students down too much. I make no apologies if I've loaded them down with more, because that is what you have to face if you're going to work in theater. Part of your success in the theater is having stamina and discipline. I can't teach that. I can give you the facts that demand those qualities, but I can't teach it. Don't forget it. Stamina and discipline are most important.

Some of my students think I'm mean. I'm not. There isn't a mean bone in my body. They mistake my passion for "mean." I'm incredibly patient as long as I see the actor working. I'm impatient when I sense the actor is not doing the work, and my passion is aroused when I feel that the rigor that the theater and the rehearsal process demand is not being observed.

GAYE TAYLOR UPCHURCH (Director, Former Student):
As a teacher, he could be really hard on you. We lovingly called it passion, but what it might have looked like to a casual observer was a man screaming at students in a room. But we all understood that it was his passion. It was what he was trying to impart to us. And it is how we learned those lessons.

I place a high premium on professional discipline, not because of its authoritarian echoes, but because it is a means of eventually releasing the creative impulse of each individual.

This is the backbone, the spine, if you will, of my approach to actor training. One must have a way of working, fostered with discipline, learned techniques, and good work habits to release individual creativity. On the way toward maturing, the rules may seem restricting, but they will eventually be the key to unlocking one's special talents. The skill and challenge for the teacher/director is to instill the discipline while nurturing the spirit, individually, of each student.

Learning How to Learn

Gerald didn't just teach craft for the theater, he taught the tenets for learning: initiative, readiness, and self-awareness.

You may be a college student, but this is not a usual college. This is a conservatory. This is your first step on the path through the art of theater to your creative self. As a past drama student said, "You experience what it means to train as an artist." Another described it as "learning to think as a creative human being." Another saw it as "learning how to learn." All of it requires mindfulness.

Look for what you are learning, not for what is good or bad.

I feel my obligation is to make you self-conscious about whatever the problems are. The workplace is where you should be self-conscious about problems, so that when you're in a performing place, you don't have to worry about them.

That's what we do: isolate different areas of the craft, look at them, try to analyze them, and then find out how we can improve them.

You must get in the habit of being ready and volunteering right away. You must not hesitate. Get up. If you're taking an acting class, you fight to get your name on the board. You're paying a lot of money. You want to get up there and be criticized, otherwise there's no point in paying the money for the course. If you are at an audition, you want to be seen. You're not going to be any better ten or fifteen minutes from now. You have to be prepared beforehand. Get in there first. Don't hesitate. Make it a habit.

Half of you sink in your chairs right away. You give up. You should all be on the edge of your seats, thinking. When I say to you, "Don't act like students," or, "Get out of the student mentality," what I mean is take responsibility for yourself. The student part of it, the learning part of it, we do always, forever. I hope I'll be eighty, I hope I'll be ninety, and still be learning. You always learn, hopefully, if you keep your mind open. But self-knowledge, and opening up, and allowing yourself to be vulnerable and available, that's tough.

GRACIELA DANIELE (Director, Choreographer):
You have to have such tremendous technique to throw yourself into it, and not be afraid. It requires study, and that's what keeps you young! Continue studying. Don't ever feel like you have to stop.

I love to keep learning. That is the point of my life. And the reason I took this position, in the second place, was for new experience. Not because I think I know everything about it, on the contrary.

JERZY GWIAZDOWSKI (Actor, Former Student):
He has this fearless, adamant embrace of what he does not know. Gerald was not only always doing work, but working on the way he worked. Working on new techniques and ideas and points of view. That to me is the greatest skill and gift, and the best thing I learned from him.

Questions and the Search for Answers

Gerald encouraged questions because they foster an ongoing spirit of investigation. Answers, by contrast, can breed complacency and stagnancy. In Gerald's school of thought, there is always more to dig for in the work. There is always another question to ask. There is always further to go.

It's not about answers; it's about asking questions. I love questions. Questions mean you are looking for answers. Never be afraid to ask questions. Look for answers for the rest of your life.

Don't be students. Think like actors! I want you to learn to think for yourself.

JOHN DILLON (Director, Guest Teacher):
The main thing he did was make sure that everybody was present in discussion. He made sure that everybody discussed communally, so it wasn't just a matter of the great master on top of the mountain, dispensing his wisdom to all, but rather, "What do you think, and what do you think? How would you solve this problem?" So it was everybody collectively figuring out where the ball laid and how to hit it.

Do not hesitate to ask questions. Don't be afraid to speak up. The more you test it and talk about it, the more you'll find out. You get a better answer with that, far deeper. It's not about being right. It's about the creative imagination. It's how you put the *doing* together.

Stop trying to be right. Right cuts off impulses. Questions! We are offering you elements, teachings, skills, that will open you up, free you. Your body, your throat, your breathing, your coordination, your thinking, if you will allow it! If you will stop being "right" and become more aware, self-aware, and honest in your evaluation.

None of you can feel "finished." At best you have some tools—perceptions, skills, the ability to ask questions—with which to move on.

No teacher or textbook will provide you with "the answer." So why bother? It's about learning how to *search* for the answer. How to ask questions that will lead you closer to the answer. Don't look for answers out of this work. This work is all about asking questions.

There is no answer. Write that big on the wall. Part of your difficulty is that you want answers. And I'm telling you that there are none. So you have to give up that idea. Because the imaginative quest is all about the quest. And if you want to be an artist, that's what you have to be willing to do: go into unexplored territory. And that's hard.

The questions are the catalyst. They start the thinking.
The answers are the goal.
The search for the answers is the payoff.

The struggle *is* the answer.
The search *is* the work.

The problem is, you ask questions and you feel like you've got to have answers. And so it ties you up, rather than advancing your quest. Keep looking. It's about the investigation that leads you to a better idea, a more complete idea. Often, actors will start editing and negating the work before letting it flower. I don't mean you can't find a working hypothesis, a working idea about how to go at it. That's what you *want* to do. It's not about forcing. If you have to force, there's something wrong with your work or your thinking.

While you're asking questions, you can't be immobile. You can't. *Quest* is part of *question*. So whether you're sitting down and your mind is moving, or whether you're up looking, questions are about action, which is about doing, which is what acting is about.

If you run out of questions, that means you're dead. There are always questions about what you're doing. When we finish this discussion, I don't want you to go away thinking you have the answer. This is not the answer for the rest of your work. This is the beginning.

Measure for Measure is about the power of sexual energy in man - the human, the animal, the life-bursting, the disorganized in conflict with the law, the rigid, controlling, boundary-making force set-up to control the former.

Sexual energy out of control is lost, without moderation it is bestial, destructive physically and psychically - it is the unbridled id.

The law, without compassion, removed from humane thinking is equally destructive - murderous and sadistic. Saint! Man is in a desperate struggle to moderate these forces. He is afraid of the unknown, dark, nameless forces that he is driven by and much of this is collectively labeled "the sexual urge". He has created the idea of law to channel and force this energy into a controllable and positive force. To "civilize" man.

The pendulum between excess and repression swings back and forth. But the forces are always in contention.

Shakespeare says, or believes in, a moderating influence in the use of both. The law and sex must be applied with compassion and self-knowledge. If you are aware of these "dark" forces within yourself you should be able to understand them and the use of them in others. But above all they are "human" urges and are meant to be controlled by "human" social and legal structures as administered by "humane" judges.

Man is imperfect as presumably are his judgements. Fallability is a constant. On earth as it is in heaven. The Dark Angel was cast out of heaven but he was not destroyed.

Isabella must learn this as Angelo must.

The Duke is aloof from sex and love - but at the end he sues for Isabella's hand. Claudio has been through a fearful trial but he is alive at the end.

KURT ESLICK

G. ALLEN AYCOCK

LEFT: A page of Gerald's text work on *Measure for Measure* from his 1981 production at the Old Globe.
TOP: Gerald at work on *Ohio State Murders* with Ruby Dee in 1991.
BOTTOM: From left: Gerald leads directing class with guest artist Joe Mantello and students Tre Garrett and Matt Cowart at the University of North Carolina School of the Arts in 2003.

CHAPTER TWO

BREAKING DOWN THE SCRIPT

Gerald Freedman's work was deeply rooted in the text. This chapter focuses on text work from the actor's perspective. Whatever your role in theater, this work can help to strengthen your particular craft.

Breaking down the script can be done before collaboration with other artists begins. It helps you get your insides in touch with the insides of the play. It gives you a way to dig in.

CAROL LAWRENCE (Actor, Singer):
It isn't just, "Oh I understand the words on the page." It has to go so much deeper than that.

Acting can be fun. It is also your work, your chosen profession, and the way you will earn your living. These are some tools to help you.

These are the instructions to get your instrument in a place for action, to do it. In rehearsal, we're all faced with this blueprint: the script. There's nothing there beforehand, but there has to be. That's what you have to supply.

This is a convenient way to help you think. That's the usage. This gives you a nice form to put it into, a nice box to hold it. This is language we can learn by. It's an organizing method. It helps you organize random thoughts.

This isn't the only technique in the world. There are a lot of great actors who don't use this terminology, who don't even know how they go about their process.

If you want to be an artist, to control your craft, this is a way. Some of it will seem very difficult. It gets easier as you do it over and over and over again. A lot of it seems to be a head trip, because you have to think and write and examine what you do. But it is a head trip to make you act, meaning *do*. It's not about the head stuff, it's about how the head stuff gets you to work with your muscles.

CHRISTINE BARANSKI (Actor, Former Student):
When I first started applying what Jerry was saying, it was a more plodding kind of process. You have to learn how to read a script. There's an art to really learning how to read a script, and how to analyze it. As the years go on, it does become easier.

As you exercise, the muscles get stronger. This work is about muscle memory; you have to exercise in order to get better at it. Doing these exercises helps you understand the play, the layers of the play. It helps you get to it.

RICHARD TROUSDELL (Director, Former Student):
He respected the text, not in some deadly literal library way, but as a living thing that you could get in touch with. And this was his way of getting in touch with it.

You want to get to a place where this work will activate you. So it's not just actor talk, it's actor talk that relates to who you are as an animal. This way of working does not preclude imagination or intuition; it should be a springboard for these talents.

This work is not to close you off, but to open you up. It's not an obstacle to rapport with other artists. It's not something that freezes you. If it does, you're not using it correctly. It's something that fills you up and prepares you, channels that energy, focuses it into areas that you control.

The bottom line for all of this—once you comprehend what I'm talking about—is common sense. Don't leave your common sense at the door. Bring it with you. Also your sense of humor.

Read the Play, Write Things Down

The basics of breaking down the script are reading the play and writing things down. All subsequent work stems from the discoveries made in this initial phase.

First things first: read the play. Now, that sounds so obvious. Who needs to hear that? *How* you read the play, that is the key. It is the most important thing you do. All the answers are in the play.

STACY KEACH (Actor):
Jerry's always been very good about the text, the importance of the text. It's all in the text. Whatever you're looking for, it's all there. It's in the words. You just have to find it.

Read the play three or four times, and let it live in you. Don't just read your part; read all of the play consciously. It's not about automatically reading the play. Once you've read the play once, often you feel like you know it, so in going back, you tend to skim over certain things, and focus more on your own role. So to read all of it three or four times, consciously, is not as easy as it sounds. Really read the play. If you find yourself slipping away, refocus. You have to work to keep your full attention on it. Make yourself come back to the play. You uncover all kinds of things you didn't know were lurking there. There are mines of source material that are not immediately apparent. The answers are there.

BRIAN MURRAY (Actor, Director):
They're all in the play. The play's the thing. You really have to trust that. The answer is always there.

As you read, all of your thoughts, feelings, images, and responses of any kind can serve you in this early work. Pay attention as you read. Do you *see* images? Does your inner ear *hear* the play? Are there physical responses? You may feel your lip curl with disdain, or you may notice a frown on your face, or tears may form. This is not the time to *do* anything about these responses. Simply notice them, or, better yet, go ahead and write them down.

As you read and examine the play, you will have spontaneous thoughts and questions. Write them down, too. Later you will find that's your subconscious work. It's very, very helpful. If you write it down, however vagrant it may seem to be, it will be a clue for you later on.

JOHN LANGS (Director, Former Student):
You read the play until it talks to you. Jot down images that come into your mind while you're reading it, even if they don't make sense at the time. In the reading of it, you're getting another layer. You're getting thicker and deeper.

Each time you come back to it, you add another layer. Don't rule out the possibilities too early in the game. What you don't want to do, while learning to do this, is shoot down ideas. What you want to do is open up ideas.

Each time you turn back to Act I, Scene I, Page 1, you will discover that these subjective responses change as you gain more information. Keep re-reading as much as possible, as more possibilities make themselves felt each time.

PATTI LUPONE (Actor, Former Student):
I really just keep reading the play, because all the information is there. Jerry said all the information's in the play. Jerry taught me to just keep going back to the script. Jerry said to me, "Dig deeper." I said, "I think I've done as much as I can." He said, "Dig deeper." I'll never forget that.

Write it down, write it down, write it down, so you don't have to try to remember the great thought you had. I don't mean a thought for every line. Just whatever comes to you. It's great if you can write it in your script, because then it's there when you need it.

If an idea is only in your mind, it evaporates, it leaves very quickly. There are hundreds of stimuli every day, one of them being the work. It's hard to remember. Why leave it up there? Why not put it on paper so you can look at it? And not only that, writing it down allows you to see the evolution of your thinking.

Remember that you are beginning a relationship, here. You are gathering information in a subjective way, in order to take your knowledge of the play to the next, more objective step in the pre-rehearsal process.

Having *experienced* the play in many different ways, you are now in a position to *think* about it.

Vocabulary

Once you have read the play a few times and noted your responses to it, you are ready for the following fundamental steps of Gerald's process for breaking down the script.

To work, you need intelligence. You need vocabulary. I use specialized jargon, but it's only so we have a convenient way of communicating. I want us to get clear about language so that we mean the same thing when we're talking to each other.

DANE DEHAAN (Actor, Former Student):
Gerald gives you a very specific vocabulary when he teaches you acting. It's not a universal vocabulary, but the main principles are principles that a lot of people strive for; they just go about it in different ways. If I didn't have that vocabulary, I couldn't listen to them and interpret it and turn it into something that I could actually use.

What I don't want you to get stuck on is that there's any magic in the words themselves. There is not magic in these words. They are only a way for us to communicate.

GIVEN CIRCUMSTANCES:
The conditions revealed in the text. The *who, what, where, when,* and *how.*

STORY:
An objective telling of the story in your own words, four or five sentences in length.

SLOGAN:
A short phrase, theme, or bumper sticker that succinctly sums up the spirit of the play for you.

SPINE OF PLAY:
A single active sentence which motivates everything everyone does in the entire play.

CHARACTER SPINE:
A single active sentence which motivates everything the character does in the entire play.

OBJECTIVE:
What the character wants.

ACTION / INTENTION:
What the character does to get what he/she wants.

These are not definitive definitions. This is meant to serve as a quick and simple guide.

Nothing about what I'm saying is linear. I can only give it to you in a linear manner. So you're working on the story, and you're thinking about character spine. Or you're working on the spine of the play, and it goes back to the story. But the only way I can communicate, the only way I know how, is in this linear manner.

When you do the story, you're working on the play. When you start to figure out the slogan, you're working on the play. You're coming at the work in tangible ways that will free your imagination.

In order to clarify some of the terminology, I am going to imagine a hypothetical play that has not been written yet. The play is called *The Drama Crusade*. Let us call one of the leading characters "Dean." Dean is a director who has worked in the commercial and not-for-profit worlds of theater and comes to a conservatory training school to teach.

In this hypothetical play, Dean's spine is:

To challenge the existing order without creating a revolution.

In the scene we are considering, Dean is talking to some students about a process to add new and effective tools to an actor's development.

His objective is: **To have you buy into the program.**
His action or intention is: **To change your mind.**

As he and the students begin a dialogue, he uses various tactics to achieve his objective:

"It should be easy for you." *(His intention is to flatter.)*
"You're the only student not doing it." *(His intention is to embarrass.)*
"I won't be able to give you good roles." *(His intention is to intimidate.)*

With this hypothetical exercise, I am trying to illustrate and clarify the terms. People behave with objectives and actions. That's what life is. We're all doing it right now. (Your objective is to learn what the hell I'm talking about, and your action is to look alert, or be receptive.) It's the nature of being alive.

Given Circumstances

The given circumstances are just what they sound like: the circumstances given to us by the play. The who, what, where, when, and how. Answering these questions can help to specify your work, ground you in the reality of the play, and build a framework for the exploration that will follow.

Given circumstances are the key, the beginning point.

There's no substitute for belief in the given circumstances. If you fill in your givens, you know what's going on. If you go from the given circumstances, you have more interesting choices.

BILLY MAGNUSSEN (Actor, Former Student):
Gerald taught me about using the given circumstances. It's like when you play a basketball game, you have the rules: there's a court, you can't double dribble, you can't travel. And you have to find that with the play. You have your court, you have all your rules, and then magic can happen in it. Anything can happen as long as you play by these rules. Once you discard the rules, or go out of bounds, it's very apparent that no, that doesn't work. Because those are the rules. That's given circumstances.

The given circumstances ground the actor, and that includes understanding the period, the clothing the character wears, and the cultural influences.

To discover the given circumstances, ask:

WHO am I? (Gender/Age/Profession/Spine)
- Man?
- Woman?
- Old?
- Young?
- Rich?
- Poor?

WHAT do I want? (In Life / At This Moment)
- A drink to quench my thirst?
- To win an argument?
- To overcome my opponent?
- To beat the competition?
- To overcome an obstacle?
- To beg?
- To comfort?
- To threaten?
- To dance?

WHERE am I? (Country/City/Neighborhood/Room/Environment)
- The country?
- The city?
- The neighborhood?
- Inside?
- Outside?

WHEN is it? (Time/Day/Month/Year)
- Year?
- Season?
- Date?
- Time?

WHAT am I wearing?

HOW do I go about getting what I want? (Activity/Behavior)
- Seduction?
- Physical Force?
- Welcoming Love?

Actors tend to feel, "My scene starts with the first line, or when I walk in the door." It doesn't. It starts before. What are the given circumstances? Where are you coming from? To do what? Believe in the situation, not the line. The line comes out of the situation.

Story

The story, as Gerald defined it, is the essential, fact-based action that occurs in the text. To tell a clear story, one must first determine what the story is. That's not as simple as it may seem; we often layer our own subjective, emotional responses on the story before allowing the objective truth to become clear.

In your own words, compress the story into a short paragraph of four or five sentences. Just facts. No opinion, no psychology, just the story. It's not a reduction of the plot. It's not retelling the story so I can understand it. It's compressing the story into one paragraph.

Use no adjectives, or as few as possible, in telling the story. When you use adjectives, you're already conditioning your telling of the story, which will in turn condition your choices. When you use adjectives, you already have a preconception, rather than finding out the adjectives through the process. It's not that you can never use an adjective, but think about how predisposing adjectives can make you in telling a story.

QUIN GORDON (Teacher, Former Student):
You want it as barebones as possible, the idea being that in making those choices as to what's really important to the story, you actually learn the story so much better. You want to really adhere to the facts of the script, and not sully it with anything that's not in the script, or any opinion, because it will start to limit you choice-wise in a way that is probably not helpful yet.

It's not a matter of right and wrong. There are no laws or rules here; there is only what it serves.

As you work on the story, think *Dragnet*: "Just the facts, ma'am."

Without editorializing, just state the facts:
- Date
- Place
- Time
- What happens

Not a rehashing of the plot.

MOLLYE MAXNER (Director, Former Student):
Plot is the events that happen along the line of the play. The story is about what's really going on.

I will take you through my process to arrive at the story for my production of *Hamlet* at Great Lakes Theater:

Hamlet, Prince of Denmark, is told by his friend Horatio that the ghost of late King Hamlet is outside Elsinore Castle. Hamlet learns from his father's ghost that he was slain by his own brother Claudius, now king. He begs his son to revenge the murder, and Claudius's hasty marriage to Gertrude, young Hamlet's mother and the late king's widow. Laertes, son of the Lord Chamberlain, Polonius, warns his sister Ophelia against Hamlet's advances. Ophelia tells her father that a very disturbed Hamlet has visited her. Polonius tells the king that Hamlet is mad for Ophelia's love. Hamlet has actors perform a play in which he reconstructs Claudius's murder of the late king. Claudius's reaction to the play proves his guilt to Hamlet. Polonius, hiding behind a curtain, is fatally stabbed by Hamlet, who says he mistook him for the king. Frightened, Claudius sends Hamlet to England. Ophelia is driven to insanity, commits suicide. Hamlet returns, and Claudius and Laertes plot to kill him. Laertes, seeking to revenge his father's murder and his sister's suicide, mortally wounds Hamlet with a poisoned foil, but the rapiers are exchanged and Hamlet kills Laertes, then the king. The queen, having taken poison intended for her son, also dies. The play ends with Hamlet's body being carried off in honor.

This seems too wordy, not condensed enough. I'll try again:

In the winter of 1601 in Elsinore, Denmark, the ghost of the murdered King, Old Hamlet, confronts his son, Prince Hamlet, and demands to be avenged. Hamlet traps his Uncle Claudius, who is also the new husband of his mother, Gertrude, into revealing his guilt. By mistake, Hamlet kills Polonius, the King's counselor and father to Laertes and Ophelia, and is exiled to England. Claudius's plan to kill Hamlet is thwarted and Ophelia goes mad and drowns. Laertes returns from France to avenge the deaths of Polonius and Ophelia, but in a fencing match staged by the treacherous Claudius, mortally wounds Hamlet with a poisoned foil, who in turn stabs Laertes and Claudius to death. The queen, having taken poison for her son, also dies.

This exercise is valuable because it reminds me of the story: the essential element of communication, after the acting problems have been worked out. Your character's name may not figure prominently or at all in the telling of the story. In this exercise, Rosencrantz and Guildenstern aren't mentioned in the story, although they do figure into the plot.

ROBERT BESEDA (Administrator, Former Student):
I found that so helpful when I was an actor, to really do that homework and see where my character fit into the story. It really is enormously helpful when you're playing roles like Rosencrantz in Hamlet, and you're not playing Hamlet. It helps you to realize what your character's job is. It can be liberating to know who you are in the story.

MANDY PATINKIN (Actor, Former Student):
It doesn't revolve around me. It's about the story. And if the story's not working, everything fails.

Slogan

The slogan—or "theme," as Gerald used to call it—is a succinct phrase that gives a sense of the world of the play. It should serve as a quick reminder of the play's style and tone.

The slogan is the short reduction of the spirit of the play in a few punchy words. The slogan should help you grasp the tone of the play by distilling its essence.

Reduce the play's message to a slogan. Phrase it like a theme, bumper sticker, or sampler, in words that catch the spirit of the play, and stimulate you, the actor.

Capsulize the play's message: what the playwright is saying. This slogan should come from the story. It should be stated in words that reflect the tone of the play. Try to find the purest and most pungent words for your phrase.

The slogan is a living thing that comes out of our discussions and the search; it's not an answer. It's an evolution to really pinning down the tonality, the spirit of the play. That's the use of slogan.

QUIN GORDON (Teacher, Former Student):
Slogan is another way into the play and the world of the play. It's a concrete thing that you can do to start to distill it down to one central, unified idea. This is the world of this play, or this feels like this play. It's that process of paring down to this one central idea that forces you to know the play on a deeper level.

A good slogan reminds you of the style of the play. It gets you back where you need to be in a little time. Now, you have to put in work to get to that place, of course. You have to take your good, earnest work and put it into the appropriate package.

I will take you through my process to arrive at the slogan for my production of *Hamlet* at Great Lakes Theater:

Readiness is all.

Is that really a good encapsulation of the play? Does it help me *grasp* the play? I'll try again:

Thought colors action—and should.

This seems like an *idea* to me. It may be right, but it doesn't get me going.

When politics and power prevail, it devours the human heart and spirit.

Too long. Not compressed enough. Since my point of view for this production was the casual way young people were sacrificed for power politics, this last theme's statement had the most turn-on for me. Notice that the change in wording makes you feel differently about the play. Try to find the fewest pungent words for your phrase. I finally arrive at:

Politics/Power kill heart and spirit.

Concise enough to fit on a bumper sticker, and remind me in an instant of the essential tone I'm going for.

Here are a few examples of my work on slogan from *The Importance of Being Earnest:*

Sincerity simply cheapens style.

Style is insincerity in earnest.

To improve my name by perfecting its spelling.

These are not just accurate, but are written in the style of the play.

Each time I phrase a slogan, I ask myself, "Is that a really good encapsulation of the play? Does it help me grasp the play?"

I used to call it *theme*, rather than *slogan*, but *theme* got in the way; it meant something different to too many people. *Slogan* seemed to be just a better, clearer way of saying it. I don't care what you call any of these exercises. They're just ways of communicating amongst us.

It's in the looking for the slogan that you come to a deeper understanding. It's the search for it that helps you get to the core of the play.

The Spine of the Play

The spine of the play is the forward momentum that drives all of the action in the story. It is what unites every single character in the play. It is what makes that world go round.

In Gerald's process, the spine of the play is discovered by investigating what everyone in the play is doing. What does all that doing add up to? Try to articulate an answer in an active sentence. This is the spine of the play.

I am first concerned with the discovery and understanding of the life of the play, beneath the surface of words and form.[2] Every play has something that gives it life, that breathes life into it. Up until actors get a hold of it, it's just pages, dialogue lying flat on a table. We give it life, we give it breath. The spine of the play is the breath of the play. It's the generating motor of the whole play. Every character is moved forward by this spine, active verb, breath, life force, or forward energy. What is the life energy that is shared by all the characters in the play?

Create a short sentence that generates the life of the play. Don't give up easily. Think about the action of the whole play, not just your character or the main character. The spine of the play, when you really get it, has to encompass all the actions in the play.

Keep asking:

- "What is the life of the play?"
- "What makes it move forward?"
- "What is the action which unites all the characters in the play?"

When I say "unites all the characters," it has to be from the servant to the master, from the somebody who has no lines to the somebody who has all the lines. You'll get closer to it faster if you don't think of the main characters.

QUIN GORDON (Teacher, Former Student):
You need something that unifies everybody. What's a basic need that all the characters have in a play? It can't be too general. Like, we all want love and acceptance. That's true to all humans. But within the world of this play, what does everyone seem to be striving for? And everybody goes about it in a different way, and often in opposing ways.

Find a common verbal action for all the characters in the play that binds all of them to the story. Try to put it into words. Keep refining the verb until it jumps off the page for you. Remember, there is no "right answer," only what engages YOU.

MOLLYE MAXNER (Director, Former Student):
You know you've found the spine of the play when the world starts talking to you through it. You start seeing it and hearing it everywhere. The world starts resonating back to you.

To be helpful, the spine of the play should be phrased with an active verb. *To be* is not active. Finally, you have to test your word, or your active verb, or your idea, against the play. It has to be what the play really does.

An example of a statement of the spine for the whole play of *Hamlet* might be:

To grab hold of life at every moment.

In *Hamlet*, this spine must be true of Polonius and Guildenstern as well as Hamlet himself if it is to be useful for you. I think the one above is pretty good for *Hamlet*. Although a play as complex as *Hamlet* might be subject to other statements of spine which would be just as apt and true. You have to test it for every character. If it is accurate, and really is the spine of the play, you can see how active this phrasing could be. "To grab hold of life at every moment" is a spine that does away with the contemplative, do-nothing Hamlet stuck in thought and inaction, which did *not* correspond with my idea of the play.

I did a *Hamlet* that was more about Hamlet's personal torture, and then fifteen years later I did a *Hamlet* about how society chewed up young talent and young people. I think they were both true to the material, to *Hamlet*, to what Shakespeare intended, but they were differently centered. Every scene would be different, and it was different. Not in a big way, but in all the subtle ways that make theater.

If you have worked at finding the right articulation and words for the spine, it will then inform every decision you make for the play. The spine helps you make choices. It gives you a framework to operate from.

JOHN LANGS (Director, Former Student):
Story teaches you what it is. *Theme* teaches you what it's about. But *spine* teaches you how it works. How it really works. It's the bones and cartilage that all the flesh and muscle is going to get around.

I prefer to use the word *spine* rather than *super objective* because it has resonance, and an essential, organic quality. To me, *spine* is a more useful word than *super objective*, or *spinach*, or *horse manure*, or whatever you want to call what we're talking about.

I don't say, "The spine of the play is THIS," but if you do it, you've done the kind of work that grounds you in what it's all about.

Now that I am starting to see what the whole play is about, it begins to give my character dimension.

The Spine of the Character

Like Gerald's journey to the spine of the play, the spine of the character is discovered by examining all of the things that character does, in order to reveal what motivates them.

The spine of the character is what drives the character through life. It informs everything they do (or do not do). The spine of the character helps the actor make choices. It is a guide for doing.

The spine is the central armature around which the body is organized. We say someone has *spine* when we refer to a gutsy, determined person. Conversely, someone with *no spine* is considered a weakling. That's everyday language. In my training, I use the word *spine* to answer the question, "Who am I?"

Whatever the role, the actor is always dealing with the human psyche. The character that you imagine, the life that you imagine, is finally anchored by the events of the play. Spine is derived from all the actions of the character—not by what they say, but by what they do.

As one of my many wonderful teachers has made clear to me, the choices you make distinguish you as a person. Well, they also distinguish characterization. Why does this particular character make this particular life choice? What you are, what I am, is perceived by other people by the choices we make—our choices in life, our choices of career, our choices of food—so that *is* characterization. When you begin to see the choices Jerry Freedman makes, you can begin to characterize him. You can begin recreating my character without having to imitate my voice or my physicality, but through my behavior.[3]

What is your character's spine? Just go through the actions. That's the beginning of getting to a spine. Don't think that it's an esoteric question, or a mystery. Don't make problems for yourself. I look at what the character *does*, in addition to what he says, or in spite of what he says. I note all of that carefully, pin it down, write it down.[4]

I'm not interested in the *why*. I am only interested, and I want you to be only interested, in what the character does. Because what a person does is who they are, not what they say. Why does the character do what he does? I can't tell you; I don't know enough answers. I don't know enough material behind "Why?"

This process of investigation is external. The external will lead you to the internal. Actor after actor tells you this. Don't worry about the *why*. Worry about, "What do I do?" Work from that into the inner life. And that will begin to tell you who you are.

The spine work has to encompass all of the actions of the character. What does the character do? You don't know everything the character does, everything he's capable of doing, until you get to the end of the play. In life, we don't know our spines until we're dead, because we don't know, really, what we are capable of, until we no longer are capable. You might say, "Oh, I would never do that." But faced with a certain situation, you might. Every day, we are in the state of becoming, so you cannot properly talk about a living person's spine, because we're still becoming whatever we are.

In a play, given a beginning and an end, that is the life of the play. A character in a play has a beginning and an end. We can define a character's spine, as we cannot in life, by adding up all that character's actions in the play. This summation is the life of the character. The rest is speculation. This is all the author has given us.

You can only find spine in terms of the events of the play, but then you have to phrase it in a way that gives it life beyond. It is a bit paradoxical. On the one hand, you can only know about a character's spine because a character has a beginning and an end. And on the other hand, a spine should give you the life of the character beyond that beginning and end.

It doesn't matter what happened to the character before the play or what the character does after the play. We can't know that. We can invent those events to help ourselves, but nobody knows. They're not given to us.

If you want to give the character a life, an essential core, they have to exist before and after the play, but not in terms of events. Just as a life. That again is paradoxical. And it is so that, during the time of the play, you have a fuller character. A more original character. A character that has a total life, a core that justifies more than only the events of the play. So that's the big bundle. That's why spine work is useful and important.

MATT BULLUCK (Teacher, Colleague):
Jerry's way of looking at spine is not just the play. What is driving this person through life? Before the play, during the play, and after the play. And we can't really come to a clarity on it until that person's life is over, but as we're working on these characters, the play will take care of the play; your job is to figure out who this guy is. What's really driving him?

"What does he do?" Not, "What does he say?" Not necessarily what other people say about him. But what does he do? What are his actions? Your character might say one thing and do another. For example, Scrooge in *A Christmas Carol*—you can't say he's just a mean, twisted old misanthrope, because at the end of the play he's a generous, reformed person. That is who he was. Something of what he was allowed him to change.

MANDY PATINKIN (Actor, Former Student):
His belief was that if you really figure out the spine, it plays in every single moment of your character's life, and that if you pull back the arrow, and you shoot it, if it's true, it runs right through the spine of your character's life; it never misses.

Find the most active verb that justifies *every* action of the character, from the first moment to the end of the play.

Avoid stating it as *to be* or *to become*, as these verbs are inherently inactive.

Hamlet ruminates a lot, but he also fights a duel with Laertes, writes a play, stages a mad scene, and displays other *active* choices. If you are playing Hamlet, your spine must encompass all of this in order to help you.

MANDY PATINKIN (Actor, Former Student):
What does Hamlet do? He questions. He mines. He delves. He fights. He wrestles. These are actions, these are things you can play.

State the spine in a short sentence, with an active verb, and possibly a qualifying *how*, or conditioning phrase. What does he do? And then, how does he seem to do it?

A spine might include a *how* or *without*—a character limitation which makes this character unique in their behavior. Look at the manner in which—the *how*. How do they go about it? Or, what is the manner in which they conducted these actions?

To be useful, your character's spine should relate to the spine of the play, so that you are part of the whole. It should not restate actions of the play. You check back with the play to see, "Is this really the character who would live this life?"

I will take you through my process to arrive at Hamlet's spine:

I don't see Hamlet as melancholy; I see him as tremendously active.

Hamlet: **To face every moment and do what is right.**

To face is too general. I like the word *survival*, but by itself it doesn't mean much.

To confront every choice in life and act out what my mind and heart tell me is right.

You can see that I've now conditioned every general word in my first spine statement, in an effort to be specific and charged. *Confront* is more active than *face*, etc.

To think through every decision and determine what is the appropriate action.

To think through goes backward; it's less active than *to confront*.

I'm trying to illustrate how one must keep working over and over and re-working words until you find the phrasing that really activates YOU.

If your spine is phrased effectively, it should stimulate you as an actor. It should help you weed out choices in behavior from the many possibilities that every scene and line offer.

Spine tells you *what* you do, but it leaves out the *how*. To discover *how* you fulfill your spine demands actions.

Let's say your spine for Hamlet is:

To confront every choice in life and act out what my mind and heart tell me is right.

How will you *confront*? By sword, by deception, etc. But *confront* seems very active and fun to play. Keep testing it at the table work, and when you get up on your feet.

A spine is something to keep refining until it becomes what guides your process of discovery, from your preparation, through rehearsal, and into performances.

My spine for the play: "To grab hold of life at every moment," works well for most, but how can I make it relate to a character like Ophelia's spine, when she seems to be more passive?

Ophelia: **To question everyone's action without direct confrontation.**

Question isn't specific enough. Instead I try:

To observe and overtly question everyone's actions without direct confrontation.

In the profession, I don't ask actors what their spines are. But I do the spine work. I do it, and I know the kind of security it gives me in directing it. And I know the kind of security it will give you in rooting yourself in a way of working.

Spine doesn't limit you. It doesn't say *you can't*. Usually, it opens you up to possibilities. Spine enables you to make choices from an endless list of possibilities. You can't really act a spine. Do you hear that? You can't act a spine. It helps you make choices.

In my second year at the University of North Carolina School of the Arts, I learned a way of testing a character's spine from my teacher Matt Bulluck, which he'd learned years before from Gerald as his student at Juilliard: How would a character with this spine buy a bottle of wine? Would they do a lot of research beforehand, then go in and order the exact thing they wanted? Would they ask the shop clerk for advice? Would they look for the cheapest bottle, or the most expensive, or would money not matter at all? Would they pick the bottle with the picture they liked best? Would they maybe even steal the bottle, or hold the store for ransom? As Matt summarized, "Hamlet would go about buying a bottle of wine differently than Ophelia would go about buying a bottle of wine." If you have a character spine that works for you, it should help you to imagine the choices that character would make when buying a bottle of wine, or behaving in any other situation.

All this stuff about spine, you can very well do without. But if you want to be a better actor, or a more proficient actor, or a more interesting actor, this will help you.

CIGDEM ONAT (Teacher, Colleague):
I never felt that I actually could say, "This is spine." I still find it elusive, but at the same time, I always use it. Spine helps you become more specific, and gives you a map.

WILL ROGERS (Actor, Former Student):
Getting to a spine isn't the goal. The goal is continuing to ask the questions, so that you're continuing to discover what this person will do.

Remember, this is all an exercise. It's a way toward the bigger job of communicating, of relating. It keeps you connected to the life of the play. You start thinking about the character, and it leads to questions. It keeps you thinking and searching in an active mode.

Spotlight: Gerald's Text Work

Below are two more examples of Gerald breaking down the script: The Cherry Orchard, *from his 1993 production at Great Lakes Theater; and* Measure for Measure, *from his 1981 production at the Old Globe. Both work samples show Gerald using the tools described in this chapter, but neither follows one precise, prescriptive method. They reveal a man whose work is always in process, who never stops asking questions, and who never arrives at a final answer, but uses text analysis as a live, active tool with which to dig deeper into the plays he directs. These two examples have not been edited; they are laid out here—roughly at times—as closely as possible to how Gerald put them down on paper for his personal use.*

The Cherry Orchard

STORY

Mme Ranevsky comes home on a cold spring day in May to her estate in Russia in 1904 from a five-year stay in Paris. With her is her daughter, Anya, and a governess, Charlota, who had come to get her, and a young valet named Yasha who had accompanied her from Russia from her earlier days. She, and her brother, Gaev, will lose their estate, including a famous and beautiful cherry orchard, unless they can pay their debts at an auction in August. After a summer of remembrance, idleness and procrastination, the estate is sold to Lopahin, the grandson of a former serf of the Gaevs. Mme Ranevsky goes back to her lover in Paris, Varya, her stepdaughter does not marry Lopahin as expected and Anya leaves with a student, Petya Trofimov, to study in Moscow. Gaev goes off to a job as a banker to which he is ill suited. Firs, an elderly servant, is carelessly left behind in the deserted and locked-up house, as the cherry orchard is being cut down with axes.

THEME

- Change is inevitable
- Growth and change are not the same
- Growth and change are not synonymous
- Personal growth and change may not come together
- Change needs adaptability

SPINE OF THE PLAY

The demands for social change cannot be stemmed, stopped.
(needs of)

1. Everything (family loyalty, friendship, symbols of the past, beauty, principles) is sucked into a vortex of change; sacrificed if necessary to the sea of progress.

2. Everyone will drown in a sea of change if they do not adapt or seek help or the Sea of change will drown you. The rising of the water is inevitable. What will you do about it?

MME. R. cannot stop loving the wrong men. She knows what she must do. She knows what is expected of her. She seems to have the education, charm and intelligence to do the right thing: save the land, marry her daughters. But it would mean sacrificing her own emotional needs (?). She seems consumed by the telegrams. She doesn't want the house or the land. It has too many bad memories. She <u>has</u> the good memories right where she wants them. In her consciousness where she can control them. (For telegrams read passion, love, emotional needs, hunger for.) Lyuba is essentially selfish and self-serving. Her generosity is undiscerning and indiscriminate.

GAEV is a child. He's always being pampered and taken care of. Firs is a stand-in for mother, governess, sister, servants, friends. Gaev seems totally pliant, pleasant, charming, cultivated. He was not educated to work. He is at home in the nursery. Indolent, playful. I like his sentimental and somewhat tendentious perorations. I find them touching. Why do the others shut him up? What are his private thoughts? Is he a thoughtful person or shallow? Why did Stanislavsky want to play him? Lyuba is the "star" of the family. Why? When Gaev is older and a man-child? Is he simply not trained to <u>think</u>? Should I know more about billiards? (Preston research)

ANYA – I take Chekhov at his word. Young, happy, childlike, intelligence enough for compassion, sensitivity, goodness.

DUNYASHA – shrewd, practical, flirtatious, adaptable, ambitions to better herself. Healthy, sexual, uncomplicated.

VARYA – complicated. Foster-daughter, out of place, emotionally needy, guilty to earn her place, justify herself. Work and responsibility are her payments. God is her stability and refuge. She is vulnerable because she doesn't truly know where she belongs. (Cousin) and she cannot afford to indulge herself, because she finally only has herself and god!

CHARLOTTA – also a foster child. She entertains to maintain her place. She has no emotional attachments. She invites none. Does she realize that? She seems to distance people. Uses the tricks to alienate as well as ingratiate.

(Now the thought comes to me, that these people are all adrift. They seem to have no families to go to. The Gaev home was the anchor [Lorain—and the Sepsenwols] Some incredible security, beautiful image is gone. Now, we're fragmented. Broadway was our Cherry Orchard. We keep thinking about it. Longing for those days. How far can I go with this?)

Lyuba-Natalie, Aunt Rose	Lopahin-Uncle Abe, Max
Gaev-Barnie, Itz?	Charlotta-Caryl Crane
Anya-Losideane	Trofimov-Gerald
Varya—Fannie, Aunt Emma	Pishtchik-Uncle Harry, Larry L
Dunyasha-Aunt Anita, Lucille	Epihodov-Bobby
Yasha-Cousin Arthur Rosenthal	Firs-Grandpa Freedman

Centrifugal force. Change. We are all whirling away from the center. Some adapt. Some can't. Does anybody change in the course of the play? Anya isn't formed yet. Everyone else seems to be already cast in their future guise.

PISHTCHIK – Why does he fall asleep? Insomniac? Too easy? Is he not really <u>there</u> when he's talking to you? Like a humming bird flitting from flower to flower till it gets enough nectar. Always hovering, never staying. Why the horse image? Because the original was so bizarre? Not to be taken seriously? A little foolish? Is there more?

YEPIKHODOV/EPIHODOV – he is another Gaev. I like him. He has sweetness and he seems harmless. True, he does not seem very effectual. Does he have dignity? Not like Medvedenko in Seagull or Kuligin in Three Sisters, both of whom he resembles. He is pathetic and self-aware. A bit like a dog who is always in the wrong. Slinking around waiting for "it" to happen or be discovered.

TROFIMOV – it seems to me to be all there. Idealistic, visionary, sexually shy. Student more than activist. The moment in Act III with Mme. R, "I feel sorry for you." "No, not like that" suggests that he is reserved emotionally. At least, uncomfortable.

YASHA – opportunist, ambitious, sexual charm, makes me think of servant in Miss Julie. Gauche, not sophisticated. Sneering competence. Somewhat naïve.

FIRS – dedicated to Gaev's well-being. True to the "old way." NO question of adjustment or change.

LOPAHIN – he is still justifying himself to his father and grandfather. He is still guaranteeing his place in the new society. No one seems impressed with him. They are not giving him "position." Only his money can do that and, therefore, he needs more. He seems to be saying, "look" at me. First as a friend, advisor and equal (on some level), then as a profit of doom, and finally as a capitalist. Trofimov "sees" him, truly. Varya "sees" him as a way out. Yasha seems to want to emulate the Gaev's not the new merchant's, the new entrepreneur.

Changing realities in society demand adaptations of behavior, adjust or die (Firs?). Adjust or disperse. Adjust and succeed (Lopahin (?) Too obvious and not really what the play seems to be about. There is a natural growth and inevitable decay here. There is no struggle.

SPINES

MME R. I will clutch to sexual passion and an elegant quality of life at the risk of my life. Even if they take me down to the bottom.

GAEV. It is my obligation to live and behave like a gentleman even if I must drown/blind myself to the truth. A gentleman sums up for those present. Crystalizes the moment.

LOPAHIN. I will/must hang on/pile up(?) on the money to carry me through the currents of change or I will sink. To accumulate more money and build an island of refuge against the currents of change or I will sink.

TROFIMOV. I will swim against the current with all my strength and change its direction.

ANYA. I will hold on to Trofimov because he seems to have an answer even if it means leaving/separating from home and family.

DUNYASHA. I will cling to any man who will keep me afloat and if I can like him.

VARYA. I must behave like a lady to gain respect or I will be thrown back into the sea of change even though I know hard work and determination will save me. God will preserve me.

FIRS. I will go down with the ship. Serving all to the end, as I have been taught.

YASHA. To ingratiate myself to anyone who will save me from sinking and float me out of here.

PISTCHIK. To build a raft from a lot of small scraps and not depend on any one person to save me.

YEPIKHODOV. To flow with the current and hope for the best.

CHARLOTTA. To drift from raft to raft by making myself useful and entertaining. (She does not seem to have a strong desire, but she survives. She does not ask much.)

Measure for Measure

Measure for Measure is about the power of sexual energy in man – the human, the animal, the life-bursting, the *disorganized* in conflict with the law, the rigid, controlling, boundary making force set up to control the *forever*.

Sexual energy out of control is lust, without moderation it is bestial, destructive physically and psychically – it is the unbridled id.

The law, without compassion, removed from humane thinking is equally destructive – murderous and sadistic. Social Man is in a desperate struggle to moderate these forces. He is afraid of the unknown, dark, nameless forces that he is driven by and much of this is collectively labeled, "the sexual urge." He has created the idea of law to channel and form this energy into a controllable and positive force. To "civilize" man.

The pendulum between excess and repression swings back and forth. But the forces are always in contention.

Shakespeare says, or believes in, a moderating influence in the use of both. The law and sex must be applied with compassion and self-knowledge. If you are aware of these "dark" forces within yourself, you should be able to understand them and the use of them in others. But above all they are "human" urges and are meant to be controlled by "human" social and legal structures as administered by "humane" judges.

Man is imperfect as presumably are his judgments. Fallibility is a constant. On earth as it is in heaven. The Dark Angel was cast out of heaven but he was not destroyed.

Isabella must learn this as Angelo must.

The Duke is aloof from sex and love – but at the end he sues for Isabella's hand. Claudio has been through a tearful trial but he is alive at the end.

THEME

- The Law is fallible therefore it must be administered with compassion
- Man is fallible therefore Man must be Compassionate
- Mercy is the Instrument of Compassion
- The Law and Compassion Must Be As One.

SPINE OF THE PLAY

- Morality
- Sexual Coupling
- Control of Sexual Drive
- Seeming and Being in terms of the Sexual Drive

Humans are driven by sexual urges which must be controlled (and moderated by marriage or lawful bonding)

Sexual Urges drive humans forward and must be understood and accepted for the good of mankind.

$\longrightarrow$ Since the Law is an impersonal instrument, Humane judges must administer it.

ANGELO: I must bind up my ferocious lust by ruthless application of law and order in all things.

ISABELLA: To submerge/deny my sexual feelings by total immersion in religious law and order.

To disguise my sexual feelings even from myself in Nun's robes and rigid religious thinking.

my sexual desire for Claudio

DUKE: To become a whole man in accepting my role as a husband and my full power as The Duke by dropping my disguises.

CLAUDIO: To live/experience life at its fullest by/and becoming an older and wiser man.

MARIANA: To complete myself by coupling with Angelo.

JULIET: To free Claudio by marrying him.

LUCIO: To say anything and do anything, without moral judgment, that will keep my life free and fun-loving.

                    defend the "business" of sex
POMPEY: to keep the business of sex going without getting caught
             by the law.

OVERDONE: To stay in business even if it is sex.

PROVOST: To serve my fellow man compassionately by using my
             good sense and good humor.

ESCALUS: Now that I am beyond sex, I have infinite patience for it
             in others.
             To second/serve the highest will be it God, Duke or the Law
             by keeping the inner man in view.

BERNADINO:

ELBOW: To do the right thing in the right way within the limits of
            the law.

The insects in Measure are mostly hard brittle.
They look dangerous. The softest are the Duke, Pompey?, Juliet.

ANGELO   A Beetle – Black Iridescent
                Brittle Carapace, Soft Inside. Pincers.

ISABELLA   A Larvae – Encased in White
                The real Isabella only emerges at
                the very end. Is she struggling
                to get out or stay in?

DUKE Seems common 'till wings are opened.   A peacock. Only truly
          Then he is huge and his markings noble. majestic when angered and
          Special. Stronger than a Butterfly   reveals his tail in its full
          and not decorative.   glory.

CLAUDIO   Butterfly. He is a beautiful and fragile
being. He has not long to live and
must find the right flowers.

ESCALUS   Grasshopper. A little dried up, brittle.
Angular, testy. Not dangerous. He will
nibble away at the grain until it is gone.

PROVOST   Black Ant. Steady, industrious.
Try to divert him, he always finds
the path home.

POMPEY   A Bee or House Fly. The Bee is
more benign and industrious.
The Fly more parasitic and
bothersome. They both buzz
around. The Bee around Flowers.
The Fly around garbage. That says it.
He's a fly.

OVERDONE   A Venus fly trap – Looks good.
Smells sweet. A spot of honey to
attract the other insects.

ELBOW   Caterpillar – steady, plodding.
Crawling through life.
He will never be a Butterfly.

ABHORSON   Tarantula. Steady. Heavyweight.
Looks Dangerous + Dumb.
Maybe he is a <u>Maggot</u> living off
of dead flesh.

LUCIO   A Dragon Fly. Iridescent, changeable.
Transparent. Brittle.
A little sting in his tail.

FROTH   Lice. A Flea. Nips around.
              Not very dangerous. Not very helpful.
              An annoyance.

BARNADINE Cockroach – Ubiquitous

MARIANA   Is a bloodsucker

Centipede
Bee
Wasp
Ant – Black-Steady – Provost
Fly – Pompey?
Dragon Fly – Lucio
Butter Fly – Claudio
Grasshopper – Escalus
Spider – E
Tarantula
Red Ant – More Threatening
Moth – Duke
Caterpillar – Elbow
Cockroach – Barnadine
Mosquito
Flea – Lice

Objective

The objective is what the character wants. As Gerald upheld, everyone wants something, all the time, all day long, at every moment.

After figuring out who you are in a play, you ask, "What do I want?" I call that an objective.

Wants are the very energy of human life. You would be dead if you didn't want. We always want something. It's difficult to see that all the time because we don't think we want something. For instance, you might think that right now, in this class, I don't want anything—that I'm just talking to you, just trying to explain. Well, I want approval from you, I want understanding from you. I want to see that you get it. It's not enough just to teach; I need feedback! Am I getting anywhere? Is this reaching anybody?

Objective: What do I want?
What do I want to achieve?
What do I want to *get* from the other person in the scene?

Keep asking, "What is my objective in each scene?"

Monologue is a dead end. It will kill you. You don't do anything alone. You always have a partner. If you're alone, you might be talking to yourself, or to God, or to the audience, but you always have a partner you want something from.

MISSI PYLE (Actor, Former Student):
It's in the other person. It's always in the other person. You've done your work, and now, what do you want from the other person? That's the basis of acting.

One can get into the habit of asking, "What do I want?" instead of "What do I want from YOU?" The latter will make things *happen* onstage, activating what you want through your partner. The objective is not what you push for in a scene; it's what brings you back to your partner.

Action

Action is another word for doing, an essential ingredient in Gerald's school of thought. An action is also commonly referred to as an intention.

In 2006, I assistant directed Gerald's production of Beckett's Happy Days, *starring Cigdem Onat, another master teacher of mine. The play was to be presented in Cigdem's home city of Istanbul. After a few days of table work in English, Cigdem rehearsed the play in Turkish, as it would be performed. One of my responsibilities was to be on book, following along phonetically in a language which neither Gerald nor I spoke a word of. To my amazement, Gerald was usually the first to know when she missed a line. He didn't speak Turkish, but these two masters were communicating fluently in the language of doing.*

The next question is, "What am I doing?" And usually that's "What am I doing to get what I want?" And I call this an action.

Action is the *behavior* you use to achieve your objective: the *doing.*

CIGDEM ONAT (Teacher, Colleague):
To teach action is very difficult at first, because the young actor is not aware that they act, that there is a whole vernacular in them of action. It's not just behavior. It's what you do. Always. We are always doing. Everybody is doing, in one form or another. It's impossible to be otherwise. It's so powerfully essential.

Action: The process or state of doing. Or, feeling alive.

"What's my action in each scene?"

Break down each scene into actions and beats, all written in the margin so it is available to you.

MANDY PATINKIN (Actor, Former Student):
[At Juilliard with Jerry], the game was to write down in a single word, hopefully, your action. Well I'd take a yellow legal pad and write five pages, and Jerry would read my pages, and then he'd crumple them up, and there was a mountain of legal paper next to where I was sitting.
　　And then I started to get it. And I got it into smaller paragraphs, and then into sentences, and then into words. And that business of learning

that I'm coming to *attack* you, I'm coming to *embrace* you, I'm coming to *welcome* you, I'm coming to *rally* you, I'm coming to *encourage* you, I'm coming to *terrorize* you, I'm coming to *awaken* you, I'm coming to *vaporize* you, I'm coming to *love* you, to *hold* you, to *never let you go*, to *rattle* you, to *shake* you, to *arrest* you...these are words that have become *my* words, repeated over and over and over again. My vocabulary, that I have learned and assembled through my life's experience of the work, and of my mind, my memory, my imagination, and my creativity, of marrying the word of the text to an active, connective tissue in my being that lives in me, that's truthful.

We often don't come up with the definitive word, but looking for the right verb is not an academic experience; you want a visceral word that will activate you, that will stimulate you. It's not about bringing in the right verb, it's what will really excite you. Language is important because it's symbols that activate us. Period. They mean something.

STEVEN ROUTMAN (Actor):
You always need to know what you want from the other person, and why you are there in the scene. Not just in the general framework of the scene, but moment to moment. What are you trying to achieve three lines into the scene that you weren't trying to achieve when you entered the scene? How is that different from the end of the scene? Did you get what you wanted?

You can't just say a line, you must investigate every line to find out what's behind it. The words take care of themselves. *Don't act the words!* Keep asking, "Why am I saying this word? What does it mean to me?" There are no lines, only intentions that demand language. The language is the character's need to do something.

REBECCA NAOMI JONES (Actor, Former Student):
The huge thing that I learned from Gerald was that every single time you speak or do anything in a scene, it's because you want something. Within the scene, there are different beats of how you might change a tactic to get this thing that you want, and how what you want might change color in a way, but it's all gotta be really clear to you.

You should never say a line without an intention. Why repeat a phrase, unless there's been some change in thought, some change in intention? The less you have honed in, that's what happens; it's just a repeated phrase, rather than an additional need to say the line. Unless you've dealt with the scene, or unless you're really present, it's just a dead phrase. And you must avoid that like the plague.

The terms *action* and *intention* may often overlap; they are not mutually exclusive. What's my intention? The *tactics* I use to achieve my objective. Depending on the obstacle the other person presents, one may use different intentions or change tactics to achieve one's objective.

JOSIE DE GUZMAN (Actor, Singer):
He would make sure that we were clear in what our characters were intending to do, and needed from beat to beat. I have learned through the years that that choice can change depending on what the director wants, what another character might be giving you in rehearsal or onstage, and how your character grows and finds its way. What was great with Jerry's direction is that, because you were clear with the character's intention, it would free you up to be flexible with your choices. It would make it easier to deal with changes.

Why We Need This Work

For theater artists, breaking down the script is a way to begin—to dig into virtually any project and start to figure things out. This work gets your mind working on the play, and helps to create a clear, concrete direction forward.

Like many of Gerald's students, I wrestled with this text work for a long time before I started finding it useful. I would get trapped in my head, and mired in intellectual analysis as I grappled with the concepts. (I often still do.) But in persevering, I began to make discoveries that galvanized my work, that anchored me in the play, and that helped to get me out of my head and into the doing.

You have to articulate your craft so you can be in charge of it. To me, thinking and organizing your work is a means toward freeing your impulse, because finally it's about acting, it's about doing. The components of this work are only useful insofar as they help you act, not write a paper.

Can you act without all this preparation? Yes. Can there be great acting without ever having heard of these methods? Absolutely. If you think you are one of those geniuses who doesn't need this work, go for it. But all artists of consistent achievement need and use some way to get beyond the panic, anxiety, and chaos that often accompany creation.

All actors do this, whether they are aware of it or not. They read the play, have responses to it, and develop ideas on their path to mapping out their character. These tools help you make it a *conscious* process, so you are in control of your craft. Other actors might say, "This feels right," or "I'll just do something until it feels right." If you do not make your process of discovery a conscious one, it can lead to confusion, false assumptions, and misguided justifications for your character. CRAFT PUTS YOU IN CONTROL.

This is to give you tools so that you're not at the mercy of, or the victim of, a director. Now, I'm a director, so how dare I say that? But you have to have craft as an actor. This work is applicable to every play you work on.

There are notable exceptions. If you were working on a piece by Robert Wilson, this might not be applicable. But for all practical purposes, for the rest of your life, if you're going to be in the theater, this is a technique you can use.

Ultimately, what this work helps an actor to do is make choices. In many plays, there seem to be a thousand choices. So which one do I take? Through this work, you begin to see that there are many possible choices, but many of them are not within the framework of the play. Choices aren't arbitrary. They come from the script.

JEREMY WEBB (Actor, Former Student):
As an actor, it's really my primary function to interpret, to winnow down my choices to a group of choices that line up to that thing that the writer is trying to say, to tell that story.

These exercises are for clarity. There is no right or wrong. The clearer you get it, the more succinct, the more they will help you. This is how you as an actor can get a hold of and grasp the work, so you can enrich it and make intelligent choices and play into the play. You can't just pick up the script and be an actor. I mean, you can, but you'd be a bad actor, or a false actor, or an unimaginative actor, because you wouldn't really know what you were doing. This work gives you support, underpinning. It gives you a map to investigate, to guide your search.

DANE DEHAAN (Actor, Former Student):
It's really just a way of getting you thinking about what you're working on. It gets your mind thinking in different ways. It's a constant thinking. When I look at the story and the slogan and the spine, it's a great way to dive into it headfirst. These are important things for the project, and it's going to get me to really think about it.

Using this work as an outline gives the actor a *structure* or *form* to think about a play.

It does not matter that the answers are right or wrong; it's the questions that matter. It isn't about having the answer. It's about looking for the answers. You'll never really find the answer, even in the doing of it. If you make an attempt at looking, at trying to find out, that is the experience. That is the rightness and goodness of this kind of work: the search.

This craft gives you a way of organizing your thinking to the particular thing you're working on. Otherwise it's just, "Yeah, I'm talented, I can read, I have a feeling about this part." Your feeling may be right, but what happens when your feeling runs out?

When you get a script at a cold reading, you will not have the time to say, "What's my action? What's my intention?" But if you have exercised those muscles, it will be instinctive.

What Is Happening?

For Gerald, breaking down the script went deeper than the words on the page. He would ask, "What is underneath those words? What is happening? What is really going on?"

I always look for what is happening in a scene, and not necessarily what the scene says. "What is happening? What are they *doing*?" These are the first questions I ask.[5]

The play is about what is *happening*, not what the words say. It's often what the words don't say. That is absolutely true in modern theater. In classical plays, before Ibsen, often the action is in the words. We have to start with the words. You start with the words, and work down in layers. What is really happening? What is supporting the words? Where are these words coming from? You're going layer by layer by layer below the words to find out what made the words happen.

MOLLYE MAXNER (Director, Former Student):
You can't get everything from just the words if you don't understand how humans behave. In your text analysis, you have to know what humans do to each other, and what humans want, and why humans would do that. That's how you really understand what a scene is about. And that is a lifelong quest: to really understand human behavior.

You have to get real intimate with what's *on* the page to find out what's *not*. Don't just analyze words; you have to see through them.

Backstory

Many actors and directors use backstory—the imagined history of a character not provided by the playwright—in order to build a fuller understanding of the character(s) in a play.

You can make up a backstory, but that is not always helpful. You have to take it from the play. If you look, it's in the play. Mine every detail for information.

MARY IRWIN (Teacher, Colleague):
All of the answers are in the play, and woe betide the person who would bring something into Gerald's rehearsal that was just a high concept thing.

You can have your own backstory. You don't have to agree. All I have to know is that it does not contradict the given circumstances of the play. You may not be excited, or your instrument may not be made alive by the same factors as your fellow actors. All you need for your backstory, if you choose to have one, are things that activate you, that get your instrument going and alive.

Stage Directions

Stage directions are used to indicate action that takes place during the play, or to describe the play's sensory environment. Stage directions are sometimes more a record of the choices made in the premiere production than a reflection of the playwright's desires. Other times, stage directions are integral components of the playwright's creative vision.

Most directors and acting teachers will tell you to ignore stage directions, because they're often inhibiting. They predetermine what your response might be, rather than giving you a chance to discover what your reaction might be. I'm experienced enough now to think of them as clues, without taking them literally. Quite often a stage direction says, "Laughing." I would totally ignore that, until I discovered what the relationship was.

On the other hand, a few years ago I did a play of Beckett's: *End Game*. And he's very explicit. And I said, just as a test, that I would do everything that he says, and I worked in a totally different way. First we talked about it, explored it all through table work. And it produced a wonderful play.

Preparation, Preparation, Preparation

Gerald believed that preparation is key to a fruitful process, and that it can and should be done independently, prior to the start of rehearsals when possible. Preparation primes you for your work with others.

At a master class, the first thing I say is, "Grab your legal pad, and make three columns. On the first column, write the heading *Preparation*. And on the second column, put *Preparation*. Then on the third column, put *Preparation*." You cannot do yourself more good than preparation. Do your homework. Do the script breakdown. Do your research. Do everything. That puts you in such a positive position to deal with rehearsals. That doesn't mean you have all the answers; the dynamic of the cast and the room brings up all kinds of questions, but when I know the material cold, I can watch rehearsal with more openness. If you're winging it, that puts you at a terrific disadvantage.

In anything, in order to get to the joy, there's a price. You've got to put in the time to get to the fun. It isn't all fun. It isn't all spontaneous. The fun comes when you're making it *appear* spontaneous, after you've done all the work, when you're letting it all happen in the space. We put in all this time to get to those moments, eventually. Unless you put in the time, it can never happen.

I have patience with actors who are working, who do their homework. You have to do the homework, so that when you are together, you can explore, not learn your lines, not do your work there and then, but beforehand, so that in the rehearsal room, you can find the next phase of it.

CHITA RIVERA (Actor, Dancer):
I walk into the room knowing the script, having memorized the words and gotten the rhythm of the words. Then I have the freedom to listen to other things.

If you're prepared, if you've done your homework, if you know where to put your energy—what your action is, what your objective is—it helps take away your nervousness, because you know what to focus your energy toward.

If you haven't done the work, you're in mystery land. If you've done real preparation, it puts you in a secure place where you can handle whatever comes your way. Through experience, I see how useful and helpful it is.

It's for you. It's a map that you have worked out in order to understand the terrain. Nothing earns you more than doing your work.

GABE SCOGGIN (Program Manager, Former Student):
Gerald said to me, "Confidence comes from preparation." He is a meticulous preparer. He has his own methods, and whether you use his system or not is not the issue. Giving yourself a process is paramount. If you build yourself a foundation, then you have something to stand on, and you'll be much more confident. You'll be more capable. You'll be able to execute.

Too often, actors come to the table having done no work, but open to what the director has to say. That is not a good idea. As an actor, there's a lot of work you can do while still being open to the director's point of view.

These are steps you can take *before* you come to rehearsal, as soon as you get the script. Now, much of this work still goes on while you're in rehearsal. But this is all an actor's preparation.

Bringing Your Homework into Rehearsal

Gerald urged his students to do a whole lot of preparation at home, and then to step into the rehearsal hall and let it all go. Holding onto homework too tightly can hinder collaboration.

REBECCA NAOMI JONES (Actor, Former Student):
A massive thing that I learned from him was that you can do all of that work—and you have to do all of that work—but when you get into the rehearsal room, you also have to be willing to put that down for a minute and listen to the scene partner that you're with. You can't just pre-dictate everything in the scene without the person that you're working with, because that'll shut you down. It always is about what you want from the other person, and not just about what you've designed for the scene and how you want it to go.

Let go of the work. When you break down a script, it makes you familiar with the terrain, the landscape of the scene. Then you go out and do it. It allows you to respond to what your partner is giving you. You respond. You don't decide it all on paper. What you're doing with your homework—figuring out what your actions are, what your objectives are, and what you want—then you have to let it happen, not play that word, but do it. You don't bring your homework with you; you don't wear it like a mantle or a cloak into rehearsal.

NEAL BLEDSOE (Actor, Former Student):
A spine is just an idea. An objective is just an idea. You have to put it into action. You have to really pursue it. That is so much more of a visceral experience, rather than just to put some English on a line. It's really taking that work, making a spine so vivid, so powerful that it can't help but shoot you off of your chair like a champagne cork into the scene to do something. Until that happens, it's all just an idea, and that was the work as an actor that I think he got me to see. Not just how to break down something into beats and super objectives, because, fuck, you can read Stanislavski for that. Where I think Gerald's work is phenomenal is how

to take all that, all that carbonated shit, and how to shake it up and make it explode. That's where the work is. It's how to take those ideas and make them actionable.

You mustn't confuse the work process with the work. So, you break down a script, you break down speeches, only to put them back together again. People often confuse the process with the work, so they're still doing the process when I just want them to act it, say it, do it. Don't think the action; do it. Don't do all the thinking before a line; put it together with the words.

A lot of the process needs to be, and should be, private. Your written work is for you. You don't have to share it. We share it here in school so that we can guide you toward more knowledgeable or deeper understanding. But out in the world, you don't have to show anybody any of your work.

Other actors may not have had this work, and may not go at it in the same way, so they might ridicule it because they don't understand it. A director may say, "I don't want you thinking at all; just do." Fine, good luck.

Finally, a director—and usually a playwright—is only interested in what they see, in what you're objectively delivering to them. There are many directors who don't give a shit about how you work, or what you want to hear. Great directors. You have to understand that your process is not everybody's meat and potatoes.

These are actor's preparations and techniques. They may have nothing to do with the writer's intentions. THEY ARE FOR YOU. You don't have to agree with the playwright. You don't have to agree with the director. They don't have to know what's in your mind or in your body. This is to help you achieve a craft that you can bring to the table.

CHRISTINE BARANSKI (Actor, Former Student):
The fact that you've put in that work beforehand, and you have a feeling, a point of view, a centeredness about the work you're about to approach, is absolutely invaluable. It speaks to your own integrity as a contributing artist. You will go into a process of any play with more confidence and more clarity, even if, in working with the director, you discover other interpretations.

This is all to train your muscles to be prepared for anybody, anything. That's why it's important to me that you be *thinking actors*, rather than just trained dogs. If it's, "Do this, do that, do that," then you can't respond to anybody except your master. But if you have a craft, then you can say, "Oh, I know what you want. I know what you're really talking about." It puts you back in command. That's the bottom line.

You continually check your work against the playwright's intentions, your partner's actions, and the director's vision. You should be able to take this work into what you're doing, otherwise it's not valuable. And it is. It should be.

The Work Goes On

As Gerald reminded his students, the work isn't easy. The work is never over. No artist is ever finished learning. The work is a lifelong pursuit.

When you see a paragraph of words, don't be intimidated by it. Go moment to moment. Thought by thought. Line by line.

Because this work might be new for you, it might make you very self-conscious for a while. For the next ten years it might make you self-conscious. "Do I have to do this?" "I hate doing this work." "I'm afraid I won't have the right answer." A student might say to me, "There is no right answer! What's the point?" But I tell you, unless I do this work, unless I really sit down and do it, I don't really get a handle on the plays that I direct. I try to do what I'm telling you. I'm not always so good at it myself.

DANE DEHAAN (Actor, Former Student):
I don't know if I've ever figured out a spine or a theme. I'm pretty sure I've never gotten one that's good. But I think that's completely okay, because I've used it in a way that's helpful, that's gotten my mind thinking about the project.

Great actors of reputation and experience still find this work hard to get through, so it's not that you're going to beat the problem now, but you can start understanding now, and building some of the muscles that will help you get through.

I'm absolutely sincere when I say that sometimes, I hate doing this work. I think, "Oh god, what is this play?" And finally I start to work, to search for the words, and then the inspiration comes. The intuition starts to operate. I start to really know what I'm doing, and in rehearsal, I have room for newer invention. If I know what the play is about, and someone comes up with a great idea that I hadn't even thought of, I know that the skeleton will accommodate that idea.

If you have done the kind of work I talk about in breaking down the script, you'll learn, as I did a long time ago, that there are a lot of ways to the truth. You want a truthful journey, but there is no one way.

What I'm trying to do is paradoxical, working at both sides of a skill. I have to make you a thoughtful actor. And I have to remind you that you are always active, even while you're thinking. And temporarily, you may have to put your emphasis on one aspect of it, rather than the other, temporarily. But finally, it's about the two things together, putting it together.

The actor's creative imagination and the actor's need to work with the given circumstances both come into play. And you are constantly, as an actor, exercising both. And I want to remind you of that, as I do all the time: it isn't one or the other. This isn't head work. It's head work that leads to action. And the action can't be just anything you wish, it has to be anchored by the given circumstances. It ends up in the gut. And although you need intelligence, and you need creative imagination, you also need industry.

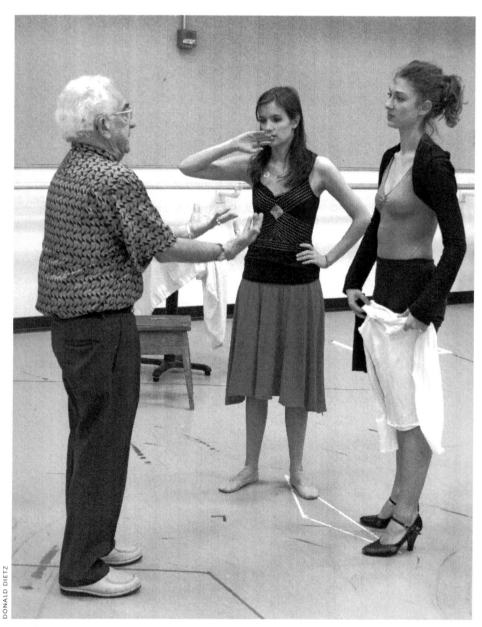

Gerald directing Anna Wood as Maria (center) and Jenna Fakhoury as Anita in *West Side Story* at the University of North Carolina School of the Arts in 2007.

TOP: From left: Gerald leading an all-school meeting with Olympia Dukakis, Mandy Patinkin, and Missi Pyle, onstage at the Gerald Freedman Theatre at the University of North Carolina School of the Arts in 2009. **BOTTOM:** Gerald auditioning students for *West Side Story*, onstage at the Agnes de Mille Theatre at the University of North Carolina School of the Arts in 2006. From left: E.J. Cantu, Nicolas Townsend, Dane DeHaan, Mykel Vaughn, Paul Duran, Gerald, and his assistant director Mark Karafin.

CHAPTER THREE

ACTING IS DOING

In Gerald Freedman's School of Doing, great acting is not just pretending; it's really doing things. Doing is authentic, engaging, and alive. Gerald's highest priority was helping actors to really do it, not just act like it.

What is this fascination to act, to bring to life a story in the form of a script or a narrative that asks to be illustrated? Is it the appeal of assuming the psyche of another, of exploring an alternative world and inhabiting another set of responses other than our own? Or is it simply a layer of pretend, of living in the imagination as an extension of childhood memories and fantasies? Whatever explanation we favor, "acting out" or "being possessed" seems to exist in every culture, and acting in front of an audience in our Western society is thousands of years old. The sharing of storytelling seems to be essential in our consciousness. An endless stream of books, techniques, instructions and instructors has been developed to help us accomplish this with greater skill, ease, and truthfulness.

The word *drama* comes from the Greek word for *draw*, meaning "to do"—an action.

I wish we weren't referred to as an acting school. We're really a doing school. I don't want to use the word *acting* anymore, though I know I will, and the world will refer to it as acting. Think about this: If you're doing something, you can't lie. You can't pretend. It's not about pretending if you're actually doing. We have expressions like, "Actions speak louder than words." It's in the common vernacular. What a person *does* means more than what they say.

PENNY FULLER (Actor):
The trouble with acting is calling it acting, like it's a thing. It isn't. It's doing, it's living.

If you're performing an action, you're doing something. Not faking. Not acting. You're doing. Don't act. You are what you do.

MISSI PYLE (Actor, Former Student):
I remember I had this monologue I was really having a hard time with, and I remember him saying, "Well, just do it! What is she saying? What is she doing? Just go do it!" And it was one of the most freeing things. I think about that a lot: listen to what you're saying, and just do it. He opened that promise for me.

When you say in life that someone is "acting," you mean someone is phony—you don't believe them. That's why I wish we didn't have to use that word, *acting*. When I say, "Stop acting," which I say all the time, what I really mean is that I'm seeing something called emoting: a superficial indication of feeling, a surface action. So what are we? First of all, we tell a story. We're storytellers. Whatever you call it, that's what we are. And it has a great tradition. It started around a campfire. How do you tell a story? When we act the story out, when we do the story, we are doing. That's how we tell our story.

DANE DEHAAN (Actor, Former Student):
He stopped me and he said, "You're just doing your idea of the scene. It's your idea of how you think it should sound for it to be a good scene, but I don't care about what you're saying because you're not doing anything. What are you doing?" I said, "I'm trying to impress this guy, I'm trying to get him on my side." He said, "Well, start the scene over, and just go about your business, and look over at your acting partner, and if you feel like the words will help you get what you want, then say the words; but if you don't feel like the words will get you what you want, then don't say them, and don't say them until you feel like you need to say them."
    That was the day that I always look back on: the day that I really started to understand acting. Up until that point, I was a smart enough person

that I could read something and say it the way I thought it was supposed to be said, and it would sound fine and good and pleasant; but acting is really doing things, and you are capable of really affecting a person.

This is about really doing it. And I will keep reminding you of that, and why this will help you up the ladder towards what you want to accomplish.

Craft

How do you go about working on a role? Whatever your answer, that is your craft. Gerald championed the study and application of craft, while recognizing that over time, through the work, each actor will discover what works best for them.

I can teach you to be an actor in fifteen seconds. Here goes: What does your character want, and how does he/she go about getting it? That's all you need to know. I've just saved you four years of your time and thousands of dollars. If you can do that well, and in an interesting and truthful manner, you can leave now.

Then, you might ask, "Why am I going through a conservatory training program for four years?" We teach you a craft that will give shape to your doing.

This is an analogy I'm fond of using: You all can hammer a nail, or have tried to. You tentatively *tap, tap,* or give a wallop and miss the nail, or bend it, or it goes in crooked, or you hit your finger. In other words, you can all hammer in a nail, but I wouldn't call you carpenters. If I wanted to build a house, or construct a frame, I'd call me a trained carpenter, because with one stroke, he'd put the nail in the right place and it would hold. The result is efficient, economic, and often beautiful, because the carpenter has craft. He's developed a skill. Craft: what to do, and then, when to do it.

Talent is not a craft. Imagination needs tools in order to shape something. How you choose to use your work, your craft, together with your imagination, what you create, makes you an artist. Desire does not make you an artist. Craft coupled with imagination makes you an artist.

It is important to learn and study a process, because that is a starting point. Having a process—or craft—enables you to put your talent to use on demand, instead of waiting for a lightning bolt to strike. Craft is a how-to. Craft is how to use what you already possess.

Acting isn't mysterious. Your talent may be. Where does it come from? How do I get it to work for me at eight o'clock every night? And craft helps you get to that point to release your talent, or to support your talent, or to open up your talent. But without craft, it is very intangible.

MANDY PATINKIN (Actor, Former Student):
You always do the work. You never don't do it. Because inevitably, you will have a particular kind of day: a lost day, a hurt day, a thrilled day, a world's-in-trouble day, an exhausted day, an overly enthused day; and it won't have to do with the work. It'll sometimes help you, and sometimes not, but that's not the job. You need to do the work ahead of time.

What I want you to do is try to apply these principles and master this process, then go out and work it. I'm not saying this is the only way, or even the best way. This is the way I teach. Some of this will stick, some of this will be useful to you. Some of you will find other ways of getting into the work.

CHITA RIVERA (Actor, Dancer):
To get into a house, you can go in the front door, you can go in the window, you can go in the back door, you can go in through the basement, you can bust the bloody wall down—but you're in there. Everybody has their own technique and their own way.

Craft does not rule out subconscious discoveries. Those happen when you set the right behavior in action. Happy accidents can happen with your partner when you stay open to respond. Craft is not the end; it is a means towards an end. There is no end to what you can discover. Acting must always be open-ended. But with craft, the artist is in control.

NICHOLAS GALBRAITH (Marketing Director, Former Student):
Craft is how you work. Craft is the ability to wrestle with something and to try to define something for yourself, even if you don't come to an answer.

I want to create a thinking actor. He or she has to know how to break down a script, how to survive on one's own (a paradox, since I believe in collaboration and ensemble playing). You have to have a way of going at a role—a craft, in short. What you do with that craft is the measure of your art, your uniqueness.

I don't have the magic to make you an actor. I'm trying to help you refine the process, to give you benchmarks to do what you do. You have the answers. Right now, you know everything there is to know about acting. But what you don't know is how to ask the questions that will get this information out of you.

Who Am I?

For Gerald, acting is about discovering and sharing who you are. As he often said, the idea is simple, but achieving it is not.

I want to demystify it all. I don't find it simple. But it is simple.

Acting boils down to three things:

1. Find out "Who am I?" both as a character in a play, and in life.
2. Learn your lines.
3. Get out of the way of the play. The better the play, the less you have to do.

It's as simple, and as complicated, as that.

BILLY MAGNUSSEN (Actor, Former Student):
As long as you have a good grasp of what your job is—what your lines are, who your character is—then you're free to play the scene, and really just live it and listen and respond.

Acting is simple. It really isn't difficult, but getting to the simplicity, to just allowing yourself to respond, that's difficult. If you recognize the difficulty, you're on your way to letting go, to making a change. It's not about a great deal of energy. Mostly it's about relaxation. Opening up. Staying open. It's about uncovering your layers. It's not about going and finding out things. You've got it all. There's so much and so little you have to do to act.

CIGDEM ONAT (Teacher, Colleague):
Theater, I found out very young, is a gift I have. I liked being in and around it, and I liked that it made me visible. But it would always be a means, not an end, the means to a question, and the question was, "Who am I?"

In order to be a great actor, you must perpetually discover, "Who am I?" That's harder to answer than you might think. Most of us are attracted to acting initially, consciously or unconsciously, to hide. To hide behind the character, to hide behind showing off, to hide behind the clown, to hide behind the smile. But who, really, are you? That takes honesty, and courage, and a willingness to face the truth. And the truth produces clarity, which I put a high value on. We all talk about truth in acting, and that starts with facing the truth of yourself, and embracing it. Now, that may take you a lifetime. But it ought to start today.

Don't frown and get anxious: "When will I find the truth of myself?" I don't know the truth of myself. It's an ongoing journey. It's also about the good stuff, your strengths, your assets, your positive take on life. Know that coming through you, through your physical being, through your mental process, through your vocal equipment, it will be different. It is different from anybody else. When we say, "Use yourself," it's your *self* that is the unique part. Find the character in yourself.

KEVIN KLINE (Actor, Former Student):
Don't hide your light. Shine it! Take the stage and go full out with it, as opposed to tiptoeing around it, or doing it halfway. You're born with a capacity to understand that idea, but it takes doing it for a while to understand what real theater energy is. Not false energy, but fullness of spirit, fullness of focus and energy, and whatever else goes into that crazy thing we do called acting.

Acting is the only discipline in which you use yourself totally: your body, voice, and intellect are your instrument. A musician picks up his violin, and with a few little adjustments, his instrument is in tune. It takes at least twenty years to get an actor's instrument in tune. It takes twenty years to understand, to absorb, to make the craft an organic part of yourself.

JAKE LACY (Actor, Former Student):
You feel like you're realizing something on your own, and then you learn that it's an echo of something that someone was trying to teach you ten years earlier, and that finally that little seed they planted is starting to grow into something.

JERZY GWIAZDOWSKI (Actor, Former Student):
Just because you're in school for four years doesn't mean you're expected to emerge a fully formed creative entity. The expectation is that yes, you are now equipped to be a professional in the world, but many don't really reach that level of facility and ability until long after. And you're constantly relearning lessons in a deeper and more truthful way. Gerald wasn't educating people to finish their education by the time they graduate. He taught us to have a foundation of skills that we will be refining for the rest of our creative lives. That's the beauty of his approach to education, because it reflects his own approach to his work.

Other artists often don't understand the difference between how they use their instrument and how we have to use our instrument. You have to be patient, because it's about your body, your intellect, and your skills. It's about you and your individual achievement. It's about being the best of you.

Facing the truth of yourself, that's the task of becoming a real actor, and the tools that I offer are meant to help you along the way. Tools to pry you open, to discover who you really are, what you really feel. To work with clarity and honesty. Not answers. Tools.

The task is to learn the tools that will enable you to pursue your chosen profession with consistency and endurance and authority.

Bringing the Inner Instrument to Life

As Gerald taught, to live a full life onstage, your inner instrument must be primed and accessible in the moment. Personal connections must be forged. It's not about manufacturing feeling; it's about freeing what's already within you.

What John Houseman used me for at Juilliard, and what Jerry Robbins used me for on Broadway, was to bring the inner instrument to life. So I would come to Juilliard, and they were very competent and had many of the outer skills—good speech, good movement, a sense of the use of Alexander—but nothing was happening. Nothing was coming from the heart. That's what I opened up for them; that's what I've taught here at UNCSA, and in general, that's what I do.

I was working with a student who was playing Octavius in a production of *Man and Superman* that I was directing. The text demands that he cries. The actor had no access to it, so I asked questions:

"Have you ever been in love?"

"Have you ever been in love with someone who didn't return it?"

"What about high school? Think about that."

And then he had an emotional response. He had no idea. *I* had no idea, but I know young people. If you haven't had that kind of experience, you're probably dead, because we all have. It was a crack in the cement of his understanding. It gave him an idea of what the character needed to do. He didn't really open himself up, and there isn't time in a rehearsal period, but it gave him some idea of where he had been and where he needed to go.

My approach lets actors look for the character in themselves: "What do I have that is like this character?" "How do I understand in my own mind the things that affected that mood of the character I'm playing?" "What about me is similar to the character?" I often help an actor understand that there is much more of himself that he can use than he may think. I try to point out the many similarities that may have escaped the actor, sometimes because of careless analysis of character. He may think, "Oh, I'm nothing like that," and then you begin to show him that he and the character are very much alike.[6]

CHITA RIVERA (Actor, Dancer):
I sang "A Boy Like That," and Jerry said, "Chita, don't you have two brothers?" I started to sing again, and it was the first time in my life that I seriously related to something that was real. I was just singing lyrics before. My brother's name and the image of my brothers came straight forward in my mind, and I started to be affected by it. Gerald said, "Keep going, Chita." And I'm going. I was living in between the two worlds. Jerry took me there. As I got more and more affected, I started to back up. I was physically trying to get out, because I was totally exposed. I had never been exposed before, the innards of myself. That was the first time I touched my subconscious mind, and I knew what real life was, and what acting was. And it was through Gerald Freedman that that happened. Then he had to

teach me how to pull back, how to not explode, and let the audience do that—not you. That stuck with me forever, because it was my first.

ANNA WOOD (Actor, Former Student):
When we did *West Side Story*, I had a really hard time connecting with the anger that Maria experienced, and the rage and the sorrow, after Tony kills her brother. I personally, up until that point, hadn't experienced any great loss in my life. And I didn't really know how to get angry. Gerald was trying to help me, pushing me, giving me tools. Then one day, finally, he was like, "You know what? We've been working and working on this. It's not happening. I'm very frustrated with you." And he asked me to push him. Physically push him. I think at the time he was eighty-two. And I thought, I could never possibly do this to this small old man. And he was like, "Do it! Push me!" And I was like, "I'm so scared to push you." And he was like, "If you don't connect with something within yourself, something physical, and communicate to the audience the rage that you're feeling, then the story is going to fall through." And I pushed him. And he kept encouraging me to push him harder and harder. And honestly, as scared as I was to push him, to hurt him, he wanted me to. And for me it was a huge breakthrough in physicalizing and communicating the rage that he wanted me to find, that I needed to find to tell the story.

CAROL LAWRENCE (Actor, Singer):
Jerry made it clear that if you can get to the visceral part of your being, and make that an identifiable place in the character's heart, then it's an easy jump to get to what really moves you, what really is the most personal.

If you can't get it into your body, it doesn't mean anything. It's about the stuff that's in your muscles and—although it sounds esoteric—in your heart. That's where it ends up. And you can't study for that, because you're absorbing it. That's what I mean by process. It's this everyday *drip, drip, drip,* "I get it!" That's why we rehearse.

Onstage, you often want to "feel" something. You are not working for feelings. You are discovering them, letting them happen. Don't work for emotion. Work for the truthfulness of the scene, and then, usually, the emotion comes.

I want to train artists of the spirit. You have to have an enlarged emotional language, a bigger outlook than craft seems to imply. So this will be a process of discovery. I know the kind of artist I want to produce. How to make that happen is the challenge.

Commit

The ability to choose what you want to do—and then follow through—is vital to a successful life, onstage and off. As Gerald urged his actors and students, take the initiative. If you hold back, you'll never know if it's going to work.

Commit yourself to a choice. Do it. There's no testing unless an actor commits. You may be reluctant to commit if:

- You're afraid of making a mistake
- You want to get it right

Just going through a rehearsal is never sufficient. You have to commit. If you don't, you can't find out anything. Rehearsal isn't less work or less commitment than a performance. Commit. It isn't difficult. Step over the threshold and *make it happen.* Then it becomes easy. Then you find out what's really there.

Be Specific

In performance, rehearsal, and discussion, Gerald encouraged his students to get in the habit of being as specific as possible. He asked that they strive for specificity in all they said and did.

[At the Actors Studio] I learned a great respect for Lee [Strasberg]'s method of criticism. He always asked the actor what he was working on, and his observations were scrupulously limited to that end. He never allowed you to say, "I liked it," or "It was good," or "It was bad." Your comments had to be specific in craft terms. This is still my method in rehearsals and in the classroom.

I put a high value on the words that we communicate with, on the exact thing you want to say. Communicate with clarity and demand it of each other. The essence of acting is to be specific, absolutely specific. The more specific you are, the more universal you are.

When I ask, "What do you want?" and your answer begins with, "Kind of," I can tell you—"Kind of" will get you no information. Be specific! Commit!

Stop using the words *good* and *bad*. Be specific. What did you see and how do you find the language to describe it accurately, not in generalizations? There's too much generalization in the world as it is. We're beginning to think in sound bites. We think we have information when all we have is sound bites. So, language is very important and you will think about it differently in my training.

JAKE LACY (Actor, Former Student):
I remember distinctly that he had such an appreciation for the words. He kept telling everyone to slow down, and to think, and to stop. Because, in retrospect, he had taken so much time to be thorough, clear, and concise about what he wanted to communicate, and had boiled it down into a single sentence, and wanted the students to be able to grasp what he was trying to share with them.

Listening and Talking

Gerald prized listening and talking as cornerstones of truthful acting. He would point out that actors often pretend to listen and talk, rather than really do it. When you're pretending, it's hard work. But when you are truly talking and listening, it's easy, because you don't have to pretend; all you have to do is engage with your partner and respond.

You find out in rehearsal what you can't find out in your room. You find that you have a partner. Add what the script can't add: the power of the actor in the space.

We need each other onstage. You cannot act alone. Your salvation is in the other actor. If you're concentrating on the other actor—listening, talking, responding—you will find the answers for yourself.

You are often *listening*, but not *hearing*. Active listening is hearing the specific items mentioned within a point of view. When we listen actively, there is a possibility of conflict, of give and take—and this is drama.

ANNA CAMP (Actor, Former Student):
I'll never forget *Man and Superman*, because it was the first time I really actively listened through the ears of my character. I remember one night during a show, it was the scene where I find out that I'm not gonna get any money from my fiancé. And I let out an audible gasp. I had no lines in that

moment, but I was really listening as Violet, who wanted money so bad, and I let out this little audible gasp, and I remember the whole audience laughed and laughed. I didn't even realize what had happened. Gerald gave me a big pat on the back afterwards, and was like, "See, see, that's funny: listening!"

The thing that separates the very, very good actors from the ordinary actors is concentration. Those people who are able to absolutely zero in on the other actor and go after what they want command the audience's attention. I don't know why that is, but you can feel it in the theater. In a generally good performance, suddenly the audience will be holding their breath because one of the actors really locks in and really focuses.

Talk and listen to each other as if for the first time, not a repeat. Make the play happen onstage! That is the essence of the performer's art. It's not about pretending, it's about opening yourself up to listen.

CAROL LAWRENCE (Actor, Singer):
His first direction was, "You must listen to every single word, every single need of the other character. Every time you look them in the eye, it has to be with interest, and you have to impart that to him as well so that it's real, and it's in the second, not in the moment." It's wonderful to think that what he gave me fifty years ago still works on the stage.

I stopped an actor and I said, "No, no, no, you're not talking to her." "Yes I am!"
"No, you're not. You're looking at her, but you're not seeing her."
"I'm looking right at her!"
And I said, "What color are her eyes?" He had no idea. Because looking isn't pointing your face in the same direction, it's seeing. SEEING. You understand the difference? And you have to remind yourself of the difference, and not fall into that trap of listening but not hearing, of looking but not seeing.

JAKE LACY (Actor, Former Student):
We spent ninety percent of our rehearsal time at the table, working on text and talking to people, and as a cast, we were like, "This is insane. We are never going to have a production." And he stopped everyone again, and was like, "You all are so upset that I keep stopping you, but if I wanted to just stage this, I could stage it in two days. We don't need three weeks. You're

not going to learn anything from three weeks of running a staged play where you're not talking to each other. What is the point of doing that?"

You'll always look better when you help your partner look better. It takes the concentration off of yourself and your problem, and shifts it onto your partner. So immediately, you have a connection. You're not just playing an action, you're playing it in order to get something from someone. It's a two-way street.

The audience's attention goes to wherever your attention is. If your concentration is on how you're producing the sound, that's where the audience's attention will be—I promise you. So when you feel your concentration slipping, get back in touch with the other character.

When you speak a line, communicate. Talk; do not emote. You get it from the other by letting them affect you.

MATT BULLUCK (Teacher, Former Student):
Talking is affecting your partner. Listening is being affected by your partner.

REBECCA NAOMI JONES (Actor, Former Student):
I think the kind of talking and listening that Gerald was referencing is allowing yourself to be fully present with what another person is saying to you, with their speech, and with their body language, and with their actions, and responding to that earnestly.

If I invest in the other person, and let it come, instead of thinking about how I will say it, that's the fun—that's where the real spontaneity comes from.

Sometimes you get so worked up about your objective ("I'm playing my objective!") that you forget to see. Once you think, "Am I doing this? Am I playing an action?" you're out of it. When that happens, you have to be brave enough to put everything in the other.

It can't all be done at once. It's not about compartmentalizing, it's about staying in the moment.

JOHN LANGS (Director, Former Student):
No acting, just listening and talking. Don't put anything on it. Just stay open to the person. Let's create a culture of real talking and listening in this room, and then it can slowly move, and then you'll develop the

moments. But don't try to put something there, because then you're not really in the room with the other person, and there's nothing more important than that.

You have to do it. I can't talk about it, you can't hear it and understand it. It's about you *doing* it. Every time you're in rehearsal or in class, ask, "Am I doing this? Am I really hearing? Did I hear the last five things that she said?" It's about exercising that muscle and knowing the difference.

ANNALEE JEFFRIES (Actor, Guest Teacher):
Listening is key to acting. It is active participation. It is generous. It's hard to do. But a good listener onstage can make an audience's eyes go right over to them. Listening is doing, too, in a big way.

Listening and talking. It's become the mantra of my training. It sounds obvious, although many of my students leave still trying to achieve it: listening and talking. The bottom line of what we do.

Being in the Moment

Gerald knew that being in the moment is what makes us fully alive. The moment is not mired in the past or the future. The moment is one of a kind, right here, right now—and anything can happen.

You have to love that each night it's going to be different. You have to love that each time you get up, each moment, it's going to be different; but if you do the work, it should still tell the story. And if you don't love it, if you don't get enjoyment out of that, it's going to be a very difficult world to live in. Because that's what it is. You have to enjoy the IN THE MOMENT experience.

MANDY PATINKIN (Actor, Former Student):
The thrill of it is that it's never the same, ever. Nothing is in stone. The accidents are our gold. They give us and teach us everything.

GLORIA BIEGLER (Actor, Teacher):
You're saying the same words every night. You're doing the same lines, the same blocking, the same thing, night after night after night. But within the structure that has been established, you have to be living freely, as though it's never happened before.

The ideal in theater is to play moment to moment. Staying alive to the people in the room to respond. It's a game. It's a trick. Part of your head knows exactly what you're doing, and part of your head says, "I don't know what my next line is."

It's *as if* you don't know what's next, what line is next. It's a trick of the art, and it can be done. But you have to keep tricking yourself. You have to constantly make those adjustments. Stay in the moment. That's work.

If you are *waiting* for an impulse, you're *generating* an impulse. Say yes to what's going on. Accept all your thoughts during a performance. Accept all your thoughts as the character's thoughts.

REBECCA NAOMI JONES (Actor, Former Student):
I remember feeling in school like I was failing if I had a thought during the work, during a scene, that was my own, that was Rebecca. But then I remember at some point in school, Gerald was like, "You're always going to be a combination of you and the character. It's gonna be you," Rebecca/ [the character]. And hopefully, most days, it's gonna be mostly [the character] and a little bit of Rebecca, but you have to bring what you know and who you are to every character.

Let your thoughts continue. Trust your subconscious; the mind is an amazing machine. It remembers a lot.

You don't know what the next moment is going to be. And every moment you have to be totally there. Just worry about how to be truthful, how to really be present. You have to be always present.

ASHLEY GATES JANSEN (Teacher, Former Student):
The big one for me is the present moment. In the theater, to be present is to be free and unlimited. And for me, that's the invitation for how to live your life. How am I showing up in this moment, and what would happen if I didn't control it? Control is what we do because we're scared. Control is the belief that "I can't just allow this moment to be, because

it will hurt me." I thought that for a long time, and I was wrong. Life isn't here to hurt us; it's here to heal us. And we're only going to taste that in the present moment.

Letting Go

The temptation is to try to make something happen, rather than allow something to happen. Gerald would often remind his students that giving up control does not mean giving up the work you've done; it means trusting the work you've done and taking the leap.

Another element of craft that few of you master in four years is *allowing*, letting go. A carpenter doesn't think about the hammer and the nail; he raises his hammer and brings it down on the nail and drives it in with the strength, pressure, and speed appropriate to the task. He counts on his craft. He lets go of thinking about it. If you're thinking, "Is this right?" while you're doing, you're automatically wrong! Most of you spend all your energy thinking, "Is this right?" rather than *allowing*, or just doing.

This does not leave out the importance of preparation, drill, practice, or learning better ways—more efficient ways—of performing a task. *Then* comes the doing and the allowing, the letting go. Talk yourself out of thinking that rehearsal needs to be good or right. There's no admission to get in. For one night, let yourself be free.

JOSIE DE GUZMAN (Actor, Singer):
He said, "I don't want you to edit yourself at all. I don't want you to think. I just want you to *do*, to *act*, just whatever comes, let it happen." So I went and I did it, and he said, "You're not doing what I'm asking you to do. I don't want you to stand outside yourself and look at yourself while you're doing this. I want you to just go."

I guess I didn't understand him the first time, and he demonstrated a little bit. But I did what he asked me to do the second time, and it was the most amazing acting experience I've ever had. I did not know where I was. I just went from moment to moment, so that everything happened spontaneously. No thought, just being and doing. It changed my life as an actor.[7]

It's all about opening yourself up to your own impulses, to the givens, to each other.

It's all about giving up control. Be willing to not have it look like anything in particular. Most actors are not comfortable with giving up control—that's another paradox. In order to accomplish some of this work, to even understand some of it, you need a sense of control, and then you need to give up that control. Trust it to be there, because you have done the preparation. Then, deal with the other person and what you want to achieve. It will happen. You simply have to trust.

MANDY PATINKIN (Actor, Former Student):
If you're really on your game, you're doing nothing in that moment, because you've done the work, and now you can forget about it, because it's you, it's in you. If you've really done the work, if you're really working well, you're able to be there for what your partner's going to do. And then you can respond and react. And then the magic happens, because you don't know what they're going to do.

Finally, the closer you get to really good acting, the farther away you are from control of it. You don't have to know what you're doing if you've done the work. Permit the experience. Flip the switch and let it go.

Staying True to Your Text

Gerald's methodology always comes back to the text. The text is your guide for every aspect of creative expression.

Always stay true to your text. Whether you're doing *Our Town* or *Piano Lesson*, *Chekhov in Yalta*, *What the Butler Saw*, or Moliere, or Shakespeare, this is the way you go about each of those different tasks. You may say, "Shakespeare acting isn't like *Piano Lesson*." No, it's not. But what makes it different is in the language. It's in the text. So if you really invest in the language, it will take you in different directions.

Don't waste the words. Make the words your own. The words endow you, and you endow the words. You can't just justify the line, you have to justify the life.

Pauses are overused by actors—in particular, modern actors, who I think are most of the time working with underwritten texts, so they have to pause to give something some meaning. But within these plays of language, and not just Shakespeare—I mean Mamet, or Beckett, or Pinter, for instance—the pauses are built in, so pauses have to be used very discreetly and creatively. In the rehearsal process, in the deconstruction of it, there are often pauses so that you can understand what the hell the text is about, so that you can understand what's happening. But then you have to put it back together, and often that step is forgotten. Let the thoughts come faster. Don't play the pauses. The pause is in the language.

Style

Gerald often referenced Sir John Gielgud's saying: "Style is knowing what play you are in." The style of a performance need not be preset; it can be discovered as a natural evolution of exploring the text.

As far as I am concerned, the best way to approach style is not to approach it at all. By that I mean, the best way to achieve a play's style is to achieve it honestly, from the bottom up, from the heart out, not to superimpose it, not to apply it like varnish.[8] Style is what emanates from working honestly from the specific material. It comes *from* rather than settling *on top of* character.[9]

DANE DEHAAN (Actor, Former Student):
Gerald taught that there are different styles, but what it boils down to is really doing things within the world of the play.

I think style is what emanates from the language and from the structure of the play, from working truthfully from the material. The style will emerge; it should not be thought of as being appliquéd. Obviously, if you read a scene from *West Side Story*, it has different texture, a different weight, a different size from a scene in an O'Neill play. The difference doesn't mean one should be treated with less reality, with less truth.[10]

There's no need to predetermine a stylistic quality that makes for the difference. With either show, you start with the initial questions and a layered or *unified* approach, so that you're always thinking of them as related.[11]

LOGAN FAHEY (Actor, Former Student):
The style is written. You don't have to worry about it. It's in the words. So in really going for what you want as the character in relation to these other people, it reveals itself.

You have to be truthful in the moment, in the situation. In the given circumstances. Commit yourself to it. It's not naturalistic, it's not about bringing it down to your reality, and it's not acting big or theatrical. It's responding to your partner in a truthful manner, in the given circumstances of the play.

PATTI LUPONE (Actor, Former Student):
It's the style that's different. I don't think the emotion is different. It may be different in as much as you express yourself according to the times, according to the period, but the heart beats universally.

Because of the clothes you wear, how that dictates your body movement, how social mores and customs dictate how close you come to somebody, how you relate to them. That is what we see as style, not some imitated movement. If one does not leap to results but lets the character emerge through behavior and relationships, a more interesting and complex person is discovered.[12]

Actors have to deal with something in which they can believe. They have to deal with many ideas, objects, and people. They have to suggest various levels of commitment. They have to move with inner logic. They cannot be made to do things simply because they fit a certain style. If their behavior is truthful to the action of a scene and to the play as a whole, and if this truth is applied as well to all aspects of the production, a style for the play will emerge.[13] We cannot deny the truth of human behavior. When you try to rule that out, that's when you get stiff acting and artificial stuff.

The pursuit of style does not preclude the absence of truth. Style comes from the text, from language, from behavior.

An Actor at the Table

Gerald's rehearsal process typically began around a table, with table work, as further discussed in chapter 6, "Directing." At Gerald's table, discoveries were not spoon-fed. He demanded that actors dig in and conduct their own exploration. The table is a place for actors to connect not only with the text, but with each other.

DEBBIE ALLEN (Actor, Director):
What I learned from Jerry that really changed my understanding about approaching theater, and any role, is the work that you do at the table. We sat at that table, and we were not allowed to get up or think about staging a scene until we had really examined that text, examined those characters, built those circumstances, knew the questions of each character: "Who am I? Why am I? What do I want?"

I feel you have to go through a lot of layers at the table that will then free you when you get up.

I hate it when people are buried in their script. I know you can read. That's not what the work is about. It's about, "What are you saying? What does it mean to you?" So you need to be looking up, and not down at your script.

QUIN GORDON (Teacher, Former Student):
He'd always encourage people to take it off the page in that first read, because the relationships start there. In the first read, you start endowing your partner as your mother, or your brother, or your lover. Otherwise everybody's face is just buried in their scripts, and then they're really just saying lines, you know? From day one it's gotta be about, "What am I doing to my partner, and what is my partner doing to me?" And it takes more time, sure, but it's well worth it.

JEREMY WEBB (Actor, Former Student):
I'm actually starting by looking at you across the table, and we have the freedom in that moment to have the discussion about what we're doing. It's like laying out the map of battle in the tent with the other generals and captains around the table the night before the war. It's where we conspire together, where we get confidential and giggle and argue about what we're doing. That's what's useful about the table work.

Let's say I'm an actor at the table. I'm looking at my next line without hearing or looking at my scene partner. How can I know until I hear? Now, of course, I read the play. I knew what he was going to say. And I know what I'm going to say. But I don't know how he's going to look. I don't know what's in his eyes. I don't know the inflection. I don't know anything about it until he's finished speaking, and then I can look down and see, "Oh, that's what my next line is."

ANITA GILLETTE (Actor, Singer):
It gave you a chance, before you got on your feet, to know what you were saying. I mean really know, in the true sense of the word, deeply, because we didn't get up until we were almost ready to perform it.

Working with a Director

There are many sorts of directors, and Gerald knew it was important for actors to learn how to interpret a wide variety of direction. Whatever their method, virtually all directors appreciate actors who understand their responsibility and take initiative, rather than waiting to be told what to do.

You have to learn to work with a director and a fellow actor, just like I have to learn to work with actors with all kinds of training. You have to translate what the director says. Don't expect them to talk in your language. It is as if you were in another country. I was in Japan with a friend who spoke some Japanese, and she was using a Japanese-English dictionary. I didn't speak any Japanese. She asked a man for directions, and he explained to her where to go. As he spoke, she started flipping through her dictionary to try to figure out what he was talking about. All I did was watch his hands, and I knew exactly where he wanted us to go. So that's what it's about. What does he really want? What is he talking about? Translate. I didn't need to know Japanese.

Some directors don't know anything about an actor's craft, and don't care. And they're great directors. They have a vision, a conceptual idea, that if you bring a craft to what they do, it'll result in a great theater piece. Many directors won't work the way I do; they won't use this language. But whatever language they do use, you often have to convert what the director is saying into what you understand. That is not because he's a dope and you're brilliant, it's because you have a craft.

Being able to take an adjustment is exemplary of true professional behavior, that you as artists have the ability to take direction—quite simply, to not get so stuck in a groove that you can't move off the dime. It's important, it's necessary, and it's something that I don't think is taught much anymore, if at all.

I do act from time to time, because I want to know what it feels like to be an actor again. And when I do, I lend myself to the director with total openness. You can say anything to me, and I will do it. I don't hold back. I don't hesitate. I just do it. They're totally in charge. It's easier than you think. What I feel an actor should be is a trained instrument.

The director says, "I want you over here now." You don't say, "Well, I don't believe her." You have to figure it out. With integrity. Yes, you have to go over there, and it can't be a blank space when you move there—you have to fill it.

Bring something intelligent and thought-through to be considered by the director. That's really what you do in a rehearsal.

HAL HOLBROOK (Actor):
I don't depend on a director to tell me what to do. I come to rehearsal really well-prepared to begin with. I know exactly what I want to do. I have a very good concept of what I want to do with a role. I've researched it and thought about it a great deal. I've properly learned all the lines, before I ever come to rehearsal. Before I come to the first rehearsal, I've done a great deal of work myself.

Working with Hal Holbrook, who was very well prepared, I was still able to open him up to additional thoughts that he had never had, or that he had buried deeper, so that some of it was still an area of discovery for him. He still had significant things he hadn't thought of, because they were too personal. And he was very grateful for that. And I think it changed his way of working. I gave him something new. He hadn't worked this way before. He was open enough to realize that and put it to use.

As an actor, you're presenting your choices, or you should be, for the director's observation. And if they don't say anything, you must be on the right track. So then you can start adding things. And that's another one of those paradoxes: as an actor, you have to be both passive and active.

ROBERT STATTEL (Actor):
He said, "Take over. As opposed to being an obedient servant," which is what I had been until then. He really freed me. I remember him saying that, and I had never thought of it before: "Start being the disobedient one. Take over. Let your spirit shine."

LEE GRANT (Actor, Director):
All of my favorite directors said, "Surprise me." If you're secure with a director, then you can go any place with them, and you do surprise them. That's part of the joy, that you take it to a place that they didn't expect, and that you didn't expect. Jerry takes your hand, and says "Go. Fly. I'll pick you up if you fall. But fall if you want to. Don't be safe." And what more can an actor want than to fly?

As actors, really at rehearsal, you're working. That's your work time. That's when we say you can't be wrong. And you can make a fool of yourself, you can ask a dead-end question, but you can't be wrong. That's the workplace. Oh, did I offend you? Oh, did I go too fast? Then we learned something. So now I know something more about this moment than I knew before. But if you wait to be told, nothing can happen.

CHITA RIVERA (Actor, Dancer):
You have to forgive some things that happen in rehearsals, because you're exploring. That's your time to make mistakes.

Each rehearsal, you have to bring something. You can't just go home, come back, and start where you were yesterday. What happened in rehearsal today that you have to bring back additional work on tomorrow? That takes time.

RAY VIRTA (Actor, Teacher):
Be fully prepared. Bring ideas to the table. Understand that when you go into rehearsal, if Gerald asks you to run a section again, he's not asking you to repeat; he's asking you to develop. Gerald demanded that you take responsibility, and that you do it.

Only you can know what you're doing. I can observe you, I can tell you what I'm seeing or what I'm hearing, but only you know what your inner mechanism is doing. You are in charge! Not the director, not anyone else. And this takes practice, too. That's part of disciplining yourself.

Making the Work Your Own

Gerald had no interest in training automatons who would blindly follow his code. The ideas in this book have no value if they remain merely words on a page. When you read them, and think about them, and wrestle with them, that's when they become useful. Try to bring these ideas into your work. Forge them anew in your own language. Find out how they live in YOU.

The work doesn't mean anything unless you internalize it and personalize it. It's not enough to repeat my wording of something. You have to understand what it's about. You can repeat it back by rote, but what do you understand from it? You have to *apply* the work.

WILL ROGERS (Actor, Former Student):
He's often said, "The homework doesn't matter if you don't personalize it. You can do all the homework in the world, but if you don't have imagination, then it doesn't matter."

Now, you can't do all of it at once when you're learning it. And you can't do all of it at the same level when you're learning it. But what can I do, leave something out of the training? No. You have to at least hear it and know it, and it will fall into place, hopefully, eventually.

JEREMY WEBB (Actor, Former Student):
Jerry's approach, or my version of it, has become my approach, completely. His feelings about art and acting and what's important about them have become comingled with my own instincts, and my own impulses, and my own ideas about theater. Over time I've turned it into something that's more personal that works for me.

There's a time in all this work, this work we're doing here, where you're very self-conscious. You're watching yourself all the time. You're trying to become aware. And you have to commit to that in order to get to the next step. That's what this work is meant to do. It is to get conscious of what you're doing. It's the paradoxical thing again. Finally, it's about letting go. I've had people—actors—write to me three years later to say, "Now I understand what you were talking about." Suddenly, in the process of working, they found out what it meant. And I'm grateful. I'm thrilled that finally it landed. I know it's valid.

Auditions

According to Gerald, the key to auditions is to focus not on booking the job, but on sharing who you are and what you can do. Whether someone likes you or thinks you are right for a particular role is out of your hands.

You have to go in and do your best. People almost never do their best work [at auditions], but if you go in, and you've prepared, and you learned your stuff, and you did the job, that's all you can do. It rarely is the thing that's going to sell you. It's a combination of how you look, how you read, your intelligence, and your behavior that gives somebody the confidence to give you the part.

You may not be what they're looking for that day for that project, but if you impress them by being a good actor, they'll remember you for the next one. That's the important part.

You may not get the final callback for a lot of reasons, none of which may have anything to do with your talent. They may need someone who's six feet tall, or who's got to be really short.

Don't try to be what they want. Make a strong, honest choice, and then *do* it, and let the chips fall where they may.

JOHN CULLUM (Actor, Singer):
When I'm working with an actor who's getting ready to do an audition in New York, people try to figure out, "What is the role? What are they looking for? And how should I approach it so that I can convince them that I'm right for this role?" And so they spend all their time thinking, usually, about how they can please the director; and what I say to them is, "Look at this role, figure out what you like about the role and what you think you can do with the role, and do it that way. That way, if you go in and do what you think you'd like to do with the role yourself—without thinking about what you think the director wants, or the producer wants, or how it's going to be done on Broadway—if you go in with your own idea, everybody benefits. Because you're not trying to create something that you're not fit for. You're creating something that you think is right, and you will do the best job you can to show them what you have to offer. That way the director may not agree with what you're doing, but he sees you, and he sees what you can bring to it. So you're bringing to the role your best quality. And don't worry about what he thinks. Worry about what you think. Go in and do what you think is right. Then they know what you can do."

They are looking for someone who will make them look good. Everybody at that moment is in a risk situation, and although you may not approve of it, money is a big factor. Everybody's at risk at that moment. It may not be the greatest artistic statement, but everybody is putting themselves on the line. They want to be sure that they're right, that you're right. But they're looking for help, in a sense.

When I went to auditions, I went for people with talent, not for their names, ever.

Nobody wants to be told that a scene is bad or that it doesn't work. They're casting this. They're involved. Your job is to do it. If you make it work, it's because you brought something to it, not because you were critical of it.

Sometimes a director will throw you an adjustment just to see if you are flexible enough to adjust. It may not even be what they want, but they've got to see if you can take a direction, if you can pick up on something, rather than repeat the same thing.

Try not to psych them out. Just be there, hear what they're asking, and do it. When you start to try to figure it out, it inevitably leads you in the wrong direction—I can almost guarantee it—because you're misreading what they're saying. Just do what they're saying. Try not to edit or reconstitute or think they want this or that. Just do it. Let them make the decision.

Make a strong and clear choice, not an arbitrary one. It's not just to be different; that doesn't get you anywhere either. It's within the logic of the scene.

As readers, you're not acting in the scene. You're giving as much as will help the other person.

Outside of the Rehearsal Hall

Gerald always knew that being a great theater artist requires more than just working in the theater. In order to create a character of depth and substance, you must be one yourself.

As an actor, you have to remain curious. You can't be an interesting actor or director if you're not an interesting person. You must read; be aware of what is happening in your world. Go to museums, hear concerts, observe dance. You have to expose yourself to a lot. If you're not curious as an actor, I don't think you'll be very successful. You have to understand that the world is made up of a lot of people, with a huge range of experience. It's our job to hold the mirror up to nature.

Reading is essential. You can't be an actor just by living off your inner life. It is a stretching and an exercising of your imagination, and your imagination is stimulated by painting, by music, by dance, by literature, by history, by archaeology—by everything, in short. An actor needs to be an enriched human being. It is the inner resources you draw upon as an actor, not a narrow group of surface techniques.

KEVIN KLINE (Actor, Former Student):
It's important for actors to expose themselves to the best that there is to see. If you just have a steady diet of sitcoms on television, and that's your point of reference, then that's going to naturally influence your work. Exposing yourself to the best that's out there, it will influence you. It's learning what to do with that influence. It has to be distilled into something that is yours.

You have to enrich your cultural understanding and your education all the time, because you pull from so many places that you don't even know of, all the time. If you have nothing to pull from, then you have nothing to contribute.

Gerald directing Jordan Brown as Tony in *West Side Story*, with directing student Nicolas Townsend observing, onstage at the Roget L. Stevens Center in Winston-Salem, North Carolina in 2007.

CHAPTER FOUR

TECHNIQUE

Working organically with the text, talking and listening, and really doing things are the central tenets of Gerald's training. But Gerald knew that strong, specific, consistent acting also requires technique: a precise, result-oriented way of working technically from the outside in. Ultimately, Gerald's goal was not for technique to remain separate or external, but rather for it to become innate, to fuse with and support the doing.

We're talking about technical achievement, not truthful acting, not natural instinct. We're talking about mastering techniques that will enhance your ability. Don't confuse it with acting. It's not acting.

It is not antithetical to the truth. It is not antithetical to character work. It is simply a skill, like finger exercises. You have to do finger exercises to get your fingers limber before you can play a Chopin étude. Then you have all the problems of the étude itself: what does it mean, how do I feel about it, how am I going to phrase it? But you still have to get your fingers going with the agility that will enable you to play the piece at all. You do exercises, whatever will stretch your fingers. That's what this is. Look at it from a skill point of view.

When you take tennis lessons, you're very conscious of the grip and how your hand is and where your body is as you swing, but when you're playing a game, your eye is on the ball—and if you've practiced enough, your body is doing it. Do you understand? As you do your exercise over and over again, it gets in your muscles and you don't have to think about it. In performance, you shouldn't think about it. You can't anymore.

I know this sounds artificial. I'm asking you to sound artificial so you can isolate the technique. This work is about raising your consciousness of what you're doing. These are self-conscious exercises to make you aware. An artist must be aware before they can be fully unaware.

There is no great mystery about it. If you do it more often, you will get better at it, like anything else you do.

This is breaking down into technique what we already do naturally in life. It's being broken down to a place where you can control it, and then master it, extend it, and do incredible feats, because now you understand the process. It's getting control of your art. That's what it's all about.

When You Learn a New Technique

Gerald knew that it can't all be done at once. He cautioned that when you focus on a new technique, other elements of your work may fall by the wayside. Ultimately it's about putting everything together, but as you are learning, give yourself permission to isolate one piece of the puzzle at a time.

Technique's imposition may cause truth to take a temporary hiatus. When you learn a new technique, you tend to forget everything else you've learned, and I understand that that happens. This is all a layered approach. It's another layer to add.

You work on comedy, classic text, and camera work consciously. That doesn't mean that you don't do inner work, that you don't have to know where you're coming from, what you need, what you want from the other character, what your intention is, et cetera. The overlay is technique—how to enhance it, how to sharpen it. So we're working at both ends. It's a little bit of a seesaw until you become really adept at it. And when you're really adept at it, you lose your self-consciousness. It's in your muscles.

These are *techniques*—skills. As you work on them, they will seem artificial and untruthful. They need to become part of your muscle memory, so they become like breathing: natural, organic.

You sensitize yourself to one aspect at a time, and then eventually put it all together.

These are purely technical exercises. There are things you really can't talk about; you have to do them. It's all in the doing. If you observe the effect of it and you become aware of it, then you'll become more adept at it.

This is consciously taking technique and incorporating it into truthful acting. Don't play the technique before the truth. Technique *reveals* the truth.

COMEDY TECHNIQUE

Gerald formed these techniques from his training with Alvina Krause and his own experience and observation. While these techniques lend themselves most readily to comedy on the stage, they can be applied to many modes of theater, television, and film.

Comedy technique is a skill in delivering comedy.

All comedy depends on surprise. It's not knowing what is going to happen. That's what makes us laugh. Even a slip on a banana peel—we usually laugh at that because it comes as a surprise. We didn't expect it. Surprise releases a response that is usually laughter. (If somebody falls and doesn't get up, that becomes something different.)

The same is true of lines. The twist at the end, a word, or an unexpected response—it's the release of it. You may not want the audience to know where you're going, and then you give it a flip at the end, a surprise at the end. That has often to do with a rhythmic trick, as it were.

MATT BULLUCK (Teacher, Former Student):
What he said to me about comedy a zillion times is, "It's all based on surprise." Now, when I say that to students and they say, "I agree," I don't even like hearing them say "I agree." It's like telling them there is such a thing as gravity and having them say "I agree." It's not a matter of agreeing to gravity, it's a law, just like surprise in comedy is a law.

WILL ROGERS (Actor, Former Student):
The biggest rule with comedy is surprise, and that comes down to not being ahead of yourself, allowing yourself to be surprised. It's not just about surprising the audience, but allowing yourself to not see what's coming, even though you've done it eight shows a week. Really, when it comes

down to it, you can only say your lines one word at a time, and you have
to be acting on the line. If the punch line is coming in the next sentence,
I can't know it's about to come; I have to fool myself into just believing in
that one moment right then.

In a live performance, I could point all these things out, like with
Carol Burnett, or Lucile Ball. Most of this is verbal humor, rather than
physical humor, dealing with lines. Maggie Smith is one of the true and
great practitioners of this technique.

I think of these as acting exercises. These are technical things that I
learned, and that I still find valid. Although they're used in any dramatic
text, I think they're particularly useful in comedy. They are technical
things that can enhance your ability to play comedy.

There are always exceptions. In comedy, different people come up
with original ways of doing things, or they have special, unique proper-
ties of their own rhythms that we learn to accept as funny; but these are
broad, general techniques that will work for you.

BRIAN SUTOW (Actor, Former Student):
Because I was someone who already thought I had some comedic instincts, I remember initially being somewhat resistant to what Gerald was
saying. In retrospect I realize that I was feeling a little threatened. And I
think it's a struggle that a lot of funny people go through, because your
comedic voice is unique and personal. "Aren't these outsider's tools going
to mess up something that's so specific and unique to me?" But of course
that's ridiculous. An athlete doesn't assume that going to practice and
running drills is going to diminish their natural abilities. Just the opposite!
And it's the same with these skills. The more I've worked with other artists
and taught other artists, the more I've realized how essential these skills
are in helping to clarify, share, and enhance someone's comic abilities.

Lifting the Important Word

Lifting the important word is about giving it an extra boost so that the
audience registers it. If every word has equal emphasis, the audience
really understands nothing.

The whole idea is to lead me through your thought process, whatever
it is. Go to the important word. I do it in everything I say. I can't help it
when I'm trying to communicate an idea.

We all do it naturally in conversation. We just naturally go to the important word we want to emphasize. Because we're talking in ideas, not text. But in reconstructing that consciously, when we start with lines, we sometimes give every word equal emphasis. Emphasizing the important word is a technical thing that you can learn—and should learn—in order to communicate sense. When you look at a line, what is the important word? Target the word or phrase that made you start the thought in the first place.

What is the nugget, the *target*, in the whole speech that gives it shape? When you merely lift the whole sentence off the page, you do not convey the information. You lose the power.

Pick out the words from which the audience can guess the rest. Find more economy. Push more of the language under the rug. Go to the important word. Throw away everything but the important word. Don't surrender to general lyricism.

BRIAN MURRAY (Actor, Director):
Very often, if you don't put the right emphasis on the right word, you won't get the laugh.

Lifting the important word is not always about inflecting it up. Lifting just means you make some kind of distinction, lifting it above the ordinary or average. That could be emphasis. That could be rhythm. It means distinguishing that word from the others, as opposed to only an upward inflection. Change in pitch is often the most useful in emphasizing the word. Volume is often the least effective way.

Technique is only the illusion of what we do in life. When you're talking to me, you *are* lifting the important word. It's not a theatrical thing; it's a true thing. So it's only when you think, "I have to lift these words off the page and make them my own," that you get messed up. And you have to get over it. It's about what we really do.

In English, the important word is usually a little before the last word, but your energy has to go to the last word. Even though you're going to the important word, you have to carry your energy to the end of the line and, really, beyond.

Carry Your Energy to the End of the Line, and Beyond

You have to go to the end of the line, and that's a skill. That separates the men from the boys, the women from the girls. Really carry your energy to the end of the line, and beyond the end of the line.

What I hear often is actors dropping the end of the lines. That's because we don't take our energy to the end of the line, and beyond, so you don't hear the last word. In real life, people talk like that all the time. They let their energy drop. But in stage life, it's important that everyone hear the last word of the sentence, even if you're throwing it away. That requires vocal, physical energy—muscular output. How you do that—lift the important word and still carry your energy to the end of the line—is a technical trick. It is something that you can practice and learn, and then you just do it automatically. You don't think about it, you just do it.

GLORIA BIEGLER (Actor, Teacher):
I do a lot of teaching now, and I say the exact same phrase he said to me: "Gloria, you have to play through the whole poetic line." Your energy has to go all the way through the line, not dumping the end of the line, and not dumping your energy partway through the middle of it.

Don't let the energy leak out of final words; use inflection and pitch. I often ask actors to go through the script and look at the last word of every sentence to see if the meaning will support lifting it in pitch, so as to put the emphasis there.

Your energy must go to the end of the line so that the audience hears the very last word. The only way they can hear the last word is if you keep your support and your idea going beyond where the author has put the period.

Accelerating to the End of the Line

Listen to the end of a joke, and often you will hear the speaker accelerating in speed to the end of the line. As Gerald often pointed out, when the rhythm picks up, it helps the final word to pop, and usually it helps the joke to land.

Another technique is accelerating to the end of the line. It's a hard one to talk about, and it will seem very artificial to work on it, but in real life, it is what people do.

Accelerating to the end of the line helps you get there ahead of the audience.

This exercise has nothing to do with rushing. Rushing means going faster than you can handle. Acceleration is control. Acceleration is moving the tempo along quickly to the important word. It's really a rhythmic exercise—slowing down, and then accelerating to a release.

JERZY GWIAZDOWSKI (Actor, Former Student):
You're setting things up so that they can fire effectively. Once everything is set, the most effective launch is accelerating through the end of the line. That's something comics do, it's something comic actors do, and for Gerald, that was paramount. One of the ways that we would work on this is the beanbag exercise.

Beanbag

Gerald often used beanbags as a teaching aid in comedy technique. He found tossing them while speaking to be an effective way to practice lifting the important word, carrying energy to the end of the line, and accelerating to the end of the line. Tossing the beanbags helped to physicalize what he wanted actors to achieve vocally.

One of the techniques that Alvina Krause used to use is what she called *beanbag*. You'll need a beanbag, or something else that's easy to toss, that won't roll away.

The beanbag is a tool. It's a way of helping you understand. It's an aid to the final result. And it's fun.

STEVE VINOVICH (Actor, Former Student):
It's literally forcing you to throw the line and the beanbag, so you're actually putting effort into it, you're putting energy behind it, and also giving it a lift so you're not letting the line drop.

You have to arc it. What is the important word? There are sometimes two and three emphases within a line; you have to choose where you really want to release the energy. Arc it, don't throw it. Arc the line, up and over the last row. Save it for the most important release in the line.

TIFFANY LITTLE CANFIELD (Casting Director, Former Student):
It was a way to physicalize how you approach punch lines. You would throw a beanbag the way you throw a setup line. When you physically did it, it would remind you and get into your muscle memory of how you were going to actually do it. Then you take the bag away, but you're going to see what that feels like when you throw a punch line.

You don't have to aim the beanbag. It's aiming the intent of the line. The line has to land somewhere. It's a skill. It is completing a moment in a technical sense—finishing it off, making it land.

More often than not, the idea is to release it toward the end of the line. The release rarely comes in the middle of the line, and it almost never comes at the beginning of the line. You don't construct lines that way.

Timing Business with the Line

If you're going to bring behavior into comedy, you have to time it. Timing business or action to a line heightens the effect of a line, and sharpens the audience's awareness of a line.

BRIAN MURRAY (Actor, Director):
To be able to time a line, it's obviously even more important than having a sense of humor, because if the line is funny, and you time it right, you'll get a laugh whether you think it's funny or not.

In rehearsal, you might just be doing a naturalistic task, but if you have comedy lines, you start to organize that behavior so that it will emphasize the line, make a comic point, and release energy at a certain time.

Sometimes it can be very subtle. Crossing one's legs is timing business with the line. Particularly in comedy, doing it in the middle of the line might screw up the line.

An object is not a foreign thing; it is integral to how you say the line. When do you put your cap on? If you only work through organic behavior, it can happen any time. But in comedy, you have to know exactly where you're going to put your hat on. And you have to use it. It's the knowing gesture, as opposed to the unaware gesture.

BRIAN SUTOW (Actor, Former Student):
I've found that one of the most important aspects of timing out business is *buttoning*. Buttoning is essentially doing some little bit of business at the very end of a joke or thought—even the smallest little gesture, like putting your hands down on a desk, crossing your legs, or a slight turn of the head. I want to do it at the end of the line. If I do it before the end of the line, it obscures the thought and feels confusing. Somehow, a little physical button at the very end helps to clarify to the audience that it's the end of the moment, and gives them the thing they need to release their laughter.

JERZY GWIAZDOWSKI (Actor, Former Student):
It puts a punctuation mark on the beat—or the scene. It allows us to breathe. It allows us to know that was the end. It's like a musical theater button that releases applause. It's a reinforcement of the line and the idea. Your behavior is another tool at your disposal to help the audience follow the thought.

You can punctuate a line with an object, with when you pick up an object. It's about a conscious awareness of how to use the objects, as a technical exercise.

Something that might start as a naturalistic piece of behavior, you then technically stylize: "I will do it at the end of this line," or, "I will do it on this word," because you get a laugh that way.

Interrupted Action / Interrupted Thought

Comedy is all about surprise, and as Gerald taught, an interrupted action is a great way to share surprise with the audience. It's about timing behavior or activity—tying your shoe, pouring a glass of water, dusting off your sleeve—so you can be interrupted in the midst of it when the surprise occurs.

MATT COWART (Director, Former Student):
Something that's very difficult to do onstage is to act surprised. Interrupted action is a wonderful technique for communicating that you're surprised without having to do any acting. Instead of having to listen to you and then gasp, I simply just have to be doing something, and then stop doing what I'm doing, and the audience understands that I've received the information. In comedy, you often need the audience to know what specific information you heard was the most important. So, if we're doing Feydeau, and my mistress is here, and my servant comes in and says, "The paper has arrived sir, and your two o'clock appointment will be here on time, and your wife is here." After *your wife is here* is the moment that I would stop ruffling through my papers, so the audience knows that that is the thing propelling the rest of the play forward.

JERZY GWIAZDOWSKI (Actor, Former Student):
There's also interrupted thought, which can be useful in any number of ways. You're about to make a point, and there's a realization or discovery that stops the current thought. You can only ever do one thing at a time. So, you commit to having one thought—and then switch.

Turning Out

Turning out is Gerald's shorthand for turning one's face out to the audience. He knew that when the audience can see the actor's eyes, their appreciation of the humor intensifies. Usually, an actor cannot just turn out for the sake of the joke, but must find ways to justify the choice through behavior and the given circumstances of the text.

What generally enhances your ability to get a laugh onstage is not only the release of the surprise, but the audience's ability to see your eyes. When they're able to see your eyes, when they're able to see the expression on your face, it enhances the line.

BRIAN SUTOW (Actor, Former Student):
With so many jokes, the reason they're funny is because of what they mean to the character. It's the character's emotional reaction. Well, we don't really understand what your emotional reaction is unless we can see your eyes. Think about a comedy like *The Office*, or really any mockumentary. A huge part of why they work is because characters can do a turn out to the camera. Anytime a joke ends with someone making eye contact with the camera, that's a turn-out.

You'll get a better laugh if you turn the end of a comedy line out front. You can increase a laugh threefold by learning how to use behavior to turn the end of the line out front.

Now, this is where the test of your ingenuity is the greatest. How can you be truthful? How can you do honest behavior that you can believe in, and still technically turn the line out front? To use a naturalistic behavior on the stage to make that happen is the art of it.

You have to find a clever, truthful way of handling this technical problem within your character. It seems awkward sometimes at first. When you get adept at it, it can be fun, and when you get really good, you're not even thinking about it anymore—you just do it.

If you have direct address, there's no problem; you just turn out and talk to the audience.

Topping & Underplaying

Gerald was a masterful director of comedy. It was evident in his work that finding the humor is usually about more than an individual line or action; it's about the buildup of longer sequences. Topping and underplaying are key techniques he utilized in such comedic interplay.

Topping is coming in a little higher than the speech before you to keep the energy going and to create a sense of excitement. The line comes on top of the other line, so it builds.

Again, it is what we do naturally. When we're in a discussion, we top each other all the time. That's what we do. It is using that as a conscious technique to build the energy of a scene.

When you are topping, you have to take your breath before the other person finishes, because your ideas are coming that fast. Your idea comes before somebody gives you the cue line.

MATT COWART (Director, Former Student):
It's not only about coming in quickly after the other person's line, it's about topping them, and there's several ways to top them. You can top them by raising the pitch of your voice. You can top them by raising the volume of your voice. You can also top them physically, if they do a gesture, by doing it back to them with more energy and emphasis. The idea is allowing the momentum and energy to build to the point where you control when the audience releases into laughter.

Pick up the impulse in the line. It's what we do in life. In breaking down the process of acting, you sometimes lose that sense, because you're not permitted to talk until I'm done.

The antithesis of topping, but sometimes just as useful, is underplaying. So the scene builds and builds and builds, and when you can no longer go any farther, the way to top is to go under, to underplay it.

Making an Entrance, or an Exit

The entrance of a character is often what shifts the scene and propels the action forward. Gerald would tell actors that when they entered the space, it was up to them to grab our attention and pull us along for that ride. Both entrances and exits are rich opportunities for the application of comedy technique.

You have to take the stage with your first word. Whatever that first word, you can literally do this.

PEGGY LOFT (Teacher, College Classmate):
It's Alvina Krause: take the scene on the first word. If you have to make an entrance on a line, the tendency—and it still is today—is to barely say the first word, to move up into the line.

What I'm talking about is grabbing the stage with the first word. It's just taking hold of the stage. That's a technique. But that can also be done in terms of an intention: What do you want? Why are you coming on-stage? You don't only have to address it technically, you can also address it in an acting way.

Always make an entrance. Be there. Say the first line clearly.

JERZY GWIAZDOWSKI (Actor, Former Student):
Entrances and exits are incredibly effective. Whether there's an archway, if you're popping up from behind a bush—but especially if you've got a door. A nice latch that slams really loudly. Which way does it open? Can you stick your leg out? Can you stick your head through? When you exit, do you pause in the frame of the door to deliver the line and then slam immediately after? Do you deliver your last line through the closed door? Do you deliver your line first and then do a whole bit of exiting the room? A door is a one-stop shop Swiss Army knife of comedy tools. Gerald was a master of demonstrating them to his students. We would spend entire rehearsals and classes on the doors.

How to Incorporate These Techniques

Gerald often said that to fully understand comedy technique, it must be seen, heard, and learned in the muscles through experience. After reading and thinking about what's written here, watch some Lucile Ball, Carol Burnett, Monty Python, Arrested Development, or Marx Brothers, and see if you can recognize their application of comedy technique. Then pick up some Noel Coward, Oscar Wilde, or George Feydeau, and try some for yourself.

Much of what we teach here are skills. They must be done over and over again until they are in your muscles. Repetition is part of mastering them. Once is not enough. You identify the tool, and then you master it with repetition so you can use it with authority and confidence. When to use this or that tool, that is your choice, that is the art of it. That is when you move from a technician to an artist.

MATT COWART (Director, Former Student):
While any number of techniques can work in any given moment, there often is one that works best. So, you know, one night, I try putting the teacup down at the end of that line, and it gets a small laugh. Alright, the

next night I try turning out at the end of the line, and it gets a bigger laugh. And then the next night, I try turning out and taking a sip of my tea at the end of the line, and the house goes wild. So much of what we do is not result oriented, but the application of these techniques, specifically inside of comedy, can often be pass/fail. And so much of getting good at them involves testing and experimenting in front of a live audience.

When you have mastered these skills, the idea is to not let the audience see them. You'd never want to see a production where actors were this conscious of the technique. As you grow in artistry, it becomes second nature. It's just what you do with the line. You don't have to think about it.

JEREMY WEBB (Actor, Former Student):
Gerald is at home telling you passionately that you need to find the truth of the moment, you need to find the thing that makes it specific to you, and sets you on fire. He's equally at home turning around and directing a scene from *The Importance of Being Earnest* and talking about the virtues of technical comedy, and taking a line out to an audience, or speeding up to the end of a line, or upward inflection. Someone might say, "Aren't those ideas directly antithetical to one another? They seem like they are in complete contradiction to each other." What I would say is, it's merely an understanding of the facets of performing, of the layers of performance. What's happening underneath is important. What's happening on the surface is also important.

If an actor is lifting the important word, and going to the end of the line, that's about the intention. It's not just technical. They may interpret it as technical, but lifting the word helps you to clarify what's really going on, so it's not just about technique. It's about clarity.

MATT COWART (Director, Former Student):
The thing that I remember most clearly about Gerald's comedy technique class, and he would yell this at us over and over again, "This isn't about comedy! This is a technique that can be applied to all kinds of theater." The actor's primary responsibility is serving the story with clarity, and all of these techniques, the reason they work so well in comedy is because comedy has to be so clear. Every moment needs absolute clarity for it to be successful and funny. But you need the same amount of clarity if you're doing *Hamlet*. Gerald taught it through the idea of comedy technique, because that's the way to see the clearest result the fastest: either you get a laugh or you don't.

JERZY GWIAZDOWSKI (Actor, Former Student):
If you're playing Oedipus, if you're playing Hamlet, if you're playing Othello, if you're doing *Death of a Salesman*, these are all still appropriate, useful tools for an actor to direct focus, to enhance performance, and support the work that you've already been doing. So, they were introduced to me as comedy techniques, but I use them and teach them for every discipline.

I'm not asking you to abandon a sense of truth. Really, it's about how to incorporate these techniques into honest acting.

Actors will often assume outer manifestations of characterization—a funny voice or a distorted physical position—and miss the truth of the character. The surface without the inner truth just doesn't interest me at all.

CHARLOTTE RAE (Actor, College Classmate):
There are certain techniques in comedy that you learn along the way, but it has to come from the truth, that's all there is to it. Truth is the basic ingredient. If you don't have truth, it's not funny.

Truth always trumps technique, but technique enhances truth. Technical work is all in the service of your ability to communicate onstage, when the proper work at that moment is relationship, following through on your intention, et cetera.

MARY IRWIN (Teacher, Colleague):
A lot of people will analyze the text in a dry and clinical way, and they might go through and lift exactly the right words, and get through to not drop off their voice at the end of the thought; but if they're not using it to pursue their actions and objectives, it just sounds like sound and fury signifying nothing. It's just pretty speech. Adherence to form is a necessary support to good acting, not a thing done for its own sake.

It's a lot of what you do naturally, but in breaking it down, it will seem awkward, it may seem not an honest way of going at something, but eventually it needs to be incorporated in the whole fabric of what you're doing. It may not happen for a while. These are not techniques that you necessarily master in a term.

There is no end to the polishing one can do in comedy.

Spotlight: *The Lady from Maxim's*

In 1990, Gerald directed George Feydeau's The Lady from Maxim's *at Great Lakes Theater, and wrote an article about his process entitled "How Freedman Inspires 'The Lady's' Laughter," which originally appeared in the Great Lakes Theater Festival Newsletter. The article is a veritable treatise on the specialized area of comedy known as farce, and it is reprinted here in its entirety with permission.*

I don't like to use labels, to oversimplify. But *The Lady from Maxim's* is a farce—a gloriously funny and extremely well-crafted one.

Farce is an elusive label. You instinctively recognize the difference between Feydeau and Shakespeare, or Feydeau and Strindberg. But there is a precariously thin line between farce and tragedy.

We all laugh, for instance, if someone slips on a banana peel. It's an action full of sheer, unexpected physicality and energy. But if somebody breaks a hip it becomes a tragedy. The same action. So it's the consequence of the action and the level of the consequence that really define an action as farcical or tragic.

Our Feydeau farce celebrates marriage and fidelity. There's a constant tease that something naughty could be going on between the respectable Dr. Petypon and the Moulin Rouge dancer, La Môme Crevette, known as "the Shrimp." Farce relies on an element of danger and discovery; something has to be at stake. In this case, it's a marriage. It may be very common for a French man to have a mistress, for instance, but not in the Petypon household.

So when Dr. Petypon wakes up under the couch one morning, with the Shrimp unaccountably in his bed, even the appearance of infidelity is not admissible, and he's got to rid his household of her to save his marriage. It's not an inconsequential situation; it's very consequential. But, in a period farce like this one, nothing can have actually happened. If something had, the consequences would be too serious. You walk a fine line between the outrageous and the serious, and the uneasiness is what makes us laugh and gives us fun. If it tips over into serious consequences, it's no longer fun.

Though farce has been around since the Greeks and Romans, it's practically a lost art today. It's very hard to write. People tend to denigrate it as a lower form of theater, when in many ways it requires a high level of skills and craft. Farce relies on complicated and heightened physical situations—hiding under tables, sneaking in and out of bedroom doors, mixed-up identities, disguises. Then these elements accelerate rapidly as the play progresses, demanding a higher and higher energy output from the actors in the play. A farce has to be very well-constructed, and Feydeau is a master at sustaining very complicated plots and interweaving such comings and goings.

In a play like *King Lear*, the resolution of a moment is in a confrontation of character, but in *The Comedy of Errors* or *The Lady from Maxim's*, the resolution usually involves the movement of a character from one place to another. Farce requires the physical solutions be found very quickly. That need for speed challenges the director. Every action has to be very carefully etched. If you want the audience's eyes *here* but they're still over *there*, you're dead.

When I did *The Game of Love*, there were elements in the dining room scene that were farce, and it was all split-second timing—tossing and catching plates and so on. The actors have to have great physical agility and timing: the appropriate action at the exact second of execution. The Marx Brothers, in their team playing, are a perfect example.

The Boys from Syracuse, which I staged here [at Great Lakes Theater] in 1987, is another. The musical number in which the two servants mirrored each other's actions took untold hours of rehearsal. George Abbot, who wrote and directed the original production of *Syracuse* in 1938, had a wonderful, really unparalleled instinct for the timing and pace that farce requires. It was inspirational to watch him direct *Broadway* at the Great Lakes Theater Festival that same season.

As Abbott always says, farce is not just physical clowning. It is built on character. Think of Laurel and Hardy. A farce has to have dimensional characters, not cartoons. *The Taming of the Shrew* is a farce, but you must have real people up there or it doesn't work as it should. The comedy is heightened when you have two people who are madly in love with each other—and then get into outrageous physical situations. In addition, the comic business you invent, the style of the production—all have to be true to character.

I taught a style course at Juilliard in the early 1970s, and my approach was somewhat controversial. I feel that the style of a production has to come from the text, whereas many people tend to think of style in terms of externals. I worked on *The Rivals* and *Mother Courage* at the same time with the same group of actors, which included William Hurt, Mandy Patinkin, and Patti LuPone, and I showed them how you do exactly the same work and preparation for both texts. As far as I'm concerned, style doesn't come by appliquéing externals; it comes from a true understanding of the internals—the life of the characters and what the play demands.[14]

VOICE TECHNIQUE

*Comedy technique can be successfully applied to many types of perfor-
mance. The same is true for voice technique. While Gerald was not a voice
teacher, he recognized that voice training was essential to an actor's development, and he championed its integration.*

MARY IRWIN (Teacher, Colleague):
Gerald has a strong belief in the foundational importance and value of all
voice and speech work in the actor training process, and as Dean, always
gave it ample time, both in time allotted for classes and in his own rehearsal processes. He understood that learning another accent in a way that is
technically accurate, yet organically truthful to the speaker, requires time
and patience. Gerald believes passionately in voice, speech and accent/
dialect work that is organic, that encourages and enables student actors
to speak from themselves, in their own voices, even when their character
speaks in an accent different from their own. Through his own example,
Gerald instilled in the students a respect for the voice/accent/dialect piece
of their process.

Breathing is three quarters of the battle in everything. If you haven't
taken a breath in preparation, if you don't have the breath to operate on,
you honestly cannot really act. You can't do all the other things you really
want to do: play an intention, focus, concentrate. Breath is life itself. We
think of it as a technical thing, but think of what happens when you have
no breath. You are dead. Breath, to me, is what we call soul. Without
soul, you really can't do anything. Breath and the proper preparation are
key. That's why eastern philosophies put so much emphasis on it, and
begin and end with it, actually—because they know the secret better
than we do. It is so essential to what we want to do. For an artist, getting
control of breath is what makes all the difference. It is the essential ingredient on which to build.

What is existence without breath? It isn't.

BARNEY HAMMOND (Teacher, Colleague):
Your speech muscles become your acting muscles. The muscularity of
your speaking is not separate from your acting; it is your acting. He and
I fully embraced that. He would say in his direction, "You've got to have

clearer consonants," or, "I feel your voice is coming from a shallow place, therefore the action you're playing is coming off shallow. The breath has to be low in the body, so that the action comes from a grounded, deep-rooted place." He never saw it as compartmentalized. He never saw it as separate from the acting process. It is a vital part of the acting process.

If you are working with heightened language such as Shakespeare, Chekhov, or Molière, you can analyze and identify your voice and diction issues as part of your preparation. All of these can be found, marked, highlighted, and worked on before rehearsal begins.

The ability of the human voice to really project is an athletic feat; it's wondrous. If you're onstage, one of the glories of the human instrument is to be able to project. Today, you rarely hear the beauty of the human voice as an instrument—the full spectrum, the direct, resonating vibrations of the voice which communicate truth and nuance. If you use a mic, you rob us of that kind of virtuosity. I think of the microphone as steroids. I have heard theater artists in musicals and plays, in these same New York theaters, without amplification. Ethel Merman did not need a microphone. There are Congressional investigations of steroids, but no one seems to protest microphones.

CAMERA TECHNIQUE

Acting Is Acting Is Acting

Whatever the acting medium—whether it's film, television, or live theater—the primary goals of Gerald's training endure: really doing things, pursuing an objective, and talking and listening. In other words, truthful acting. While there are specific techniques that can be utilized for the camera, the fundamentals remain the same.

I feel very comfortable talking to you about film acting, and about theater acting, and about acting for television. And there are some differences—there are great differences—but everything that you are being taught at the School of the Arts is applicable to film acting. More than you can possibly realize.

If people talk about acting for film, or acting for TV, you must not believe it's another craft. Because acting is acting is acting. You're being trained to function anywhere as an actor. Acting is about the illusion of truth, whatever the medium. The search for truth in acting takes a lifetime. By contrast, learning to adjust that process to a small room, or a stadium, or a camera lens, can be learned rather quickly.

TIFFANY LITTLE CANFIELD (Casting Director, Former Student):
Truth has no size, and I think Gerald was the first to teach us that. If you're a terrific theater actor, if you are a truth teller on the stage, and you know what it is to be in the moment, to drop in, to not anticipate, to listen, then you will do well on camera.

Don't forget that we are all students. We are learning a craft. You are learning the craft of acting for the theater, and we are lending ourselves to adjusting that for film acting, but they're not really different.

Don't listen to people when they try to separate these skills. People want to because it's convenient to talk about it that way, just as it's convenient for us to break down the process, but you have to put it back together again. And you mustn't forget that it's the together part that we're working toward, not the separate part.

I want you to understand there isn't that great a separation at all, at all, at all. The big difference is projection. You often don't need to project on camera, because there's a mic right over your head, or when the frame gets smaller, you need to limit your physical actions so you stay within the frame, but you always have to be a truthful actor, whether it's in the theater or in front of a camera.

DEBBIE ALLEN (Actor, Director):
Onstage, your voice must project, and you have to talk to the back of the house. In film, you can be as intimate as a mouse, and the camera is right there. The approach to the work is the same, but the technique is different.

It's not a question of being less real in the theater and more real on film, or bigger in theater and smaller in film. You have to learn how to act, period. Then, if you're smart, on the ball, and lucky enough to get a couple of jobs, you learn how to make that adjustment.

You still have to learn how to act. You have to learn how to concentrate. You have to learn how to breathe. You have to learn how to use yourself. You have to learn how to come up with an emotional sense of the scene when you're asked to. That is why I believe in classical training. It is the toughest work—the work that prepares you for anything, as far as I'm concerned. Whatever you do, the rigor of theater training will help you.

So don't think, "Why am I wasting my time doing all this theater acting, all this classical shit?" It is to learn how to act at all. What you need to know, what you can never do without, is a sense of truth about relating to another person. That is key, whether you're in front of a camera or in the theater.

DANE DEHAAN (Actor, Former Student):
Ultimately, if you know what play you're in or what movie you're in, and you're within that world, and you're really doing things, that's it. That's all it boils down to, so it's not so different from one to the other.

I don't care what medium you are in. It calls for honest, truthful acting. The really great artists, the people that move you in any of these mediums—and I've directed in all of them, and I've worked with great artists in all of them—are the ones who do truthful acting, whether it's opera or theater or film or television.

There is a difference, not in acting but in technique, and a few little clues that will help you. At best, this is introducing you to the ideas that will be presented to you as film actor problems. If you use your intelligence with a little adjustment in skills, you'll be ready for anything.

Theater vs. Film

Gerald worked extensively with actors onstage and on camera, and he knew firsthand what set the two modes apart. In theater, rehearsals can sometimes go on for months. In film, the actors often get no rehearsal at all. In theater, whatever the actor does in the performance is what the audience gets. In film, there can be endless takes, and the actor's performance can be shaped and refined with editing. There is indeed variance between genres; the key, Gerald said, is being aware of the differences.

I was in the movie industry, and I left. I didn't want all those layers between me and the final product. I want more immediate gratification, and I get that in the theater. The rehearsal process in theater is very exciting and fulfilling for me. What I didn't like about film was that after I did it, it took six or eight weeks before it all came together, and I couldn't go back and change what I had with a rehearsal. The rhythm of theater suits me; it has immediacy, a greater sense of control, and more creative freedom.

I could handle all the technical things in film, but it didn't give me a kick.[15]

A theater performance is alive, effervescent, *in the moment.* No one can measure the power of live, one-on-one communication, but power is what is being transmitted in the presence of a platform speaker or in a theater. The significant difference is what we call "real time." You are in the same room or hall or theater for two or three hours *together.* We are experiencing each other—we are affecting each other—with our focus and attention and energy and heartbeat.[16] We get a true, human experience. It is yet another reason why the theater will not die.

The theater has a magic that I think is eternal. I think it has its roots in the needs of human beings. We need to feel and touch and be in communion with other human beings in order to read ourselves. I cannot foresee a time when the theater won't be there, because I think we need it. And finally, all I can say is that I need it. I need to be in touch with the actor and the audience. It exhilarates me.

Some actors don't enjoy film work. That's why they come back to the theater. I hear it over and over again from experienced actors who work both in film and in the theater. They do film, if they're lucky, to make the money to afford to be able to do theater, where they get their real charge.

ROBERT FOXWORTH (Actor):
I get much more gratification working in theater than television and film. It's just a different animal for me. There's a richness. The environment of the rehearsal process itself to me is one of the great joys of life. It's an experience that I wouldn't trade for anything. I'm one of those actors for whom the performance is kind of the icing on the cake; it's really the rehearsal process that I love. Jerry was instrumental in getting me into that place.

In theater, there's the time to rehearse, there's the time to work, there's the time to reconsider, and there's another day to return to the scene. Usually, none of those things are available in film or TV. You just have to keep turning it out.

It very much depends on the director. There is no standard way. The big difference is money. It costs so much money to hire a bunch of high-priced actors and put them on a film set. It's a lot of money. You've got to be sure you're going to earn that money back. Maybe if there were a difference in economics, they'd rehearse more, but there isn't.

There are all shades of directing and filmmaking, so I can only generalize. The extreme example is a director like Sidney Lumet, who would rehearse the entire script for weeks, and then put it in front of the camera. But those are rare occasions, and rare directors.

Often you don't do any rehearsing at all. You've learned your lines, you get up, and you do it. If anything, what you have is a rehearsal for the camera.

You don't know how it's going to get cut together. You're not really responsible for your performance; you can only be responsible for that moment, and the director says, "Cut, print"—and you expect it's what they want. That's all.

As an actor on the stage, you're a little more responsible, because there's nothing between you and the audience. But in a camera situation, there are dozens of technical things between you and the final product. There's the camera, there's the lighting, there's the director, there's the editor—all of whom may have other ideas, which they may not have the time or the language to share with you. They might not even know what they want themselves until they get into the cutting room.

In the theater, the actor can control the comedy with timing. In film, the editor controls the timing, and they often screw it up very badly. Often, they don't understand where the joke is.

In film particularly, because the editor or the camera chooses what to look at when, it's a totally artificial manipulation. In the theater, where it's all in front of you, the audience picks who they want to watch, and, if you're skillful, they choose what you and the director chose for them to watch.

Film is so much less in the actor's control than theater acting is. The focus in film is totally determined by the editor and the director.

Working with Film Directors

Gerald taught his students that for film directors, technical considerations are abundant, ever present, and begin long before the actors ever walk onto the set. It often falls to film actors to do a great deal of preparation on their own, and they must be prepared to follow the film director's course.

Film is a director's medium. The director is the supreme authority on a film. Period. You are never, or hardly ever, to ask why. You just do it. You do what they ask. You bring your skills. They know why. They usually have spent months preparing. They know just what they want, or think they know what they want. And you do not know what they're going to do with this film when they get it into an editing rom. You cannot tell what a director or an editor may be doing. It's blind faith. It's blind trust. You just function.

What's important for most directors is the movement or the position of the camera, not the acting. They think they can create the acting, and they can, in the editing room. The director can often create a performance by the juxtaposition of images. The audience will create the emotion in a scene by what image is put next to what image.

You always have to keep in mind that you are working with directors who may have very little experience working with actors. You may know more about acting than they do, but they know more about the result they want, that they have in their mind's eye.

The technicians rule the day. They have as much, if not more, riding on the result than you do. So you have to trust.

The Camera

For all Gerald's focus on process, he knew a performance didn't fulfill its purpose if it didn't reach the audience. In film, the camera is the audience. Like a particular audience member, the camera has its own distinct perspective. To master working on film, the actor must understand the camera's point of view.

In general, there are three shots: a long-shot, which covers the whole sense of the scene; a medium shot, which might be just two people together in a frame; and then I would want to do the same again, in a close-up, with the camera just on one actor to get all of that actor's reactions as tightly as possible, and then do the scene all over again with just the other actor. Often, a close-up is to give something importance.

A lot of the time, the angle of the shot makes all the difference. It can make a difference in how somebody looks, but it can also make a psychological difference. The angle of the camera says things emotionally to those of us in the west who inherit a certain kind of visual language. We are all accustomed to seeing a fixed point of view. We are conditioned as to how to look and what to see. For example, looking from below may suggest something ominous, or it may suggest a child's point of view.

If you're shooting in film, there's always something they call the *key light*, which is the light that defines the modeling of the face—and that is very carefully placed: how high, how low, and from what direction. When I first got into the movies, I worked with a lot of famous names. Female stars could demand their own camera man, who always knew where their key light ought to be.

The camera catches you mercilessly. It will catch everything you do. Often what happens on camera is things seem closer—and it adds weight. A film camera adds about ten or fifteen pounds to the way you look. Even the sense of depth is different. That's a technical problem; it's not an acting problem. As part of your craft, you have to become aware of those things. But it doesn't really interfere with the prime thing that nobody else can do, which is to act truthfully.

Less Is More

A performance that plays perfectly for a house of a thousand people may indeed overwhelm the camera at close range, but Gerald saw that the solution was not as simple as shrinking the performance down. The power of the doing must endure, no matter the scale.

WILLIAM DANIELS (Actor, College Classmate):
A lot of actors who act in movies are mumblers. They don't know how to project. You couldn't put them on a stage. That takes another kind of conviction that I don't think they have, to be perfectly frank. You have to be able to project to the back of the house. And that has to do with diction, and with breathing, and with enunciation, and you know, just, power.

And for film, if you would do that, you'd be seen as overacting, as being too much, or somebody would come to you and quiet you down and say, "Listen, you don't have to talk that loud," or something like that.

A film director will often say to an actor, "Do less. You don't have to do so much." Language like, "Don't do anything," or, "Make it smaller," makes me nervous. The intensity is the same. The adjustments are simply technical considerations. The intensity of the moment is still the same.

If your voice is too loud for the microphone, or your gestures are too big for the camera, you can adjust that, but it's not simply a case of doing less. If anything, your concentration has to be greater. Your inner life has to be more focused, more concentrated. So it's not about doing nothing, really. It's about adjusting where your energy is focused, where it's expressed—whether it's in body language or just in thinking.

It's not doing nothing. It's being as simple and economical as possible, but you're still doing lots inside.

WILL ROGERS (Actor, Former Student):
The exciting thing about the camera is how little can be enough.

If you're told you're doing too much, it's not that you adjust by doing any less emotionally—you just don't need to show as much. That's the only difference. That's technique.

KEVIN KLINE (Actor, Former Student):
With the camera, your audience is closer. It actually increases your acting vocabulary; you can make choices that wouldn't play past the second row in the theater. Sometimes you can just think the thought, and the camera will capture that.

What You Are Thinking

It's what you are thinking that is important, and the camera catches it like crazy. If you are dishonest, if you have not a thought in your head, it will all show up like a mountain on film. So what you have to be in touch with most are intentions, actions, and behavior—as you should be in theater acting. On film, it's what you're thinking, not what you're saying, that is important.

It's not what the writer has given you to say; it's what he *hasn't* given you to say that keeps your life active in a scene. That's the greatest advice I can give to someone who wants to act in movies: listen and react. If you're thinking about lines, you're not listening. That's why you want to know your lines cold, so you're not thinking about them.

ANNA CAMP (Actor, Former Student):
I remember Gerald said, "All you have to do when you're on camera is think the thought." If you think the thought, and you are fully invested in who you are, and you're listening to your scene partner as your character, and you're good enough, hopefully people will respond and see it. You don't have to force. You don't have to indicate.

The thought comes when the thought comes. And often in film, that's when the director will want to cut to you: when he's caught you listening, and the thought comes. That's the most interesting moment, really, when your idea comes, not when you speak. What are the thoughts you *don't* verbalize as your character?

It's your reactions that are as important—if not more important—than what you are saying. You always have to be alive. You cannot be thinking of what your next line is. You have to be there, present, responding to your partner.

What I'm getting at is honesty and truth and thinking. As in the theater, you can't indicate thinking; you have to *be* thinking. I see this a lot: fake truth. You're trying to pretend that you're having a thought. Have a thought! Unless you're brain dead, you are always thinking. But are you thinking, "Oh god, what's my next line?" or, "Jeez, I'm scared shitless," or, "What do they think of my performance?" Are you thinking the character's thoughts? Or are you thinking some private fear, anger, or whatever the hell that has nothing to do with the character? All of it will register. You cannot fake in front of a camera. You cannot fake in the theater. Learn how to be an honest actor, period. When you have a real thought, you're not acting it. In your eyes, we can tell.

The Eyes

The most important part of you in film acting is your eyes. If you are in a close-up, the first thing we look at is your eyes. Absolutely, without any doubt, that's where we go. Why? They look right into you. Everything you are. The moment is in your eyes. It is true in the theater too. You have to find ways for an audience, whether it's in the theater or film, to see your eyes. And that's why you can't fake it: the eyes reveal everything. Everything. The eyes are really where the story is being told, all the time.

When you're in a close-up, the person you're playing the scene with is off camera—not being shot, but standing close to the camera so that you can relate to them. Don't look from one eye to the other, which we often do when we're talking to somebody. Look at the eye that is closer to the lens, so that more of your eye is open to the camera.

Breaking Down the Film Script

Gerald maintained that the ability to break down a script can prove even more essential on a film set. Doing so allows you to build a linear path through the story, and get to the root of what each scene is really about, so you have a foundation to hold firm to amid the flux.

Films are rarely shot in sequence. You are sometimes asked to do the last moment of a film first—because there's sun, because that location is nearby, or for a hundred other economic or technical reasons, rarely for the actor's comfort.

I know actors who map out their whole script film-wise, so they know what the arc of the part is. If they start with the seventeenth setup, they know where they have to be. And you can only do that if you know how to break down a script.

You have to understand the whole scale of a film script when you go in to do a job, which is again what analyzing a script teaches you: to see the whole thing. *Where am I going? What is the through line?* If you get in the habit of working that way, it's there when you need it.

In film, you may often have to do your work without discussing your role with the director, without seeing or meeting the other people in the cast, and without rehearsal on the set—which is different than in the theater. Unless you've done your own script work, you'll have nothing to bring except physically what you are.

When you do a sitcom, they are often rewriting the script up to the moment you do it in front of the camera. Every single day, there are rewrites. They're working so fast. What generally doesn't change is the plot or the gimmick of that episode, but the lines constantly change. You've got to be up there with them, inventive, and quick to memorize.

You Have to Be Ready

Gerald understood that on a film set, there are ongoing concerns related to technical elements like the lights, camera, and sound; the acting is the last step. Actors therefore need to learn to be their own allies, always be ready, and use the waiting time effectively.

In film, again, you shoot isolated moments, probably in the wrong sequence. And you have to constantly crank yourself up to an intense pitch of concentration on every shot—which doesn't necessarily happen in theater, where you get caught up in the rhythm of the play. Or you've worked up a lot of steam, and it carries you a little beyond—or a moment slips, and then you're back in the groove. That isn't true in film.

There is so much money at stake in film and television at every minute. They are totally intolerant and unwelcoming to any problem you have. They don't want to listen to excuses. They don't want to do it again. They want what they want at the moment they want it. All the excuses you may have are irrelevant to them. Particularly at the entry stage, "May I do that again?" is just not even to be thought of. You are expected to deliver at that moment, and to do it again, and again, if that is necessary.

Doing it over and over again does not mean necessarily that they capture your best performance. Sometimes they end up using your worst performance because technically, it may be the only one that is useable.

Sometimes you literally are racing a clock covering the sun. "I've got to get it now, right now, before the light goes." That's it. If the light goes, you have to go the next day. You can't go the next day, because another location is waiting for you, so you've got to get it now. There's no temporizing with that.

Mostly, film acting is about waiting. You have to learn how to wait, and what to do with that time. It's hurry up and wait. You spend hours waiting in your trailer, or in your chair, waiting for all the technical people to light the thing, to get the sound perfect; and then, when the time comes, how do you come up and give a performance? For three lines? When you've been waiting for two hours?

Save your real commitment for the take. Usually the first take is like a first class dress rehearsal. So they take it, but everyone still needs to do it again. Savvy actors in a feature film will often not blow it the first time, because they know that's not the take they're going to use. But sometimes, it is! You can outfox yourself.

In the limited rehearsal time onset, usually, nobody's rehearsing with you. They're rehearsing lights, camera, all the technical things. So every time you do a take, you have to be finding out something more about your character, because this may be the only rehearsal you get. It's all focused on the work. You don't just go off and chat. You can't afford to miss any of this time for yourself.

LEE GRANT (Actor, Director):
Working in film and television, the directors usually didn't care about the acting. You came in and did whatever you wanted. They didn't know about actors. They were all lights and camera. Acting was like a sidelight.

On set, there are so many technical things around you. At the last moment before filming, it's not always about the scene. It's about hair, it's about makeup, it's about light. But you have to be ready for "Camera, action, go!" You have to be ready. You have to be focused all the time.

Hit Your Marks

A brilliant film performance is worthless if the camera doesn't capture it. On set, you will often be asked to walk specific paths and to hit your marks, which are literally marks on the ground that show you where to stand.

You have to hit your marks. You have to be where the camera man wants you.

What may seem very artificial to you doesn't look artificial on the screen, because we're only focusing on a small part of you. You cannot know that.

You have to know exactly what you did so it will cut together well. The impulse can evolve, but the movement has to be the same. You might find another color. You can do that change without screwing up the technical part.

You have to take the camera with you, and it can only move so fast. When you sit down or get up, you need to be conscious that the camera has to follow you.

Be Cordial

As in most situations, if you are kind and helpful to the people around you, they are more likely to be kind and helpful to you in return. Gerald's advice for the film or television set: Be polite. Remain alert and curious about the work going on around you. Find out how you can be of help.

We come together in the theater, and we create a family. Whether we like it or not, we become a family. We come together in the film studio for a much shorter time, but there is still that interdependence. Everybody wants the project to be good. Everybody wants you to be good. Everybody wants to do their job well. So that removal, any kind of protective circle around you, is just a bad idea. It's not conducive to the kind of short term friendliness that is needed in these risk situations. Be available. You have to be everybody's friend. Be nice.

When I say be nice, I mean be cordial. Say good morning. I'm not advising you to bribe anyone by throwing your clothes off and hurling yourself at them. But if you want to look good on screen, good manners do help, because the technical people can knock themselves out for you if they feel you're on their side.

When I was working in Hollywood at Columbia Pictures, I worked on a picture with Joan Crawford. Joan would come over from makeup in a house coat and slippers, and she'd walk onto the set and yell to the technicians, "Hi, Jimmy! Hi Lee! I baked some brownies for you!" And they would just die for her. I'm not sure it was true; I don't know where she bought the brownies, but she did it. She knew after that they were going to be on her side, so they would kill themselves to light her properly, to go out of their way to be nice to her. She was an old established star, but she never lost that sense of making everybody her friend. They could make her look good, make her job easier, and take obstacles out of her way.

It's a very good idea to respect the technicians. It's one of the reasons why I've always believed that actors should do crew work, so you know the kind of support you're getting and don't take it for granted.

Keep your wits about you all the time. Don't just be an actor. That's your job, but look at what the other people do, find out what the other people know. Many actors simply do their lines, and then they go over to the coffee place, and they have no idea what else is happening on set. Let your curiosity find out, because eventually, it could help you be more of an asset on the set. Just like working in the theater.

Olympia Dukakis was here [at the University of North Carolina School of the Arts], and she said, "I used to be a pain in the ass." And she was. She was very intense, and very committed. And then she said, "I realized people don't like to work with that—a pain in the ass." You want to work with people who are fun to be with, pleasant to be with. That doesn't mean you can't be passionate about your craft, but you spend this intense time together, you want it to be pleasant and happy. So I think you need to learn how to bond with people, learn how to collaborate, that's absolutely essential. Learn how to be an attractive person, instead of a moody dark person sitting in the corner who I don't want to work with again; I don't care how talented you are.

You Will Learn through Experience

As Gerald counseled, mastering camera technique takes practice. As you work, you will continue to learn. When you watch films, see what techniques from this section you can identify.

You can't do it in your head. You can't read about it. All of that, you will learn through experience—by doing film. Each time you do it, you'll learn more. You'll learn how little and how much is expected. You'll get better and better at it the more you're in front of a camera.

Gerald (foreground) with the cast of his 1974 production of *Love's Labor's Lost* for The Acting Company.

CHAPTER FIVE

SHAKESPEARE & MUSICAL THEATER

From early on in his career, Gerald had a unique dual perspective: he directed Broadway musicals like West Side Story, Hair, *and* A Time For Singing, *and also directed classics, including numerous Shakespeare plays at the Delacorte in Central Park. Over the years, Gerald realized the wealth of parallels between Shakespeare and musical theater.*

JOHN HOUSEMAN (Director, Teacher):
Gerald Freedman is that rare combination in the American theater of a director who understands and excels in both classics and contemporary musical and dramatic works.[17]

I was doing Shakespeare in the Park and doing Broadway musicals at the same time, and I don't think, at that time, there was *anybody* who was doing that.[18]

I find myself now passing on to the next generation the knowledge and understanding I received from Leonard Bernstein and Jerome Robbins, which eventually came down from the Elizabethans, dare I say Shakespeare? And this phase of my journey is as enriching and exciting as when I was a young Turk just trying to get my foot in the door.

I do both classical and contemporary plays. I love classic theater. I love Broadway musicals. A lot of people say, "How strange you should be doing such different things," but there are a lot of similarities.[19]

JOHN MAUCERI (Conductor, Colleague):
He can sing and he can dance; he can write music and he can write lyrics.
He's from an era when that was possible. It's not just that he is a Broadway
baby, because obviously his chops with Shakespeare are enormous. I think
it's because he's so honest, and so profoundly musical.

There's a great kinship between doing Shakespeare—the way I think
it ought to be done, anyway—and the musical theater form.[20] I hope I
can show how my work in the two forms revealed useful and beneficial
similarities in form and structure, and, in the glory days of the American
musical, how one form was used to enhance the other form.

My experience with musicals showed me how close Shakespeare was
to musicals in form, in energy, and in the desire to communicate. He
also wrote for a popular audience. Both the musical and Shakespeare
had been created as popular art—public entertainment—and make no
mistake, Shakespeare was show business. He had a lot of competition
with bear-baiting circus acts and the raucous street entertainment of
the Elizabethan world. Many of the same values shaped the two forms,
which in New York in the 1930s through the '60s only *seemed* worlds
apart.

Shakespeare is outrageously important to me. I tend to take it for
granted because I've done so much of it, and because I insist that it be
part of my life. I have made life-changing decisions to be near Shakespeare's texts. To be able to produce him, I have limited my availability
to the commercial theater. I have learned from his humanism and wept
with his compassion, exulted in his language and metaphor. I have been
quite literally intoxicated by them, and I salute Shakespeare the con-
summate showman.[21]

JOHN CULLUM (Actor, Singer):
Shakespeare was not just a great poet—he was as good as any of the poets
in the world had ever been—he was basically a theater man. He knew how
to tell a story onstage.

Shakespeare would feel absolutely at home in a theater where the
leading actor demanded a final flourish to finish off his performance,
where the producer demanded some scene of spectacle, and the audience wanted a great opener.[22]

The Elizabethan stage was more or less a bare platform thrust out into the middle of an empty space, open to the weather for low working class types—groundlings—who paid very little on the one hand, and a three-level covered surround on three sides for those who could afford to pay more to be protected from the elements. That meant you had to please them both. It accounts for the complexity in the material from low comic material to elevated poetic imagery. It meant there was no opportunity for elaborate scene changes or stage machinery or lighting effects. It was performed in daylight—therefore, Shakespeare put his scenic effects into his poetic imagery, words, and often into his songs.

In *As You Like It,* when we move from the court of Duke Frederick into the forest of Arden, Shakespeare sings, "Under the greenwood tree / Who loves to lie with me / And turn his merry note / Unto the sweet bird's throat." Well, compare that to the revolutionary opening bars of *Oklahoma!*—"There's a bright golden haze on the meadow, there's a bright golden haze on the meadow. The corn is as high as an elephant's eye, and it looks like it's climbing clear up to the sky. Oh what a beautiful mornin', Oh what a beautiful day." In both instances, you know just where you are, and your imagination conjures up a scene. You don't need scenery. It's all in the lyric. It sticks because it's contained in a melody.

Almost all of Shakespeare's plays have songs in them, even the tragedies: *Hamlet,* the Scottish play [*Macbeth*], *Othello,* even *King Lear!* In addition, all performances ended in a dance. This was sometimes called for in the text, but regardless, it was a regular part of an Elizabethan performance, because the Elizabethan playhouse was a place for popular entertainment—show business—just as the Broadway musical theater is.

We have to get Shakespeare out of the books, off the page, and onto the stage. Another relation to musicals: they're meant to be heard, not read.

JOSIE DE GUZMAN (Actor, Singer):
Shakespeare is music. And if you are connected to your emotions and you know what you're saying, you can use that musicality.

The kind of actor that was originally used to doing Shakespeare is exactly the kind of actor needed to do an American musical. The pieces both need that kind of energy, that kind of direct commitment to an audience—a dynamic, visceral commitment.[23] It is much easier to go from the classic training needed for Shakespeare to the musical stage than from the "kitchen sink" drama training.[24]

KEVIN KLINE (Actor, Former Student):
I've seen actors from the musical comedy world who were right at home in Shakespeare, and vice versa. It has to do with heightened language and elevated text, and what they require.

The fact is that in Shakespeare you have to discover the music. I mean, the poetry is there, but the rhythms of it have to be discovered. Instead of being like *Bohème*, where they're written in, we have to go backwards and discover the life that makes those rhythms reasonable for these people.[25]

Other areas of recognition and familiarity that a Shakespeare text and a Broadway script share in common are the blending of one scene and the next—the effortless or overlapping transition. We use the movie term *dissolve* now.

Because the Elizabethan theater was an outdoor theater originally, there could be no blackouts, obviously, and there could be no full-stage curtains. The scenery was basically the stationary architecture of the theater: a bare platform, two pillars to support a roof over the actors, two doors right and left, an alcove called *the inner below*, and a balcony above. Scenes were written so they had a walking entrance and a walking exit while characters were still speaking. This in effect was a verbal dissolve. One scene overlapped the next. It never stopped. This allowed for great fluidity and pace, one scene melting into the next instead of a curtain closing.

On the Broadway stage in the '30s and '40s, a curtain would close, and a performer would step out in front of the curtain and sing or play a scene in a shallow downstage area while scenery was being changed behind it.

Starting with *West Side Story*, scenes began to dissolve into one another, as in an Elizabethan play: you went from a little Puerto Rican dress shop to Maria—the Juliet character, twirling in her new dress—to a rain of crepe paper ribbons that lifted to reveal a dance in full stage energy taking place in a gymnasium, which eventually melted into a brick wall of see-through scrim and a fire escape balcony, all a vista in the open.

Not very different than Shakespeare's dynamic moving from scene to scene in the same sequence in *Romeo and Juliet*. The dress shop might have come from the alcove, the inner below, and the fire escape would have been played in the outer above. You can trust me, I've staged both.

The soliloquy in Shakespeare, "To be, or not to be, that is the question"—the direct address to an audience, sharing the character's inner feelings with the audience—was not that different from Professor Higgins declaring, "I've grown accustomed to her face. She almost makes the day begin." It was an equal and character-revealing inner monologue. Ethel Merman coming down to the footlights and bawling out with clarion tones, "Curtain up, light the lights, you got nothing to hit but the heights!" was not that different from Henry V's clarion call to his English troops before the gates of Harfleur, "Once more unto the breach, dear friends, once more," and so on.

Shakespeare was writing the "close-up." A soliloquy is a close-up. Or the aria—direct to the audience: "My boy Bill! He'll be tall and tough as a tree." "To be, or not to be." They are the same thing: explaining what's going on inside a character—their inner thoughts.[26]

JOHN LANGS (Director, Former Student):
A soliloquy is a song, and it requires a lot of the same investigation and work, because it has to hold the stage in the same way.

Another of the surprising similarities: I would peruse a script for a new musical and the page would suddenly read, "And here we need a show stopping dance number." And I would think, "Oh great. What is it? What can we do that will be so dynamic, so original, so much fun that it will stop the show? We'd better come up with something." Then I was given the opportunity to direct *Titus Andronicus*, an early Shakespeare tragedy, in the Park, and in the script there is a stage direction: "Exit these characters during the fray." I said to myself, "What fray? What the hell is a fray?" Well, it turns out a fray is a small skirmish. "What am I supposed to do here?" And then it hit me, they were one and the same thing. Shakespeare was saying the same thing as the musical script: "Do something spectacular here that will hold the audience and excite them. Do a show stopping number." And I did. It was a hell of a fray, and it stopped the show. But I might not have understood that Shakespeare one line direction if I hadn't worked on musicals.

Musical Terms

Gerald believed that musical theater and opera require the same truthful, specific acting work as in any other medium. He worked with musical performers to allow the music and lyrics to inform their choices and guide them toward that truth.

"You have to be bigger in an opera house." I don't believe that. You have to be specific wherever you are. When you have music supporting you, as in opera, you feel so strongly that you have to sing an idea. It only means that your need has to be greater, not that you have to do phony acting.

PATTI LUPONE (Actor, Former Student):
Whether I'm doing a song or a classical play, it's the same process. I don't think you can sing a song unless you understand the scene.

I am comfortable with music because of my singing background and my composing. It is my second language after English. I don't ask singers to do anything that I couldn't do myself, but I do make demands of them as actors which sometimes seem unfamiliar to them. They do seem to enjoy and respond wonderfully to new direction. I cannot and will not compromise on the acting work, but I do try to translate that work into musical terms.

ROBERT WALDMAN (Composer):
Jerry was one of the few really musical directors I ever worked with. I could leave the rehearsal room and leave it in his hands, and would not be afraid to come back and find a nightmare going on.

I find that the artists respect the fact that I do know the music. And I rarely if ever ask them to do something that violates the spirit of the music, because I get all my answers from the music. I never come in and impose an idea on it.[27]

VICTORIA BUSSERT (Director, Former Student):
All lyrics were treated as dialogue, to get the actors to think about the text, not just phrasing musical phrases, but to actually be specific with the text itself, which can often get lost in musicals because many times

people are thinking about where they're going to take a breath—"How do I phrase this musically?" and Jerry would make them deal with the specificity of the words.

The music tells you everything. Where else can you find what's really happening, if not in the music—the pulse of the music?

During my second year at the University of the North Carolina School of the Arts, I was a performer in Gerald's production of the musical Floyd Collins. *Gerald began rehearsals by having the cast learn all of the songs, before doing any work on the book scenes. I asked him why. He told me: "If you're working on a play, you do the table work to discover the music. In a musical, it is already given to you. So you start with that."*

Music carries a lot of information if it's well done. It's like poetry. It's condensed tremendously, so you don't need as many words as a poet—as you do, generally, in writing prose—to say something, because there is a distillation of language, emotion, color. The same thing is true with a musical.

The singer comes with the outer shell because of the music. He's got it learned, and he has to metrically be accurate. But then he's got to go back and expand on that.[28]

You see abuses of this: stagings by directors in the theater who don't, in essence, listen to the music.[29]

Music is my language. I don't think of it as something you add to a production. It's something I live and breathe and use as a communication tool all the time.[30]

Shakespeare Today

Many people are daunted by Shakespeare. They find it antiquated, inaccessible, and irrelevant to today's world. With a little time and investigation, however, it becomes clear that Shakespeare's stories, characters, and ideas are every bit as applicable to today as they were when Shakespeare wrote them some four hundred years ago. Gerald believed that Shakespeare is for the now.

Shakespeare is, well, not only very close to me—I mean I've done so much of it—but it's never an obstacle for me; there's never been a veil of academia between me and the texts. I don't know why. Maybe I was just lucky with the kind of teachers I had or the kind of introduction to it, but it's always been immediately accessible to me, and I think that's been characteristic of the Shakespeare I've done, from the very first one I did for Joe Papp, which was *Taming of the Shrew*.[31]

Nothing would have attracted me to the theater if I weren't drawn to the classics. I want to work in an environment where I can do the great works, because they're challenging and they demand you explore yourself. These plays are more than just light summer fare. They're substantial. They're a full meal. They explore the great richness of human nature.

GREG VORE (Guest Teacher, Former Student):
Shakespeare covers so much of humankind and the human condition, all of the situations you can think of, it's covered: adultery, jealousy, love, family feuds, self-delusion, and madness. The entire human condition is contained in these plays. Jerry had a great, great respect for that.

These plays thrive because they are about ideas that deeply affect us, even as the plays entertain. These are great, thrilling plays that speak to today and we've got to do them in a way that makes people interested in them.[32] When you work on a classical play, don't start thinking "classically." You have to think of PEOPLE. Shakespeare is as contemporary as eating an apple, or making love.

BARNEY HAMMOND (Teacher, Colleague):
We shared the belief that when you do Shakespeare, you do Shakespeare in the now, and it's Shakespeare in the present. You're not doing some archaic classic that you're dusting off the cobwebs of the script to do. It's the immediacy of it—the humanity of it.

The fact that plays have lasted through decades and centuries are by that very fact important and popular. Unpopular plays do *not* last, they do not have longevity.

We do classic theater because these plays have stood the test of time, which means they relate to the human condition. I want to make those plays immediate for an audience. But we also need to include new playwrights. We can't exist as a museum theater. That's impossible today, and I don't think that concept is worthy today.[33]

I think one of the problems in working with any kind of classical literature is falling into the clichés of some powerful performance that has come down to us either through movies or apocryphal stories or through tradition. The key is not settling for those choices right off the bat, but looking beyond what may be the obvious. If you stay calm for a while, and let the character speak in the behavior and the relationships, there is often a more interesting and complex person there.

My predilection in attacking Shakespeare is not lightweight or from a decorative point of view. Shakespeare wrote at a time when the language—you can tell—is bold and often bawdy, and so even people of "refinement" or upper income use strong and vigorous language. Well, I try to get that in the behavior. So rather than it being a very elegant, sophisticated kind of badinage between maybe Beatrice and Benedick, I may have seen it as a more confrontational, more challenging. That is generally my way.[34]

Scholars now believe English as spoken by Americans is closer to what Shakespeare heard than the sound of an Edwardian actor speaking an artificial construct of sounds that evolved from the upper classes at Oxford and Cambridge over time.

STEVE VINOVICH (Actor, Former Student):
"Stop singing! Talk to each other!" Jerry was always that way. It was about communicating. It makes it much more accessible. His productions were very accessible, because you knew what was going on. The people were talking to each other. It makes a difference.

An audience shouldn't need a synopsis for Shakespeare. This is appalling to me—to take a Shakespeare play that is in English, our mother tongue, and summarize the plot. That doesn't mean that you understand every word, or that you go home speaking "Thou" or "Thou'rt." In a good production, though, the behavior of the people onstage illuminates something about the human condition that you understand and are moved by.[35] If the audience does not share that enthusiasm, there is something wrong with your work.

JOHN WOODSON (Actor):
He was a great audience person. He understood that his job was to be the audience, and to say, "I don't know what's going on here. I know very well everything that's going on, but what's going on? Tell me the story. That story." He was a master of that, he really was: clarity.

Mr. Shakespeare is a bottomless pit of challenge and inspiration. He's been very kind to me.

Breaking Down Shakespeare

Gerald drove his students to keep digging deeper, to examine and explore every word of Shakespeare's text in order to find the underlying truth of human behavior.

Shakespeare's genius guides the actor to the truth. His genius lies in his understanding of human nature, and his ability to take a contemporary and conventional form of his theater and amplify it, embellish it, imbue it with such life, such reality, that without sacrificing any of the various levels of humor, he enhances it all and lovingly suffuses it with a humanizing element. This is what has kept his works universal long after his contemporaries' plays of similar nature have simply disappeared, because they no longer mean anything to us, and their characters have become mere mouthpieces of a verbal language that has lost its power to communicate. Shakespeare, first and foremost, communicates in a human language of relationship and experience.[36]

LOGAN FAHEY (Actor, Former Student):
Shakespeare is in his blood. That kind of understanding of that heightened language allowed for him to direct on a real human level. That made it so much easier for us not to be daunted by the technical aspects. We could just focus on what was going on between two people, naturally. He really got us out of our heads of it being a period piece.

Many actors are so intimidated by Shakespeare that they don't even know how to look for the clues, particularly young actors. So you do have to point them out and lead the actors to possibilities.[37]

Shakespeare always tells you what he's going to do, does it, and then adds it up when it's over.

Usually, the first couple of lines in a Shakespeare play tell you what the play's about. In *Romeo and Juliet*, he has a narrator tell you what it's about.

Don't ignore the lyrics in Shakespeare's plays. They usually contain the theme, or comment on the theme.

Shakespeare does not always give many lines to characterize a role, but he always gives important clues that make a role alive and vital to the fabric of the play.[38]

PEGGY LOFT (Director, College Classmate):
Text work for Shakespeare is about digging out the real meaning. Actors tend to—when they hit a place where they have no information about its meaning—usually make an educated guess, and they assume they're right, and it's often wrong. It's not helpful to the acting unless you have a firm foundation of what is being said for real.

Trust the Material

Don't be too easily lured by cutting or "fixing" Shakespeare, Gerald warned, because the particularly incongruous or confusing moments may be key to a fuller understanding of the play. He reminded students that Shakespeare's plays were created for the stage, not the page; some text can only become clear in the doing.

I say tamper with the structure at your peril! "This is clumsy, let's rearrange it." "I don't understand this. It's too obscure. Let's cut it." How often I have thought those thoughts. Trust. Trust. Use your blue pencil sparingly. I am familiar with our penchant for wanting to neaten up our Shakespeare.[39]

"Why not start with the shipwreck in *Twelfth Night* and then go to the court?" How much more logical and orderly. I sweated over that temptation for a long time. But *how important* the opening moments of a show are in setting the tone and subject and getting the audience involved. You see, *Twelfth Night* isn't about a shipwreck and it isn't a tragedy or a melodrama. It's about love and lovesickness, and it's a comedy. "If music be the food of love, play on…" That's all you need to know.[40]

Sometimes neither I nor the actors know what to do with a passage, and although the footnotes very carefully explain the meaning of every word and expression, they do not answer the questions, "What is it about?" and "What makes it work in the theater?" The first reaction, of course, is to cut it. That is the easiest of all solutions when dealing with obscurity in a Shakespearean play. Even if one understands the allusions after careful study, one wonders if a modern audience will. But I have almost always found that the humor does not lie in the words. I would like to emphasize that point very strongly. The essence of an emotion in Shakespeare, in poetry, is almost always in the words. But it certainly is not the solution to comedy. In my work in Shakespeare comedy—*A Midsummer Night's Dream, The Taming of the Shrew, The Comedy of Errors, The Tempest, As You Like It,* and *Love's Labor's Lost*—I have learned to trust Shakespeare's theatrical sense. I recognize the classic base of his humor, the ageless theatrical forms and kinds of comedy that are still evident in contemporary theater, including night clubs, burlesque, television, and the Broadway theater.[41]

If a director learns to recognize similar obscure passages in Shakespeare as comic routines, he will find, more often than not, that they work with this approach to the playing. Many of the scenes in *Love's Labor's Lost* that did not appear at all funny in print were very funny onstage in our production, and related to the same kind of humor we still laugh at today.[42]

A great deal of this comedy one cannot get with the eye, from the printed page. It is comedy for the ear. The sound of the words make for great humor; the joke is in the sound rather than the sense. I am sure that *pricket, facere,* and *bis coctus* made their own fun in Shakespeare's time simply by their sound. They make the same fun today. Those who maintain that the humor in *Love's Labor's Lost* is impossible for a contemporary audience to enjoy, or try to make sense of footnotes, would save themselves both time and anguish by simply performing it in front of an audience. Trust the material. If you let it work for itself, it will.[43]

What to a reader of the play may seem clumsy, abrupt, or in bad taste, or what does not fit in conveniently with some preconceived intellectual pattern, works beautifully onstage, the place for which the scene was, after all, meant.[44]

Spotlight: Serving the Public with Papp

Throughout his years of collaboration with legendary theater producer and director Joseph Papp, Gerald strove to make Shakespeare immediate, clear, and accessible, not just to the theaterati, but to everyone. All along, his equal passion for musical theater endured, notably in his world premiere production of Hair.

JOSEPH PAPP (Director, Producer):
Gerald Freedman was one of the major artistic forces in the development of the New York Shakespeare Festival. His skill and taste place him in the forefront of directors in the United States.[45]

In those years [the 1950s] it took two or three years to get a musical off the ground. Now it takes much longer. But I needed to find work in between. I wrote a letter to Joe Papp after seeing an early New York Shakespeare production of *As You Like It* with the great actor George C. Scott as Jaques. Despite that performance, I wrote, "I think I can do a better production." Joe called me in for an interview, and thus began our amazing twenty-nine year relationship.

I told him I liked what he did but I didn't like the direction and I thought I could do it better. He listened, and I obviously spoke his language, and he heard stuff that he liked. He talked to me like I was already working for him. At the end of it, he said, "We're going to work together." I said, "Fine." I didn't hear anything from him, I don't think, for at least nine months. And nine months later I got a call, out of the absolute blue, "How would you like to do *Taming of the Shrew* in the Park?" I said, "Great!" And then *Taming of the Shrew* was a smashing success in the Park and that cemented my relationship with Joe.[46]

Joe was just establishing free Shakespeare in Central Park, and was engaged in a monumental struggle with the Goliath of public works in New York City, Robert Moses. Joe Papp, the David in this battle, won, and free Shakespeare in Central Park became established, and Joe spawned hundreds of free Shakespeare festivals across the United States.

I became part of that creative team—Joe Papp, Bernie Gersten, and myself—a year after that footprint was firmly fixed in Central Park. Bernie and Joe and I became a one. We were a little family.

Free Shakespeare makes a difference. In New York City, kids who had never seen a play—much less a Shakespearean play—came together with the theater elite, Columbia professors and sophisticated Broadway regulars. It was more like the audience Shakespeare wrote for. Outdoor Shakespeare played with the vigor and energy that Shakespeare first intended when he wrote for his Globe Theater, his wooden O of *Henry V* fame. This was new, not the refined Shakespeare of theater greats like Maurice Evans, John Gielgud, Helen Hayes, and Margaret Webster. They were all giants in their way, but inside a Broadway theater—not outdoors, free to thousands of people, competing with air traffic and band concerts and the hustle and bustle of a metropolitan park. This needed a new kind of actor, an American actor. And we spawned a whole new breed. Listen to these names—unknown, young actors at the time, but trained in the classics and eager to play the great Shakespeare roles: James Earl Jones, Stacy Keach, Colleen Dewhurst, Sam Waterston, Roscoe Lee Browne, Barbara Barrie, Martin Sheen, Charlie Durning, Morgan Freeman, and eventually Raul Julia, Meryl Streep, Blythe Danner, and my own personal students Kevin Kline, Patti LuPone, Christine Baranski, Bill Hurt, and Mandy Patinkin. They were all part of our rotating stock company at that time. These are just a few of the regulars who were amongst what was to become a pantheon of new, vital, energetic, yes— roughly spoken, new interpreters, *American* interpreters of Shakespeare's verse, as opposed to a more elegant, nuanced, refined speaker of Shakespeare, exemplified by the English models that had become the standard.

Classical theater at that time meant only sonorous voices, and a kind of phony external way of gesturing. But we were something different.[47]

JOHN WOODSON (Actor):
In my Shakespeare life, I had worked with a lot of British directors, and I loved them, but it was still very heady, very much coming from a technical point of view first. But Gerald was right in there like a fighter, just jabbing away. I find myself to be a very intuitive, instinctual, and physical kind of actor, and he was right on it.

One aspect of my directing in Central Park has been to stage the plays as if the members of the audience could not hear, but could only understand the action by what they saw. This is in no way meant to negate the importance of language, but is partly a response to the enormity of the outdoor space at the Delacorte Theater, and partly an effort to encompass an audience that ranges from a highly literate group of people, who are very familiar with the literature and background of the plays, to those in our audience who do not even understand English, or who have a very limited use of the language and a very limited knowledge of the play.[48]

STACY KEACH (Actor):
I learned more about playing Shakespeare from Jerry than anyone. He shared my own feelings about making Shakespeare accessible to a modern audience, in a contemporary way, without violating the technical responsibilities of the text. Making it understood. Making Shakespeare, which is like a foreign language to many people, completely understandable in terms of behavior, in terms of the expression of a line.

These were my happiest and most gratifying, satisfying years in the theater. With Joe, *the play was the thing*; the artist and artistic excellence came before the commerce. With his genius for producing, he always found a way to move forward and stay financially solvent. I never had a contract with him. We never talked money. I knew he would do the "right thing."

Joe felt that artistically, we had to grow beyond Shakespeare. That meant new plays. The Public Theater was born.

Joe and I wanted to open the Public Theater with a new musical—the unique American contribution to the stage. The original mission of the Public was to encourage and present new works dedicated to lyric theater: language, poetry, music. *Hair* came to Joe via James Rado and Gerry Ragni whom he met on the commuter train to Yale, where we were all working at the time. We recognized its great energy and exuberance of spirit, but it lacked form. The challenge was to give it structure without destroying its energy and originality, and to give it a semblance of a beginning, middle, and end.

When James Rado and Gerome Ragni first brought it to me, *Hair* was nothing but scraps of loose-leaf paper. I take credit for shaping the material because, quite honestly, nothing very much existed except the wonderful energy and freshness of their vision. Galt MacDermot had not even written the music yet.

I never dreamed it would have the kind of impact it had, and I don't think the authors did either, or Joe. We were lucky, I guess, I mean it made a kind of theater history.[49]

VICTORIA BUSSERT (Director, Former Student):
Hair changed the face of musical theater, and that was Gerald. That was Gerald taking bits of dialogue written on napkins and overheard on subways, and creating a piece of art with it.

JACK O'BRIEN (Director):
There would have been no *Hair* if he hadn't kicked that out of a garbage can, as it were. And I use the term advisedly, believe me. He made those kids sit up and take notice. They didn't know what the fuck they were doing. And they didn't after the fact know what they had done. He willed that into being, no question about it.

BERNARD GERSTEN (Producer, Colleague):
It was a very tense time, because it was the opening show, and God knows it was a show that was all over the lot. But Jerry kept his head when all about him were losing theirs. He was very stable. He was very steady.

Joe respected my craft and my experience, I think, greatly, which exhibited itself by not interfering, and this is family to me. Joe knew he could count on Jerry, his family, to do his job, which left Joe free to deal with a lot of other problems. So when Joe assigned a show to me, a Shakespeare or a new play at the Public Theater, he pretty much left me alone.[50]

My shows generally got very good reviews, and he would always write me a wonderful note afterwards, and the note would say something like, "Jerry, when you do work like this, it's easy for me to raise money, so I'm very grateful. I thank you."[51]

Joe had the reputation of coming in and taking over his young directors' work, or at least messing around with them. He never took over any production of mine and always had helpful insights. We would cast together. His advice was, "Take the best actor" over the best type. I've followed it ever since. He would come to my second tech and give useful observations and doable suggestions. I looked forward to his visits at that stage of the process.

He also observed, "Jerry, you do your best work during previews." I took this as a compliment. I always look forward to the audience to give me a fresh and sophisticated feedback which helps me.

Joe was so paternal, almost to an excess, and we all felt like we contributed. See, even though daddy was at the head of it, we were treated with respect. Our feelings were elicited and responded to. When you were sick, I personally didn't have to benefit from this, but Joe carried people's rent bills, he helped them with their doctor bills. There was great love and affection, not business as usual or business like anybody else conducted it.[52]

Joe Papp! What a wonderful collaborator and what a wonderful and creative time we had together over twenty-nine years.

Gerald at work with Jerome Robbins (left) and Sylvia Drulie (obscured) on the world premiere production of *West Side Story* in 1957.

KEYSTONE USA

DONALD DIETZ

TOP: At the table from left: Gerald in discussion with choreographer Joyce Trisler and producer Joseph Papp for their 1971 production of *Timon of Athens* at the New York Shakespeare Festival.
BOTTOM: Gerald giving notes to directing student Robby Lutfy in the Catawba Arena Theatre at the University of North Carolina School of the Arts in 2010.

CHAPTER SIX

DIRECTING

At the University of North Carolina School of the Arts, Gerald developed his own directing program within the School of Drama, which consisted of only a few students per year, whom he took under his wing. As one of Gerald's directing students, I studied and trained with my actor classmates throughout the day, assisted faculty members and guest directors in the evenings, and directed my own projects well into the wee hours. Twice a week, in the Drama conference room, my fellow directing students and I sat around a table with Gerald and discussed the work: what we'd observed, what we'd learned, and what we still struggled to understand. It was there around that table that Gerald taught me the fundamentals of directing that I still use to this day.

What is directing? There is not one clear answer. As Gerald often reminded us, there is no one way to direct. The subtle art of directing transforms with each director, each play, each environment, and each ensemble of artists. Despite such inherent diversity, Gerald offered ideas and techniques which can help to set any director on a productive course. As in all creative work, there are exceptions to every rule, and the greatest teacher is experience—in other words, doing.

JOHN TOIA (Stage Manager, Teacher):
Jerry taught directing in a very different way than others. Really, you couldn't learn from Jerry unless you were mentored by Jerry. As a director, a lot of your training was observation of Gerald's work. So much of it happened in the rehearsal process itself.

JOHN LANGS (Director, Former Student):
[In directing class,] we would begin a conversation about acting and the work, and we would just keep going down the rabbit hole of him letting us try to explain to each other what good acting was, what spine work was, what the role of the director was in the rehearsal. We would talk about our assisting gigs with other directors, what our challenges were, what their challenges were, what their technique was, if they had any. There was very frank conversation, and a real honor clause in that room that nothing went beyond.

JOHN DILLON (Director, Guest Teacher):
It was not theoretical work in the classroom. It was based on discussions of actual problems as they manifest themselves in the rehearsal process. And this was quite a unique way of teaching directing. Most classes begin on a more theoretical basis, and I think it's typical of Gerald that he began with a very direct working approach.

This is not *the* way. It is *a* way.

My directing course should provide an overview of what my experience in the profession has taught me, rather than the superficial examination of what is commonly understood as directing: conceptualizing a script in visual terms, and moving actors around to create beautiful or meaningful pictures.

As a director, you have to be father, mother, confessor, lover, psychiatrist, everything. And that's how I interpret the director's role; it's not about "You go here, you go there," being an autocrat and a dictator.

My approach builds on actor training. I consider the actor the director's main resource, and the keystone of my directing vision. A director must understand the actor's process, and have the tools to communicate with them.

GAYE TAYLOR UPCHURCH (Director, Former Student):
He had the directors act. And that was a great exercise, too, to make the directors get up and act, because then you understood even more about the vulnerability of being an actor, and the way that you want to be spoken to, and also all of the things that you're dealing with at once. I actually feel like as a director I should take more acting classes.

The director must also acquire the basic tools and techniques, and the appropriate craft language to communicate with the collaborative designers who help fulfill the director's vision.

The first two years of training for my directing students coincide with actor training. Their last two years branch off and distribute some of the directing load under my supervision, and include thesis projects as well as field work/internships, which are the only valid way of training directors.

In short, great directing is a combination of imagination, intuition, common sense, and the tools, which you use to solve problems.

ROBERT WALDMAN (Composer):
He believed the same thing that I did: when there was a problem, to be pragmatic. There was always a solution. I'm sure he passed it on to his directing class. That's such a talent to have, and an instrument that you have to use in the theater, and in life: being pragmatic. There's always a solution. Don't get hysterical and slam doors and close off. Let's find the solution.

I think of directing as problem solving. I think the important thing is to recognize the problems. We all may have different creative solutions to them, but you have to know how to recognize them.

I value clarity above all. Every skill and device is used to bring the text alive, to find honesty in acting, something actually happening in the moment onstage. I am fierce in my dedication to achieving that quality.

Don't Be Lured by the Gimmick; Tell the Story

Rather than devising a director's "concept" or "vision," Gerald pushed his directing students to dig deeper into the text, to get to the spine—the essence of the play, the root of what it's really about—and let that truth guide every decision they made.

There are directors who have very strong ideas and images, who want to work that way, who want to put their image on bodies and see it on the stage. That isn't the way I work. That isn't what I believe in. That isn't what I want to see in the theater, and that isn't what I teach. If you want to be that kind of director, you are welcome, but that is not what you're going to get here. I don't do visual concept things at the expense of the actor.

OLYMPIA DUKAKIS (Actor):
He was not the kind of director who we have so much today, who comes in with a concept and wants you to fulfill it, and is not interested in anything you have to say, and, as a matter of fact, would consider you a little recalcitrant if you started talking.

JOHN SEIDMAN (Actor, Former Assistant):
At the time that I was working with him, there was an unusual amount of "director's theater" going on. *Antony and Cleopatra* had to be set during the Korean War, or in outer space. Gerald had no interest in doing that sort of thing. Not that he felt everything had to be historically consistent necessarily, but his highest priority was the clear telling of the story that was there, not trying to help it along by changing its natural habitat, as he understood it. He gave the final determination to the playwright.

I'm not comfortable with directors who trample all over a work, you know, and set it on the moon and what have you.[53] I don't think, "Oh, I have a concept." I think, "How can I make this clear? How can I make this hot? How can I make this immediate? How can I make this more personal?" I think concept is dangerous, because it seems to be an outside idea that will carry the play, and for me, all those ideas are from the inside, from the text.

EDDIE KURTZ (Political Organizer, Former Student):
Gerald approaches his art from a deeply human place. He has an uncanny ability to find the heart of a story. When he directs, he begins with the spine, the most profound human drive of the play. Nothing draws his ire in rehearsal or bores his mind in performance like the lack of this drive, the lack of real communication onstage. While Gerald has often been at the helm of stunning visual productions, spectacle is just gravy in his world. The human drama is what interests him, and he has illuminated our world through his work in it.

The question I grapple with the most is, "What is the author's intent?" The first thing I ask is, "What is the author saying?" And then I want to help them say it.

I'm not interested in surfaces; I don't do gimmicky productions.[54] Don't be lured by the gimmick; tell the story.

KELLY MAXNER (Teacher, Former Student):
That was the big one for me: really letting go of all concepts, letting go of all the interesting things, all the clever things, all the very dramatic things, and getting to two people talking together. Really talking. That's true north. That's the foundation. Everything can revolve around that.

I pride myself that you do not see the director's role in my productions. The things I want to achieve, I achieve, and it looks like the actors did it themselves. The few times reviewers have written about my directorial choices, it's when I've done something stylized, like a slow motion fight sequence, which I thought was integral. But they can see that it's directorial. All the other stuff that I really invest my whole life and my guts and my passion in, they don't see it, because it doesn't reflect me, and it shouldn't, in my opinion. Really, I'm only trying to serve the play. And I personally just don't like when a director presents himself.

PAUL GEMIGNANI (Music Director):
It was not ever about him. It was about the whole, the project itself, and how to get this group of people running down the same road.

ROBERT FOXWORTH (Actor):
What I love about the kind of work that Jerry does is that you don't see the work. You don't see people working at it; you see it happening. It's not like you see actors working. You see actors being and doing.

I want the audience to get the subject, as I see it, but not me. The answers all stem from the same source for me: I'm making an almost contained motion, a circular outline, because it's like the whole theater experience is contained around language—the author's words. And that to me is prime.[55]

JACK O'BRIEN (Director):
I thought the work he did for me [at the Old Globe] and the work that I watched him do over the years was varied, and balanced, and intelligent, and always true to the text. Incredibly true to the text. If it wasn't on the page, he didn't really support it. He wasn't so interested in making an impression, as he was getting the actors to be the very best they could be.

As a director I ask myself, "Where did they come from? What are they doing? What can I do to make them and their relationships clear for an audience, supportive to what the words tell me?"[56]

What Do You Think?

Gerald encouraged his young directors to invite everyone's full, creative participation. Why stifle subordinates with answers, he asked, when you can inspire collaborators with questions?

Let the artist explore, through a method of questioning, guiding their search.[57]

A play is a collaborative effort, not an authoritarian, dictatorial vision that somehow got bludgeoned and bullied into shape on a stage. I think a director who has a unified vision is important, but I cherish a collaborative relationship with the other theater artists.[58]

Mostly I ask questions, because I want the actors to look for the answers. When they look for the answers, they own it. They own the material. It would be easy for me to tell them the answers, or the moves, but then I don't think the actors own it, and they tend not to amplify the answer you gave them. If you lead them to discover it, then they're already on the hunt, they're on the trail, and so their own imagination and creativity keep expanding those answers, and ideally, you get more. You get better, richer results than you would by just giving them an answer—even if it is a stimulating answer—to a question of theirs.

With that said, usually there's a deadline, sometimes maybe nine months, sometimes three weeks, and if they aren't coming up with a creative answer for whatever you're working on, then, yes, then I fill in the outline for them. But as I tell my young directors, the big deal is *when*. When do you supply that? How long do you allow them to be looking? And that's decided by experience and your own comfort level. Now, I can wait a long time, because I know that I can quickly pull a show together in a technical way. But I would rather let them wrestle with the answers.

STEVEN ROUTMAN (Actor):
I like to answer questions in my own way. I don't like to have answers or choices foisted upon me. It's really exciting and thrilling and scary to have to go through that journey, but the reward is that you know that your performance and your choices are unique to you.

Often what I'll do, instead of answering an actor's question, is counter it with, "Well, what do you think?" When they question themselves more, they already know the answer, and then they've made their own discovery.

PJ PAPARELLI (Director, Guest Teacher):
He doesn't want to celebrate how smart he is in getting an actor somewhere; he really wants to celebrate the actor's personal discovery, because he knows that's going to stand the test of time, rather than an actor's reaction to direction. While he gives great direction, he really tries to encourage the actor to let that light bulb go off for themselves, because then they will start to trust that instinct.

When I was younger, I guess I was afraid that they would never come up with the answers, but now I know they can. Of course you have to help them by asking loaded questions.

AMY SALTZ (Director, Former Assistant):
He taught me to look for the right question to ask, that it's not just arbitrary questions. Finding the right question that will help someone to think deeper, or help to point them in a direction, or help to open up a window for them.

It is not just a matter of asking questions or telling people results; you have to find ways of stimulating the actor to look so that the search is fun, so that it allows for invention, so that it results in action, not just literal answers.[59]

My Idea

Many directors assume that they are responsible for having lots of great ideas on their own. The way Gerald saw it, the best ideas are born from collaboration, so there is no need to hold onto "my idea." The idea that best serves the story wins, no matter where it comes from.

I was attracted to the authority of the director. But my life in the theater has been a gradual giving up of that. I met these wonderful artists who took my intuition and my instincts so beyond me, and then I loved the collaboration. I'm quite willing to let the director's role in the theater diminish.

The mistaken idea is that the director is God, or that the director can order people around. That isn't what happens in the real world. It is all negotiation. If your idea is really better than an actor's, they'll love it. Everyone wants to look good. Everybody wants to make money. Everybody wants something to be a success. That's your *only* trump card. Don't go into a process thinking, "I'm the director, so I can do whatever I want." You can't. In a collaboration, particularly in a musical, the director can be the low man on the totem pole. The composer, the librettist, the star—if there is a star—or the person with the right voice, they may trump you if there is an occasion. And you need them, so you work with them, you work around them, you try to be creative and get the best out of what there is to offer. It's important to bring flexibility into the process, always.

I try not to impose my ideas on a scene. I know that as a young director I was afraid my ideas would get lost. That's why you write down *everything*, so it isn't lost. It's maybe delayed in the giving: "This is a good idea, but I'll hold off." Or, throw it into the pot in the moment; it may be stimulating. At the same time, you could throw out an idea, and it could die right away. All that judgment comes out of experience.

This happens so often, more often than I like to think: you have a great idea, and it *is* a great idea, and you present it to the actor, and since it didn't come out of real exploration for them, they never do it effectively, and it lies dead. This happens a lot in comedy—it was a good idea, but the actor will never believe in it, and it'll never happen. So, all this is very pragmatic stuff.

Bad ideas just die. They won't go anywhere. They have no life. But you have to have a critical eye that can appreciate when something truthful is going on, as opposed to something that an actor brings in that's just acting, and has no real energy or vitality or life to it. And that again will grow your sense of what is truthful. If an actor says, "Gee, what do you think of this?" I say, "Do it. Let's see!"

CAROL LAWRENCE (Actor, Singer):
Jerry Freedman would always say, "Try it. See what happens. Go for it. Go!"

If you cut an actor off, then it becomes an ego thing, and you have more problems than when you started. If you keep saying *no* and *my idea*, it just creates a bad room to work in.

Okay, now it's all devious. It's all tactics. I don't want to fight you; I want to listen to you. I want to suggest something to you. I might say, "Let's try it," and if it's not valid, it will die of its own invalidity, whereas if your idea has some validity, it'll stand up and I'll want to use it! It's better!

GREG VORE (Guest Teacher, Former Student):
Let them try all of the ideas. Don't say, "That's not going to work," before they have a chance to try it. Yes, you may know that's not going to work, but the actor doesn't know, and unless they eliminate that possibility, they may hold onto it. If you let people explore and experiment, then they'll eventually come to the same conclusion as to which idea is best.

I try not to impose a vision onto the acting. I want to collaborate, I love the collaboration process. I get more of what I want by being flexible than by being stubborn. You get a lot more accomplished by saying yes than by saying no.

ROB RUGGIERO (Director, Former Assistant):
He was very open to trying anything the actor wanted to explore, but that included all of his own ideas as well. And I think that is absolutely right. In the exploration, we can try anything an actor wants, but the director is afforded that same courtesy.

Working with Actors

Gerald has helped many of the greatest actors of the past seventy years do some of their finest work. What is the secret to such success? The work begins with profound empathy, meeting actors where they are, and learning how to supportively push them further. Helping an actor achieve a great performance requires respect, courage, honesty, permission, and trust.

KEVIN KLINE (Actor, Former Student):
Jerry really has dedicated himself to actors and acting. He's deeply invested in it, and really cares about it: the art of acting. He's a real actor's director in my book.

Too many directors come from a place other than an actor's background. And they work, and they're successful, but they don't often get good performances from actors, I can tell you.

When I first came into the theater, I thought the director was an authority figure, and told actors what to do. I had a language that came from my great acting teacher, Alvina Krause, and within her program at Northwestern we all used the same language, and everybody knew what it was. She would say, "Crystallize the moment. Hold. Beanbag that line." Those were like code words. Then I went to New York, and started working in the profession, and I started to say to actors, "Crystallize," and they didn't know what the hell I was talking about. I realized I had to learn their language, not give them mine.

I started taking acting classes from different schools in New York because I wanted to know what they were doing. I wanted to be able to talk in whatever tongue an actor needed.

When I work with actors, I'm not trying to convert them, I'm trying to elicit collaboration, and finally, get some kind of an ensemble unity out of it.

I love actors and I respect them in spades. I advocate the disappearance of the director. I think it's warranted sometimes. But definitely, with what's evolved in the theater, I think directors are useful in editing actors, and in collecting the points of view, so that it isn't anarchy. But quite often, I think actors can do without us directors, and do very well.

At the Actors Studio in New York, I learned how unimportant, in a sense, the director was.[60] The emphasis was on the actor and his or her creative process. I understood how the actor could use his own instrument, fill an author's intention—that there were more ways to the truth than just my vision. I came to be a *guider* rather than a *director*; a collaborator in the true sense of the word. I became more appreciative of the actor's contribution and richness through observing there. And I learned to be more patient, allowing them the time to do really necessary work.[61]

MATT BULLUCK (Teacher, Former Student):
He was great about keeping his point of view away from actors in a positive way. You sensed he had what he was trying to get to, but he was also aware that it was best to let the actors find it themselves. He viewed his actors more as collaborators than most directors did.

I welcome the contribution of the actor. I do everything to stimulate his imagination and personalization—to empower the actor, while guiding the result. This is primary in my rehearsal method.

It's about getting the best of you, and when I say *the best*, I don't even know who you are. I'm discovering as we collaborate together. And I want to get it without intimidating you, without hitting you on the head, without comparing you. Who are you? What are you? What can you offer? Never deny yourself who you are and the possibility that something, however crazy, is intuitive.

KEVIN KLINE (Actor, Former Student):
What it comes down to is, he wants *you*. What are *you* going to bring to the party? What is *your* take on this character? He encouraged the actors to make it their own, and find their own way.

If you have a frightened animal, you have to coax it out of its hiding place; it's about winning their confidence and drawing them out. I feel the same is true with actors, not patronizingly, but genuinely creating a safe environment: "You're gonna be okay. You will." Open them up to their intuition. Reassure them that they can't make a mistake, so they can fall all over the place, and do horrible things. And you might be thinking, "God, how can this talented person be doing these ridiculous things, making these terrible choices?" But you can't embarrass them that way. You have to support them, protect them. That resolve comes from experience.

VICTORIA BUSSERT (Director, Former Student):
He gave the actors permission to take risks that they might not normally take, because they felt there was such a strong hand underneath the production guiding them.

I challenge rather than demand. I might say, "I don't know how to do this, but this is what I want. How can we get that?"

I think the director's job should be to help actors make selections. Stimulate them toward choices, maybe fresher choices, less conventional and more truthful choices.[62]

I'm acutely aware every minute that I must keep actors interested, stimulated—entertained, in a way. I feel that is part of my job; that's part of my process—keeping them looking farther, deeper. And I take pleasure in that, not in coming up with answers so much as coming up with the tasks.[63]

I hate when directors say things like, "It's like your belly's on fire." You cannot talk like that to an actor, because they won't know what the hell you are talking about. Just ask them, "What do you want? What are the stakes?" And their belly will get on fire. Anything that doesn't help them get to the guts of it is, I think, dangerous.

ASHLEY GATES JANSEN (Teacher, Former Student):
The simplicity and the frankness with which Gerald often speaks is refreshingly nuance-free, so I don't have to guess what he means, I don't have to try to deduce what he's saying, and it resonates.

Early on, I learned that actors love to talk a moment to death. They love to talk, talk, talk, anything to delay the doing. So, I often say, "Show me. Let's not talk about it." They ask me, "Well, what do you think?" To which I reply, "Show me. It may be a great idea, and if it's great, we'll do it."

RICHARD TROUSDELL (Director, Former Student):
He doesn't make a big thing out of theory. It's more in the actual doing of it that he does it, which is great.

I like to be upfront and be very honest. If there's a problem, let's talk about it. That's how I've worked. I think it gets good work out of actors. Actors are much stronger than you think. They will not crumble easily, or they wouldn't be out there.

HAL HOLBROOK (Actor):
There I was, trying to do a scene, and I thought I was doing great, and Jerry stopped me and said, "You're acting, Hal!"
"I am?"
"Yes, you're acting. Do it again."
So I did it again. I said, "How was that?"
He said, "You're acting, Hal! You're acting!"
"I am? I don't think I'm acting."
"Yes you are, you're acting! Now do it again, and just stop acting."
I did it again, about four times, and I'll never forget that. I tried to eliminate the acting from the scene. And that was a learning moment in my life, and I'd been acting for quite a few years by then, too, but that was a moment of recognition for me that I had a lot more to learn, and Jerry Freedman opened that door up for me and invited me to go through it. Took me quite a while to figure out how to get through it, but he made me aware. In your career, you need people who are eloquent enough, brave enough, who care enough to help you in this way. To dare to help you. Our profession is filled with people who are afraid to say what they think, and afraid to hurt somebody else's feelings, instead of just cutting the bullshit and speaking the truth to each other.

He doesn't allow you to settle for anything comfortable or easy. He digs and digs at you until you get down as far as you can to the heart of the matter.[64]

In my communication with actors, it's more ballsy. It's about going for guts rather than surface. There isn't any actor at any point who can't be pushed further.

If an actor comes in on an extremely accomplished level, then you start from that point, and layer even more fully. And it's rewarding and more challenging because they come with so much, and you have to stimulate their search for even deeper and fuller expressions of character.

If you have an actor worth his salt, he is grateful that you don't settle for what he can accomplish.

If an actor finds what seems to be a reasonable solution to an acting problem, I will ask him to look further, or for the opposite, just to examine all sides of it. You know, if something is black, let's look at the white. It may strengthen that black. We might find, however, some gray, in the black. You know, look, look, look, don't cut out any possibilities.

I try to be as supportive, encouraging, and caring as I can, though I am a very strict disciplinarian about being on time, and getting your work done so others can do theirs.

ALFRED UHRY (Playwright):
He wasn't just sweet and lovely; he was tough. And no bullshit. He said what he thought. But he always made you feel like you were worth it.

You have to be honest with actors. Sometimes they'll ask me a question and I'll say, "I don't know. Let's find out!" I realize the director doesn't have to know all the answers. I can easily say to an actor, "I don't know." [65] This wasn't true when I was younger. I thought I had to know all the answers. I thought I had to go into rehearsal knowing what everybody did, what they thought, etc. I *do* have to do the preparation, but I *don't* have to know the answer…to every question.

MATT COWART (Director, Former Student):
He was never afraid to say "I don't know," or not have the answer to solving a certain section of the play, because he believed in himself enough to know that he would find it. I always walk into rehearsal with parts where I'm like, "What am I gonna do with that?" But because he didn't always know, it gave me permission to walk in with the same questions, and not be afraid, which gets in the way of finding the answer.

The way I work now produces a result that I like to experience in the theater: people taking control, people interacting—a little messy, not crafting every moment within an inch of its life. I know it's a bit of a paradox. But I don't like that other kind of theater, the kind that's only slick and superficial. You can admire the virtuosity of it, but there's no heart in it. So what I've come to is only to create what I want to see.

A production of mine is never going to be a perfect thing, but it's going to be a *live* thing, and it's going to be always working toward some important level of communication.[66]

STEVEN ROUTMAN (Actor):
I'm sure he has an idea of what he wants, but he doesn't make choices for you. He allows you to bring them in. He edits you. So you feel your interpretation of that character is unique to you. You're making choices that nobody else would make, as opposed to many directors I've worked with, who come in with the choices already made, and you don't have an ownership of the role like you do when you're working with Jerry. He's the smartest and the most collaborative director I've ever worked with. And I think those go hand in hand.

When I was a younger director, I used to talk a lot. As I've gotten older, I talk less and less and less. And I know that once you put something in the air, it's there. The actor hears it. It's part of their muscles. So when you find a better idea, they're always thinking of that other thing first. So I'm very careful about what I say. I would rather say nothing until I find the right words to help that actor.

MOLLYE MAXNER (Director, Former Student):
Wait until you know what to say. You know there's a problem to solve, but wait, let the problem be there if you don't yet know what to say, so you don't confuse them. Just let it be, until you feel you really have a good shot at addressing it in a way that's going to work.

An actor needs to find out what's in the play without being preconditioned. Often times a director's opening remarks will condition an actor's thinking. I try not to do that. I work very closely with actors, try to elicit, not tell them, but elicit their creative contribution.

You discover parameters by allowing the actors to work and try, but always being guided by the play.

Table Work

Table work is just what it sounds like: work done at a table. Gerald's table work typically began with the first reading of the play, and led into discussions, subsequent readings, and the posing of many questions. Arguably, the most important part of Gerald's process happened at the table.

Table work is the first step in discovering the shape of the play, but the discovery goes on all through the process.

The work demands different questions. At the table, you have to pin them down not to answers, but to questions. The table is where you help the actors dig.

I remember a first reading at the table. [My assistant director] sitting next to me was following the text. I put my hand over the pages, covering them. I said, "Watch the actors. You will learn so much by watching the actors. The text is printed. You can read it anytime."

I ask a lot of questions to get the actor thinking. Even for a musical, I work the lyrics as part of the text. I don't expect answers. They are questions that lead into the heart of the character: "What does the character want? What does the character need? What must the character have in order to survive?" As you break down a scene you ask, "Where is the character coming from?" I may ask, "Why do you say that? Why do you choose those words?" Many answers are obvious; many are not.[67]

All those questions make them examine specifically every moment.[68] You're building muscle that will lead them to their feet in an organic way.

RICHARD TROUSDELL (Director, Former Student):
Sitting around the table, if you weren't directly in touch with someone, looking up and getting in touch with someone, it was no good. He would demand that. He would not let actors get away with glib, easy, beautiful talking. Uh-uh. "You're not talking to him. Talk to him!"

STEVEN ROUTMAN (Actor):
I love the table work that he does. You're not forced to jump into staging. You have time to process and know what you're saying. You have time to look at the possibilities before you get on your feet.

At a certain point, you take away the table, but you're still in a circle. If you have done good table work, the play should already be coming to life. The actors will make you aware when it's time to move on. Then, with the circle and no table, the actors are already motivated to move.

VICTORIA BUSSERT (Director, Former Student):
You never knew when it would happen, but at some point, somebody would just get up out of their chair, and the physical process would start. Somebody would get up because they needed to go say something directly to somebody's face.

The first part is discovery. Then, as you get on your feet a little more, it is about testing those things, it really is. Exploring. It's still discovery, but the discovery now becomes interaction.

RAY VIRTA (Actor, Teacher):
I've always felt that his slow, meticulous, moment by moment, word by word, phrase by phrase development through the text made our work onstage almost redundant; it was obvious who you were speaking to, when you were moving, how you were moving, precisely because you'd done so much work on the text around the table.

Gerald sometimes chose to truncate or otherwise adapt his table work in order to best serve the story being told.

ROB RUGGIERO (Director, Former Assistant):
With *Lady from Maxim's*, we were at the table only a day or two, and then we got up. It was all about the physical life in the comedy for this play, and that needed to be choreographed technically, because that's what a farce needs. Jerry instinctively knew what a play needed, and how to get from that first read to the production with great skill.

Staging

Staging, as Gerald saw it, is a natural evolution of the work done at the table, not a separate step. As actors moved away from the table, he would continue to open-mindedly encourage their impulses and insights.

I don't use the word *blocking*. The word itself stops the flow. When you start "blocking," the actor always starts thinking about, "Where should I go?" rather than "What do I want?"[69]

What I believe in, what I've demonstrated in my work, and what I teach is—it's about relationships and truthful behavior. Composition is a factor; you have to be aware of those things, but there are no formulas.

The important thing is to get them thinking in character, instead of acting, instead of doing your little toy soldier ground plan. If you feel a piece of staging is crucial, do it, but I would advise you *not* to do it in the first rehearsal. See what may come out of exploration.

MARK LAMOS (Director):
When they begin to inhabit the role in their bodies, they will surprise you. They will do things that you haven't thought of, just working on the text. And that's when it becomes magic, because they begin to embody the play in ways that you didn't even begin to imagine. And then you can grow on that. Then you're inspired by their work. And that's really what needs to happen. You have to encourage the actors to feel confident enough to inspire you, to direct them well. It's a funny process, but that's what it is.

When they get on their feet, I let the actors do anything they want, go wherever they wish as long as it is in the service of telling the story clearly through relationships. There is no "staging" at this point. I want to see that actor's impulse. I want to see, "Do they understand the character?" rather than my telling them what to do. From there, the play actually stages itself.[70]

And then, when you get closer to the delivery date, it becomes pattern setting. Now, I delay pattern setting as long as possible, and even then, it's *still* about the discovery. Rather than forcing an answer or even an arbitrary choice, I try to keep myself and the actor looking or staying alive to the possibilities as long as possible.

I was doing *Henry IV Parts 1 & 2* in the Park. Stacy Keach was playing Falstaff, and Sam Waterston was playing Prince Hal, and at the very end of the play, there was a moment that I'd never been happy with. It wasn't truthful. It wasn't happening. At dress rehearsal, I still wasn't happy with it, and I stopped at that moment, and I made them examine it again. It got closer. We got somewhere, but it still wasn't fulfilled. We did it again, and the actors thought more deeply about it. At last, there was a wonderful breakthrough. Well, the headline of the *New York Times* review was about *that* moment. In spite of the terrific scrutiny that you get in New York, I felt that because I was confident with the actors, we could still try to crack that moment, and we did, and it was important. I just wouldn't give up. What I'm getting at is, the discovery process for me was still going on at dress rehearsal.

That has to do a lot with your confidence, and your judgment. Again, that grows. And you will learn by your mistakes.

Rehearsal

As the director, it was up to Gerald to set the tone for the rehearsal process—to establish the priorities, style of approach, and plan of action that would most productively lead the work forward.

More and more, I realize that what I'm doing in rehearsal is creating an atmosphere I want to live in.[71] I work best in a warm and collaborative atmosphere. I'm not someone who likes to create tension in a rehearsal or class.[72]

GEORGE HEARN (Actor, Singer):
If an atmosphere is creative and people trust each other, you're going to get a lot more work out of people than if you bully and push. Jerry was such a gentleman, and created such a beautiful atmosphere to work in. Jerry really taught me—the best way to create is in an atmosphere of trust and fun.

Rehearsal is discovery and a deepening process. It's a time for you to discover your relationship to the text—your ability to reinvest the text with your sense of life and truth. And we discover that together. So it can't just be my truth, and it isn't just Shakespeare's or Miller's truth. So [with *Death of a Salesman*] it becomes Hal Holbrook's and mine and Arthur Miller's. It has more investment than any one of ours by itself. So when I start this way, it means that in the theater you're experiencing a new synergy. It's what actors know to expect, what I've set in motion from the very beginning. It's all fresh. All using the text.[73]

I try to make clear that the rehearsal period is a period of investigation, not a time to record anything on stone or film.[74] If we don't use rehearsal to discover, what are we rehearsing for?

ANNALEE JEFFRIES (Actor, Guest Teacher):
I thought I was being so good at the table read of *Hedda Gabler*. Tears sprung to my eyes, and I thought, here's something that I can build upon. And we get through with the table read, and he looks at me and he says, "Don't make it your first choice." It was probably one of the most brilliant things that was ever said to me. He didn't want people to ever hit something too early. Always keep your options open for other things, because there's so many other wonderful artists around you that you have no idea what you're going to get out of them, because they're bringing to the table something you could never have thought of.

Don't let the idea of a finished production intrude on the work. Producers get nervous, they want to see it UP right away, but that's not the way I work. A lot of my rehearsals do not indicate how the production will work.

A lot of times people observing my rehearsals say, "God, it's so obvious. They're doing the same thing wrong! Why does he let them do that?" It's because I don't think it's time to address that problem yet. I don't want to spend time on something I can easily fix, or they can easily fix, when there is a much more profound and basic question that I want them to uncover.

GREG VORE (Guest Teacher, Former Student):
Rushing the process and pushing towards an end, a preconceived notion of what things are going to be, is not going to guarantee success. Rushing and pushing, more often than not, will guarantee failure, whereas the other way—trusting your preparation, trusting the actors, trusting the process—gives you a chance at success. I think that lesson crosses over into everything.

I stay in touch with the work. Discouragement comes from inadequate preparation, from focusing on the wrong values. Then you have to refocus. It's really a lot easier when you recommit, when you rededicate to clarity and excellence. I search for clarity in the theater.

Allow a process to happen. Allow something organically to evolve; it will happen. Let the rehearsal process take over. Allow yourself to find answers, not just give easy ones.

I'm just out there receiving. And part of the problem is to stay alert— to receive and then give them back, mirror back the information. To train yourself to really be present is damned hard. The discipline is to stay where you are in the moment, with total concentration.

When I rehearse a play, I like to go all the way through it each time. We read all the way through, then we read and start talking about it, but all the way through. Then we start breaking down intentions and objectives, all the way through, because the end of the play always informs the beginning. I can't know about the first moment until I've experienced the last moment. Then I can go back and redo that. I keep on being informed. It keeps getting richer and richer.

Giving Actors Freedom

Gerald loved giving actors freedom. By doing so, he invited their creativity into the process. He created the possibility for surprises, discoveries, and rich new insights.

My way to work is to let the actors mush around, explore behavior from which I draw or often draw the ideas for the scene, provided they are appropriate. It gives the actor freedom to use his imagination rather than imposing on him, and you sometimes get an original or fresh idea you hadn't thought of to add to the scene. It works best when the actors listen to each other and play into the objective of the scene. It often results in an unfocused mess from which I can still extract a moment or two. It also shows me where an actor wants to go and if they understand the scene.[75]

I think I know enough to stand out of their way. I mean, if you have a very gifted actor, you help them, you reinforce them, you try to be supportive to them, you give them ideas that will enhance their talents, and then you let them create. I think I'm known as kind of an actor's director because of this kind of approach I have.[76]

ANNALEE JEFFRIES (Actor, Guest Teacher):
He gave us that permission to create. That sets him apart from a lot of directors who don't trust who they have cast. By him not holding so fiercely onto every moment, and thinking he was the only one, it made him so strong.

You have to be brave. You can't give it to them and then take it away. You can't give it to them and the minute they show you something, freeze it. It's a matter which you can only learn through experience.

CHARLOTTE RAE (Actor, College Classmate):
He was a very astute director. He gave you plenty of freedom to pursue. He wouldn't step on top of you right away and tell you his concept and what he thought your character had to be. He gave you the space to find your way, and if you needed guidance, he would give it to you.

I can stand back, allow them to work, and—when they need help—reinforce them in their own terms.[77]

When I give them freedom in rehearsal, they do sometimes intuitive things in relating, and then later I can pin it down. They don't know why they were doing it, or even what they were doing. And sometimes it's just physical moves, sometimes it comes from an emotional place they didn't understand or realize—if they remain open.

GLORIA BIEGLER (Actor, Teacher):
He made an atmosphere that seemed free. If you got a new idea, you didn't think about whether you should try it or not, you just tried it in the moment. If something came to you in the moment, you felt perfectly free to just do it. That's not the case in all rehearsal rooms.

I try to point out the moments in rehearsal when interesting results occur from this process, so the actors can see the value of it and can see how much they are involved in directing the process.[78]

BOB FRANCESCONI (Teacher, Colleague):
Gerald gave me confidence in the approach, which is to try to give your actor freedom to work, yet be structured enough that you're constantly guiding and moving him or her forward.

My way of doing it, which looks very permissive to an outsider, is very calculated, and it's very devious in a sense. It is exercising a kind of control by not seeming to. By encouraging them to move around, I'm not always giving them the kind of freedom they think I'm giving them.

RAY VIRTA (Actor, Teacher):
Gerald's mastery of developing a play with a hand that is unseen by all, even those who are being guided, remains one of the greatest gifts I can possibly think of for an artist. Working on a show with Gerald always felt inevitable. Where it ended up was inevitable from where he guided it. And I didn't ever feel like it was being imposed upon me. It was coming out of me as inspired by his vision.

JOHN SEIDMAN (Actor, Former Assistant):
I always had the impression that Gerald was nudging it along in this direction or that, but only as a matter of keeping the actors thinking. I never had the sense that he was removing anything from anybody. He was just always adding. So the actors always felt extremely empowered and free.

It isn't that you never give an actor a result, it's about when it's the proper time to do it.

I can tell you that if you give actors this kind of freedom, let them explore well into the rehearsal period, they'll do anything for you, because they feel more in control.

KEVIN KLINE (Actor, Former Student):
Jerry kept saying, "Follow your instinct. Do what you want to do. Move when you want to move." He gave the actor the challenge, but actually it was the generous gift, of taking responsibility. That was the most freeing and exciting epiphany.

Behavior

As Gerald well knew, people in real life are never without behavior. Go ahead and look around at people anywhere: your home, a bookshop, a café, an office, a street corner. Watch anyone for a few seconds. Are they perfectly still? Probably not. They're touching their ear, picking a nail, twiddling a finger, stroking their chin, fiddling with a piece of fabric, biting their lip. When two or more people have a conversation, they rarely focus solely on the interaction. They're sipping coffee, checking their phones, flipping through magazines, surfing channels, walking around, combing their hair, tidying up, making lunch, or one of a thousand other activities. Real life is rich with constant behavior, and Gerald strove to reflect that reality onstage.

I have a step-by-step way that I think of as a layered way of working. I start with an intelligent analysis, an examination of the basic needs of the character and how the actor relates to them in his own person. As that becomes clearer, actors begin to physicalize it, get up on their feet and start to move around. You condition the movement with period clothes (whether nudity or steel corsets), with language, and with all the things that are lumped under the word *behavior*, which are the things that actor-characters actually do from moment to moment in creating their life onstage—the actor's character's life onstage.[79]

The result of my work is often a kind of a messy result. Things are going on. I enjoy a lot of life in the theater. I don't like frozen pictures, unless the situation calls for it, everybody focusing on "the point." When I first came to theater, the idea was that if you wanted to register something, everybody looked at the person who was speaking. "*That's* the point!" That doesn't interest me. It is keeping life going that interests me.

What we cannot deny is the truth of human behavior. When you try to rule that out, that's when you get stiff acting and artificial stuff.

Watch people—in the supermarket, in conversation, eating—watch how people behave. If they're having a one on one conversation, where do their eyes really land, rather than eye to eye contact? Don't base it on observing actors. Television is filled with so much bad acting. What you need to do is watch real behavior.

Behavior is consistent in my work because behavior reveals character, and again, sometimes it may be a little messy, and finally, it needs to be crafted, but first the behavior needs to be discovered. I look for it and encourage it from the actor because it reveals character. It is very seldom written into a play, so you have to discover it.

As soon as I can, I have objects for the play around the rehearsal area to stimulate the actors and to investigate behavior.[80] It's not about bringing props; it's about filling up your life.

VICTORIA BUSSERT (Director, Former Student):
Particularly with Chekhov, it was critical to Gerald that all the real props be there from the beginning. Everything had to be there so that everything could be used as a part of behavior. Watching how that evolved was so exciting, because you never knew what was going to happen.

ANITA GILLETTE (Actor, Singer):
We were surrounded by the world. He put us there so that we didn't have to work for any of that. We had it every day at rehearsal. We used the props we were going to use. We worked in the kind of clothing we were going to be wearing, so we felt comfortable, first of all, just being in that era and in that period. He created that in the rehearsal room, and we so appreciated that, because those colors gave the fullness to the performance that we needed. We didn't have to go anywhere to work for it; we just were there, from the very first day of rehearsal.

The clothes affect the behavior, so I need someone who will help an actor or instruct an actor on how someone might move in a corset or high-heeled shoes, which are different from shoes that we wear today. Lace around the cuff affects how you might eat at a table, for instance. A corset affects how you hold yourself, how you stand up and sit down.

What does costume do to the body? How does that influence character? Really, how does period influence character? And then, how do age and economic circumstance within the period affect that?

On one hand, I want the behavior to have some quality or integrity to the period that will be truthful to the period. On the other hand, I don't want the behavior to consume the sense of the play.

WILL ROGERS (Actor, Former Student):
That's the value of theater: being able to watch a full human in as truthful a circumstance as possible. And that comes through behavior.

You hope behavior comes through inner life, but behavior can also come through outer choices. I choose to take a shot straight down, rather than sipping—that's another kind of behavior. That can be a choice, and that can say something about character, definitely. The revelation of character through behavior and relationship—I build all my work on it.

What most actors and directors lack, in my observation, is an empathy, for not one truth, but the myriad possibilities for truth in human behavior at any one moment.

Truth

Like many artists, Gerald considered truth to be a vital component of his work. But what is truth? How do you find it, and how do you recognize it?

To me, we're on a search for truth, and truth is never safe, and often isn't even comforting.[81]

I try to find the truth. That's what I'm working toward. But I don't always achieve it. As I've gotten older, I've learned there are a lot of ways to the truth. The word *truth* is tossed around very irresponsibly in theater circles too often, and it's a very personal and maybe a very subjective thing. What I mean about it is the integrity of the material.

BRIAN MURRAY (Actor, Director):
Most importantly, it's got to be truthful. You've got to find the truth. And if you can't, you can't expect the actors to. You've got to be one step ahead.

You can hear it when actors are not being truthful, and that is key. Now, how you fix it, that can be problematic, and there are different ways, depending on the individual and the problem—but if you can hear it, that's the beginning of really good work.

I feel that truthful acting is more, perhaps, a part of the observer than the actor. I know it, I recognize it, because it includes feelings in me as I observe it. It's like plucking a string and it resonates in your soul.[82]

Actors often don't know. Even with very experienced actors, what they're doing in the moment can be phony. And eventually you have to call them on it.

You often have to settle for less than truth because you can't get at it. I know when I'm settling and when I'm not, but I've got to get the show on, finally. The curtain goes up. Sometimes I will have to tolerate a very skillful actor doing something I know isn't really happening because I couldn't get him/her there.

If it's not truthful, if it doesn't have life to it, I would abandon it and try to find another idea.

There is a difference between the truth of life and the truth of theater. You must learn not to mix them up. Usually onstage it's a heightened sense of truth.

MANDY PATINKIN (Actor, Former Student):
When Jerry talks about the truth, it's another way of desiring to be alive. In the end, it's how you're present with the other person, how you're alive.

We use the word truth over and over and I get sick of it, because what *is* truth? We define it through our discussions and through the work that we do.

Making Something Happen

In Gerald's school of thought, if something is truthful, then it is really happening. If something is really happening, then it is truthful. How do you get actors to make something happen? According to Gerald, whatever it takes. Try to open them up, free them, empower them, educate them, challenge them, encourage them, shake them, get through to them however you can. And then, expect the unexpected. When something starts really happening, it might be different from what you thought would happen.

I like to see life in the theater, rather than something absolutely created. I like to see something happening.[83] When something is happening, it's active; the actors are really doing something.

I want something to happen. As long as something is happening, I mean *really happening* between two people, as long as there is a transaction of some sort, that usually makes me feel okay. It can be on a lot of levels.

When I was younger I'd think, "Oh, I know exactly how to play this scene." Then I realized, after getting resistance from certain actors, there are a lot of ways to the truth of a scene. Most of the time, I feel I'm trying to give the actor permission to do anything, as long as something is happening.

ELIZABETH FRANZ (Actor):
He changed my life as an actor, teaching me how to get out of the way, and let things happen, naturally.

Discovering what is truthful is about opening your instrument to *receive*, not to *judge*, but to receive. And your intuition will begin to tell you when something is *really* happening, and when it just *looks* like it's happening.

JOHN LANGS (Director, Former Student):
When nothing is happening, it means that there's no talking and listening going on, that they are not affecting one another spontaneously moment by moment. It means that they are playing ideas, that they are thinking about the script still, that they are not available to move, hurt, or surprise each other, that they haven't gotten free yet. And boy, there's a huge difference, and you can call it almost immediately.

How do I know when something's not really happening? It's not because I'm so smart. I sense it, in truth. I bet you know when your friends are bullshitting and when they're coming from a real place. Sometimes you call them on it, and sometimes you let it go, but you can tell. That's what we're about. In life, that's what you're about. Your instinct for it will keep getting better. It's still happening to me. And that's the truth.

When to Make an Adjustment

In rehearsal, is it most helpful to stop an actor the moment you see a problem, or to wait until the scene has finished and then discuss? For Gerald, there was no simple answer. It's a delicate process, and both approaches present respective risks and advantages.

I respect the actor's need to follow through, and I feel it is rude to interrupt. On the other hand, sometimes *in the moment* is the only moment that's useful. I'll say, "I gotta stop you there. You're not doing it. You don't get it." Or, "No, you've done this five times. You've got to stop." It may be rude, but it may be necessary. Catch them at a moment. Make them observe it and put them in touch.[84]

Quite often, if you stop an actor in a scene and say, "Oh yes, that was wonderful, just what I was looking for," you will never get that moment again, because the actor is thinking, "Oh, I want to please you, I want to do what you thought was so good," rather than focusing on their partner and their objective. What you want to do is remind them of the setup, the given circumstances that allowed that moment to happen, not the result.

When it comes to actors trapped in habit, in most cases, you have to catch it in the moment to make them aware of it. "Now you're doing it!" In the moment is when you can change it. Then they have a true, organic sense of what they're doing: "My face is tensed up," or, "I'm pouting," or, "I'm shouting." That is how you change a habit. It doesn't happen one hundred percent the first time, but at least you've given them a clue. To talk about it afterwards will often put an actor back in their head.

It's an experiential thing you'll get better and better at, but don't be afraid of it. An actor in the moment is often where it's useful.

SAM WATERSTON (Actor):
Having good advice to give is not the hardest part. Knowing is one thing. Knowing when and how to make what you know land is another. Timing and trust are the trickiest.

Every production I do, I think, "Gee, should I have gotten to that sooner? Was this the proper time? Should I have attacked that later?" Or, "I attacked it too soon. If only I'd waited a little longer." Sometimes you have a good idea, and you give it to the actor too soon, and it's dead by the time you're in tech.

So *when* to make an adjustment is a measure of your sensitivity and your creative use of the instrument, thinking of the actor as the instrument.

Working with Resistant Actors

No matter how advanced you are in the refinement of your directing process, there is always the chance that an actor will be unwilling or unable to work with you effectively. Perhaps they do not respect you or your ideas. Perhaps there is a personal grievance. Perhaps the actor is so wrapped up in their own issues that they are unable to hear you. Whatever the cause, how do you solve this problem so that you can move forward with the work?

You can lead a horse to water. Period. You can't make him drink, unless he's thirsty. Ultimately, you can't do it for them.

Actors get into a groove, and sometimes it's very hard to get them out of it. They have the same inflection; they have the same mindset. It's not resistance—it's an inability to fully hear what I'm saying. It becomes muscle memory, and that becomes very hard to change. So what do I do?

I've made it very clear, I've repeated it, I've made it an important issue. Depending how important, sometimes I say, they're in a habit pattern and they just can't break it; or we sit down, and I take an ax to the marble and start to bust it up. Something's got to happen. When you choose which tactic, that's a judgment call.

I try to convince them as best I can that this will produce a richer result—that they'll be happy with it. I try to remove obstacles to our communicating and relating to each other. I try not to win arguments in the moment.[85]

This happened to me quite a few times when working with stars as a young director. You need to impress them to keep your job, but you can't come in being a smart ass, so what you do is prepare, prepare, prepare. It's not about showing off, it's not about bludgeoning them; it is about knowing your work. If you've done your work, you can let them talk—talk themselves blue. If you've done the work, really done it, you have things you can marshal to defend your point of view. That's why it's important.

AUSTIN PENDLETON (Actor, Director):
If there's research to be done about the text, he's done it, and therefore he can come in knowing he has all this at his fingertips, which gives him a clarity; he's not always trying to grope for it. He's thought through everything. That doesn't mean he's not open; he's very open. If you bring something in that he hasn't thought of, he lights up.

I don't necessarily feed the results of my investigation to the actor, but it means I have it at hand. I like to be at least one or two steps ahead of the actor all the time. It's not about being superior; it's about being prepared.

When you work with people of a certain caliber, they demand not having their time wasted, as it were. They don't suffer idiots too well, and I don't either. And so I've just…not made an effort to get along, I've just made an effort to be prepared for my work. And if a "temperamental artist," or someone who has that reputation, feels they're in secure hands, the temperament usually eases away and you realize they're not temperamental to be difficult; they're insecure and they want support and reinforcement, and if you're able to give them that, there's no temperament.[86]

Actors always want to look good. They are intensely vulnerable. All of them. If you're finding resistance, back off, let it sit, and eventually it'll get hungry. Sometimes it's just about leaving them alone, and then, when they see I'm doing good and interesting work with everyone else, they *ask* for help. I try not to get into a war. You never win. It's *rarely* worth it.

How do you handle an actor when they're resistant? Sometimes you can't do anything, so get out. You have to back off, or leave. If it becomes an untenable situation, you may have to leave. That happened to me several times, on big shows, when there was so much resistance from the producer about what I thought ought to be done, that there was no point, I thought, this is not going to work out. And although it was a big Broadway musical and I wanted to do it, and I knew I could do it well, I opted out.

When you're starting out as a young director, you are faced with the task of working with your peers, and those actors don't always respect what's coming from your intuition or skill. Expect the challenge, and then, you have to be clever at getting around it, making them feel at ease. Don't focus on personalities. Focus on the problems.

Cutting Text and Time

Sometimes less is indeed more. Directors may have to make cuts based on a producer's concerns, a writer's demands, or an audience's evident boredom. Occasionally cuts can be made before rehearsals begin, but the paring predominantly persists throughout the process.

The best thing to do, oftentimes, is to give the cuts beforehand.

Cutting stimulates discussions over lines that can be counterproductive. Sometimes it's best to prep a version before distribution in which the cut lines cannot even be seen. My stage manager John Toia would type up a script for me with all the cuts incorporated, so the actors did not see what they were not saying.

On the other hand, sharing the cuts responsibility with the actors can be a good move, if they're smart, because they will supply checks and balances, and know what's really important to the character.

In *Man and Superman*, I cut before I went into rehearsal. If you don't do that, actors start to say, "Oh, I need that line." One size does not fit all.

In Shakespeare, if I don't know what a scene is about, I won't cut it until I understand it—until I've got it up on its feet. Once I can say, "Oh, now I get it," then I can cut it.

Sometimes if an actor wants a line back, I'll say, "Okay, but we have to cut something else."

In college, I was working on Sartre's *The Flies*, and my teacher, Alvina Krause, said we had to cut an hour. Well, we went to an all-night diner, and we cut an hour. Anything's possible if you've got to do it and you will it.

Conversely, Joe Papp once insisted that a production of *Love's Labors Lost* I'd directed be cut by twenty minutes. But I put my foot down and refused. The critics loved it. He was wrong, and I was right, but if I hadn't been an equal partner, I might have been steamrolled.

Transitions

It's the director's responsibility to tell a clear and engaging story. Gerald firmly believed that this responsibility does not pause between scenes. A Freedman-approved transition carries the audience through it, and never leaves them waiting aimlessly in the dark. Great attention must be paid to every detail of a transition—from the choreography of its moves, to the sound, to the lighting, to the furtherance of the storytelling.

Transitions make or break even a well-acted performance. Transitions separate the men from the boys, the women from the girls. You can't have a wasted second onstage.

TONY FORMAN (Production Manager, Colleague):
[In rehearsals with Gerald] we would work the transitions. Very often, that's how we would rehearse the show, just going from transition to transition. That always impressed me. By working those transitions, it kept the flow moving. The momentum didn't stop. I think that in paying attention to the transition, you remove it as an obstacle, and it becomes another point of strength in the play.

JOHN BOWHERS (Set Designer, Former Student):
Everything had to seamlessly flow into the next look. I was proposing some things that would have taken minutes to change the set, and he would say, "No, we can't stop for that long." We needed transitions to be driven by the pace of the story. We couldn't stop to move a set. It had to feel like it was within the progression of the play.

ASHLEY GATES JANSEN (Teacher, Former Student):
The transitions can be organic to the story itself. I realize in my own life that transitions reveal character almost more than anything else. How we enter and exit a room, how we begin and end a conversation. Who we are in those moments when we don't think it's an important moment.

RAY VIRTA (Actor, Teacher):
When I think of Gerald's work, I think of the transitions in between pieces, how he would never let a needed transition go by without effectively adding to our knowledge of the period and of the world. They were never merely to get the set off. They were always conducted beautifully.

It has to aesthetically make sense, and there has to be a flow to it, something dramatic about it. And I'm good at that.[87]

A long time ago, I did a production of *As You Like It* in the Park. How do you go from winter to spring? That is the movement of the play. We ended up having the dancers throw hundreds of darts that came down on the stage, and at the end of each dart was a flower. So, suddenly, the whole stage, with one stroke, was just covered in flowers.

The only problem was, "How do I go from winter to spring outdoors? How do I do this? What do I do?" There was a conscious directorial something there, but it was all about, "How do I tell the story?"

The Audience

Gerald regarded the audience as a crucial gauge, but his perpetual priority was honoring the playwright's intention as he saw it, not the opinions of the crowds or critics.

Your play is not finished until you have an audience. An audience teaches you everything about your play. The audience will always tell you where the problems are.

You put an actor out there on the street or on a platform—the appropriate actor can hold an audience, fascinate an audience, excite an audience, without any technology. It's always been true and it will always be true.

Sure, I want it to be entertaining. I mean, finally I think all theater has a responsibility to entertain, but you can be entertained by ideas. You can be entertained by contradiction. You can be entertained by shock. Entertaining has a lot of levels. It doesn't mean a wash of enjoyment.

If I take the job, then I work under the givens, up to a certain level, meaning, the process is only influenced by the integrity of the material, rather than whom it will please, or whom it won't. If you don't like the material, don't do it. That doesn't mean I don't listen to people who suggest a better way of doing things.

I rarely have learned from reviews. Reviews tell you about the reviewer, not about you. That's their opinion. Hopefully what you did was what the author intended; other people can say what they want. I've learned not to read reviews until a couple months later, because they drive you nuts. If I like the good ones, then I've got to accept the bad ones too. And none of them are really what the work was about.

It's not that I ignore the audience, or the fact that they are a part of theater, but pandering to them or vitiating the truth of the material in order to please someone or bring more people in—that's where the commercial, result-oriented part of the process is not attractive to me, and more and more I won't participate. I'm just not interested. More often than not, being true to the material makes it successful.

The Art Pack

Gerald utilized his background in visual art to enrich his direction and teaching. In the directing classroom, he used The Art Pack *by Christopher Frayling to teach some fundamentals of visual art and discuss their use in theater.*

HARRY POSTER (Director, Former Student):
The Art Pack is a pop-up book that gives a sample of hundreds of years of art history in fifteen pages of text, artwork, and 3D motion objects that lift from the page. It's a book for students much younger than college, but is informative for anyone interested in diving into the tools of the visual artist.

Gerald looked to us as young artists, and he knew that we only had so much time together in the classroom, whereas it would take years in the field to learn what he was teaching. When he handed us this book, he was also handing us the incentive to remain curious, and to keep teaching ourselves beyond his curriculum.

The Art Pack is filled with paintings ranging from the masters of the Italian Renaissance to the work of Pop artists and Formalists in the twentieth century. The book contains articles on perspective, light, color, motion, proportion, composition, and form, replete with examples of these tools in action.

In the classroom, we would look at the composition of visual art works, and compare them to the staging we might have been viewing in rehearsals, or in the performances we saw last week.

Where do I want an audience's focus to fall? When there are many things onstage, but I want everyone to see the gun come out of the bag, how do I draw every audience member's attention there? *The Art Pack* taught us visual rules that our audiences will all be abiding by. It taught us to look at the stage picture as a composition, and to see if we could still tell the story even without the words being heard.

Through the prompts of *The Art Pack* and subsequent discussions of the work happening around us, we were able to identify what visuals might tell the strongest story, and what resources to pull from when striving for that specificity of image. We would ask, "Where is the vanishing line in the picture, and how can I draw the perspective to the main event?" Or, "There are fifteen people onstage, but I want the audience to see the park that surrounds them, and I want that to be an image seared in them before they go to intermission. How do I achieve that?"

Gerald was fond of discussing examples of storytelling not only in representational art, but also in work of surrealists and abstract artists. We would ask, "Where are the strong compositional lines? How have artists used color, light and form to show tension in the image? Why are we so satisfied when we look at Mondrian's *Composition in Red, Yellow and Blue*? Can we emulate that use of space onstage and capture that same satisfaction?"

If *The Art Pack* didn't have examples to pull from, Gerald might bring in a work of Franz Kline, and ask us to speak to where our eye goes, where it falls off the image, and where it gets caught. How do we emulate this focus of attention again onstage?

The Art Pack was given to us as a prompt for all of these questions. So much of the directing that we learned was taught through experience and conversation. There will always be a composition made for the audience. Gerald used *The Art Pack* to assure our awareness of the composition we engaged our audience in. It is one more great tool with which to specify the work.

Assistant Directing

Assistant directing is the ultimate training ground, and the core of Gerald's directing curriculum. Assisting other directors, particularly Gerald himself, is how I learned the most about directing. Working for other directors can be even more informative than directing your own productions, as it offers you an opportunity to observe what works— and what doesn't—often with a higher degree of objectivity than when you're at the helm.

GRACIELA DANIELE (Director, Choreographer):
You don't learn how to direct just through mechanics, through books, or techniques. It's the really doing it, and, most of all, working with great people. Observing them.

You need someone who has tact, efficiency, organization, diplomacy, discretion, knowledge of music, art, dance, and especially the craft of acting, and willingness to work long hours seven days a week. Who is this paragon? The assistant director.

The title *Assistant Director* is about as vague and nondescript as you can get. What actually does that person do? What is the job? The answer can be anything and everything, depending on the individual skills and talents of the personalities involved. Director and assistant develop a symbiosis that creates a new persona.

Don't come in thinking you know what the job is. Assistant directing is whatever the director demands of you.

RICHARD TROUSDELL (Director, Former Student):
There's no such thing as early in the morning or late at night; when you're needed is when you're needed.

JOHN LANGS (Director, Former Student):
You keep the room moving. You are that rover position. Think of yourself as doing anything that you can to make the environment of the art a great place to be. Your job isn't to make the art. Then, take your notes, and process each rehearsal on your own. And be ready if you're asked an opinion about something. Have opinions. Write them down. Direct your own show in your head by all means, but don't let anyone know that's happening.

TIFFANY LITTLE CANFIELD (Casting Director, Former Student): Listening is the best skill I think you can have, because when you really listen, you can start to truly understand the perspective of what the director is going for, and then even potentially anticipate and problem solve with them.

A good assistant learns to get into your head and think like you do, to help you organize your calendar and rehearsal and production time, to free you to make creative decisions.

A good assistant must be trusted to carry through tasks that require clear communication of details and creative editing of factual information.

He or she must represent the director accurately with the outside world—which requires tact, diplomacy, and charm—without flinching from getting the task done. The assistant often draws the annoyance and frustration of other collaborators who cannot access the director for time and attention.

The assistant aids the director in research, which may range from the internet to the library to a record or video store and out into the streets.

The assistant must recognize good acting, and know the play inside and out so he/she can be effective as a sounding board.

How to be a good Assistant Director:

1. Stay alert at all rehearsals. Stay focused on what is going on. You should develop a mental picture of where an actor is onstage at every rehearsal, even as it changes daily.

2. Don't act like a student waiting to be told what to do. Take initiative and tactfully push boundaries. Let the director and stage manager define these parameters as they occur.

3. Your loyalty lies with the director. A stage manager can be your best friend or become an obstacle. You should always respect and replicate the director's point of view.

4. Unless the director specifically asks you to, don't ever give an actor notes! No matter if you think you know better than the director.

5. Be a good gofer. A gofer is one who "goes for" the director. He goes for coffee, he goes for cough drops—in other words, he frees the director to work creatively. This is part of your job.

6. Take notes during performance/run-throughs. Write down whatever you have heard or think you have heard and, if possible, when in the play you heard it, for later review. Don't distract the director during a performance by asking questions.

My first year out of college, I got a job assisting the masterful writer and director Arthur Laurents, with whom Gerald had worked on the original productions of Gypsy and West Side Story. The job was going badly; I seemed to be infuriating Arthur whenever I spoke. I went to Gerald for guidance. He advised: "Arthur doesn't care what you have to say; he cares if you are getting the job done. For the next week, speak only when you must, using as few words as possible, and end it with 'sir.'" I followed Gerald's advice, and within a week, Arthur had begun to warm to me, and started to ask me, "What do you think?" What followed was a close and fruitful relationship; I assisted Arthur on all of his projects for the rest of his life, including his Broadway revivals of Gypsy (2008) and West Side Story (2009). But I wouldn't have made it past that first job without Gerald's counsel.

ROB RUGGIERO (Director, Former Assistant):
Early on in my role as his [Gerald's] assistant, I wanted to express what I thought it should be. Once I figured out that if I made my task to get into his head, to understand why he was making the choices he was making, to understand why he was thinking the way he was thinking, A) I could help him better, and B) I could learn more. So, once I did that, it became incredibly rewarding. And then I could begin to guess what his next move would be, or what he was going to ask for. I could support him more effectively, and I think he really appreciated that in our relationship.

What can I teach an assistant? I can teach them how to make priorities, where to place emphasis in the complex system of preparing and rehearsing a play, when to give a note for its maximum effectiveness, and how to handle the many sensitive artists who bring you their skill and vulnerability. Talent cannot be taught; skills can.

JOHN LANGS (Director, Former Student):
He always said, "Look at the process of what I do, and then look at the product. Only judge it from the sense of, 'Do you like the product?' Well, this is the process that got that product." So he sort of reverse-engineered your way of watching. You weren't just saying, "Is this good or is it bad?" You were saying, "How is this director doing it?"

Spotlight: Assisting Jerome Robbins

Gerald developed his assistant directing philosophy during the years he spent working with the iconic director/choreographer Jerome Robbins.

SHELDON HARNICK (Lyricist):
Robbins did not consider himself as articulate as he wanted to be, so he always got a very smart, experienced director to work with him, so that if he was not able to communicate with his actors in the way that he wanted to, his assistant would. In my estimation, it was a great honor to be picked by Jerome Robbins to be his assistant.

On set at Columbia Pictures one day, I was assisting George Cukor, and I was humming a tune from *On The Town*, and Judy Holliday heard me, and she said, "Who's singing that?" I thought, "This is the end now, I'm gone." She said, "Come here. What are you singing?" I said, "It's a show I saw, *On The Town*." We started to talk, and laugh. We became friends.

I first met Jerome Robbins in Hollywood through Judy. She was returning to Broadway to be in *Bells Are Ringing*, written for her by Betty Comden and Adolph Green. She had come to trust my eye and judgment in our work at Columbia Pictures, and she wasn't confident with Robbins and the actor's process. He, in turn, was intimidated by Judy's legendary intelligence, talent, and truthfulness as an actress amongst their tight circle of theatrical friends and luminaries. After a series of meetings, casting sessions, and lengthy conversations, he hired me as his assistant for the production. It was either to placate Judy or as insurance. I never knew which, as Jerry and I got along famously in our own right.

Jerry had the vision, and I often had the tools which helped him unlock the actor's process. I became his sounding board and trusted observer, and sometimes the emergency medic who repaired a bruised or wounded ego, or worse. I had enough music and dance background, a working knowledge of theatrical design, and the experience with actors to make our communication easy and productive. I was often used as a go-between with Jerry and his collaborating artists.[88]

DOUGLAS W. SCHMIDT (Set Designer):
He learned from the hand of the master how prepared you need to be in the light of constant change. Mercifully, what he didn't pick up was Jerry

Robbins's volatility and craziness that drove everybody nuts. Jerry [Freedman] was a picture of reason, and could go with the flow in a way that Jerry Robbins apparently was seldom able to.

I'm always asked, "What was it like to work with Jerome Robbins?" It was great for me. You see, Jerry had a reputation of picking victims and going after them with devastating results. It was true. His instinct led him to the most vulnerable and least prepared to suffer his onslaught. I was around to pick up the pieces, nurture them back to sanity, and interpret what he wanted from them.

In our first association on *Bells Are Ringing*, he took me aside after I had directed a scene with Judy Holiday and Jean Stapleton. There was some element he was unhappy with. He started to read me the riot act in something of a rage. I interrupted him, although I was trembling with an adrenaline rush; I can still summon up the feeling. I said, "You can't talk to me like this. If you have a problem with my work, let's talk about it in a quiet, constructive, direct manner, and I'll fix it." He never yelled at me again in the long professional relationship we had together.

I recall an incredibly stifling hot New York August afternoon in the fabled ballroom of the Theater Guild headquarters on 53rd Street. Jerry set the charming routine for "Just in Time" on me. He figured if I had enough physical coordination to do it, he could teach it to Sydney Chaplin, who was playing opposite Judy. It was simple and direct and based on relationship, which was the basis for all his work—in the ballet as well as the theater.[89]

On *West Side Story*, he was "Jerry" and I was "The Other One." We subsequently signed our correspondence through the years as "The Other One" in warmth and affection for that exciting collaboration.[90]

I supplied the acting coaching for the productions we worked on together, particularly for *West Side Story*. The cast was comprised of young dancers of great skill with a variety of professional experience, but very few of them had any acting experience other than carrying a few lines out of the chorus. Jerry gave me six weeks with the principals before official rehearsals started, and then, as the dances were developing, we would share rehearsal time.

I worked with Jerry on almost all of his theatrical projects or workshops in the ensuing years, with the exception of *Fiddler on the Roof*. I turned that offer down, as I felt the need to establish my own clear identity. I had begun to direct Off Broadway and at the New York Shakespeare Festival.[91]

Thirty-five years later, he asked me to work with him again on an autobiographical theater piece tentatively referred to as *The Poppa Piece*. It was for Lincoln Center. I thought twice about his invitation. After all, I was an established director on my own. Could I go back as Jerry's assistant, professionally? Emotionally? It didn't take me long though to say yes. How often does one get the opportunity to work with an acknowledged theater genius?

He invited me out to his cottage in the Hamptons. He brought out a large suitcase crammed with hundreds of pieces of paper. There were articles, scenes written and rewritten, fragments of ideas, magazine images and photographs. It represented the accumulation of years of thought and creative wrestling with his relationship to his world of father, family, work, and his Jewishness. We spent a week working through all of it; long walks on the beach, hours of writing, chatting while cooking, talking incessantly, probing, sifting, poking at the material.[92]

The workshop of *The Poppa Piece* was a miracle of creativity and frustration. There really was no script. It was all in Jerry's head. We often did not know until the night before what we'd be working on the next day. He produced a dazzling array of theatrical images I will never forget: a ballet for six two-wheeler bikes that was surreal and serene. There was a three-minute condensation of the Old Testament that was hilarious, witty and faith-filled at the same time.[93]

The Poppa Piece came to be his most vulnerable, exposed work. It was never shown to the public because he could never bring it to completion, no matter how he tried. He simply could not solve the problem of dramatizing his experience with the House Un-American Activities Committee. However, he heaped lavish praise and gratitude for my contributions and for our partnership.

The highest compliment I looked for and treasured was when Jerry would come to a production of mine in Central Park and comment on its clarity. That's what he used me for—as a sounding board, a clarity check, not for my approval.[94]

Everyone wanted to work with Jerry in spite of his reputation for long, agonizing hours of rehearsal and sometimes angry confrontations. One always thought that Jerry's fierce flame would ignite a still-smoldering spark in one's own talent that would take you as an artist to a higher level of achievement—think of Ethel Mermen in *Gypsy*, or Chita Rivera in *West Side Story*, or many other artists in minor and major roles. One always felt Jerry would bring out the best in you in his own unremitting search for truth and perfection.[95]

For me, the most salient quality of his work was his own ruthless editing in search of the best expression of an idea, or the most truthful. I remember a sassy, sophisticated three minute dance in *Bells* that ended up as an eight-bar fragment interrupted by a phone call. In spite of its charm and entertainment value, it wasn't necessary for the story. It had to go.[96]

I last saw him at Christmas 1997. Although we exchanged a letter or two a year and talked on the telephone, I had not seen him in two years. I was shocked because he seemed so tentative physically. As usual, his mind, his wit, his observations, were laser-sharp. His eyes, aimed by his thought, always seemed to pierce your outer shell like a surgeon's scalpel. He demanded a thoughtful, honest response, not an evasion or pleasantry.[97]

We sat across from each other at brunch in his home and this unarguable genius of the twentieth century theater and dance said, "No one is calling me. And all I want to do is work."[98]

I loved working with him. He was ruthless with himself. It was his commitment to excellence, to the essence of a truthful thing always happening.

I try to emulate his obsession for integrity and truth and passion in his work. We are all enriched by his many theatrical images that are indelible by their power, wit, and beauty.[99]

A Director's Evolution

What Gerald wanted from his work, and how he went about getting it, continued to grow and change over the course of his lifetime.

Theater is a wedding of language, acting, music, emotions, passions, and visual design. I love taking all the areas and putting them together and communicating with them. I think I'm at my best when I do that well.[100]

I am passionate about what I do because I think it is important to my community, and I put my whole heart and energy into it.

Theater, to me, is not a dead issue. It's alive, it's now; it's for us. When it comes to my work, what I want is for an audience to be moved for one moment in a play. In that one moment of feeling, an idea, a connection will have been made. That's enough for me.

As a director, you often work in the dark; you have no idea who you're reaching. You do *your* work. But because it's a life experience, I've found it comes back to me now in these late years in wonderfully gratifying ways.[101]

What I want is different from what I wanted before. What I wanted was a result. Now what I'm really interested in is the process and the journey.

EDDIE KURTZ (Political Organizer, Former Student):
I realized that the principles Gerald advocated in our work as directors were the very same principles he advocated in our lives. To him, an education in the theater was an education in life. The two were inseparable.

What I see when I look at the old journal I kept intermittently is that what I wanted to experience from the stage has not changed. The way I try to achieve it has undergone a metamorphosis from a rather authoritative, dictatorial, rigid approach toward the actor to a more open one. I've learned to elicit creative contributions from the other artists while still maintaining a certain controlled vision. A lot of that change came from simple necessity: the other method was not giving me the results I wanted to see. Some of it came from greater knowledge about my craft and other people's craft. And some of it came from my own growth as a person.[102]

From left, Gerald in class with Drama students Todd Loyd, Astrid Santana, Nadiyah Quander Dorsey, Misty DeBerry, Christy Pusz Decatur, Carrie Specksgoor Kayne, Jeremy Skidmore, Jim Ryan, and Alex Reznick at the University of North Carolina School of the Arts in 1999.

CHAPTER SEVEN

TEACHING

While continuing to direct professionally, Gerald spent years teaching at Yale University, Northwestern University, the Juilliard School, and the University of North Carolina School of the Arts, providing thousands of theater artists with the tools they needed to enter the field. The goal was always to help students harness their own unique talents, never to mold protégés in his own image. Gerald would do anything to help a student understand, and he wouldn't quit until he did.

I've *got* everything I want. I want to *give* more.

I've been teaching acting for a very long time, and I never have known how to use a textbook to create results.[103] I don't like to have a glib card file answer. I want you to see my struggle with it. And I want you to know that it's a struggle, and that it's not about the pat answer. I don't want to just hand off chewed up ideas from somewhere else.

I'm always desperate to be sure that you get the idea. I'm not exact, I'm not precise, but I'm trying to communicate in a way I think you all understand. I know I'm making sense, but is it registering? That's what I want to know. I'm trying to make it clearer. Out of the academic and into the real.

MOLLYE MAXNER (Director, Former Student):
We were working with him at a time where he was feeling he had very little time left, and he was ferocious in his attempts to crystalize what he was talking about, to really get us to see, to refine it to these small, phrased thoughts that would really get at what he was trying to impart. That last

year [2009] felt like he was trying to sear these things in us, for us. It was fascinating. He talked about it in directing class. He said, "I'm always trying to find out what I'm really trying to impart, and how to do it."

I'm not interested in just doing work. I feel I have a responsibility to society. I guess I'm at the North Carolina School of the Arts because something in me is always a teacher, and I want to give back some of this. I feel the need of using the theater as a really social tool, not just an entertainment one. [104]

My mission is training artists for this strange, fascinating, difficult, frustrating and collaborative art form known as the theater, which, in the last half of the twentieth century, means the stage, film, and television. The techniques may vary, but the art and the training remain the same.

JACK O'BRIEN (Director):
The quality of the work, the quality of the teaching, and the clarity, the thoroughness with which those kids come out of that program is truly astonishing. When the alumni come through the door and audition, I know exactly where they've come from. There are only one or two places in the country that have that kind of professional training, that shows from the top of the actor to the floor. There's a spark of excitement to the graduates from that program that very often is lacking in the other training programs. That's the work that the kids got down there, and that was his great gift, I think. A really great gift.

Part of my style is to remain very positive with my students, even when I don't agree with them, or when I think they've missed the point. I show respect for their point of view as I try to point to alternatives. Artists are very vulnerable people and can only learn and grow in a safe environment where they can explore and dare to fail. There must be trust.

ROBERT BESEDA (Administrator, Teacher):
In order to really go to these places that a training program is asking you to go to, you have to feel like you are in an environment where you can step out and do something. Do. The act of doing is the most important thing. And whether it's right or wrong is *not* the most important thing. If you think, "Okay, I've got to do it right," well, you're never going to do it right, because you're not doing it, right? If you're worrying about being wrong, it's the same thing. So, you've got to be able to fall down, and then feel like you're in a place where you can get back up, and do that again.

JERZY GWIAZDOWSKI (Actor, Former Student):
I remember the first show I did at school. I came to Gerald in tears and I said, "I am overwhelmed. I am not putting the pieces together. I'm trying too hard to impress, and I don't feel . . . I'm scared that I'm gonna fail." And Gerald said two things: "I don't think you will. I think you can do this." And he gave me some helpful tips about approaching rehearsal. And the other thing he said was, "But also, you might fail. And that's fine. Because you're going to learn something. And this is why you're here." In that moment, a light went on that has informed the rest of my work, not only in the acting work, but in the way I approach everything: *What are you doing? And if you fail, how was it a lesson?*

I start out by assuming everyone can do it, and then let them tell me who's better at it and who isn't. I don't start out by thinking everybody is dumb and needs to be spoon-fed. I don't assume that they can't; I start by thinking everybody can. I expect a lot from them, and then if they disappoint me, or as they limit themselves, I change my technique.

They need help. There's no rule book about this. People learn in different ways.

I have a strict code of values and ethics, and I communicate in a positive manner. I encourage my students to retain and develop their individuality, to expand it. I want them to be themselves. I don't want a lot of little Jerry Freedmans. I want them to understand where I'm coming from—what those values are—and then find their own way. I want to think of mentoring as a collaboration: a master and journeyman relationship rather than a superior and a subordinate.

KELLY MAXNER (Teacher, Former Student):
You want them to make choices, and learn their own choices. We're not creating an authoritarian dogma of "Do what I say." They're making a choice because they know that choice works for them. That is strengthening the will, and building confidence and identity, as opposed to having them fit into some prescribed definition of who they're supposed to be.

What I'm trying to teach students here are what I call tools: a system of techniques that will take the mystery out of acting, and give students a way of working that they can build on for a lifetime. In teaching them the tools, I have to burnish my own skills, and look for help if I need it— go elsewhere for the answers if need be. I share that with the students and don't in any way pretend I'm omnipotent. I very openly share my learning journey.

JOHN LANGS (Director, Former Student):
One of the really important gifts of Gerald Freedman is that he lived his artistic life so openly for us—his anger, his temper, his successes and failures—that his living became its own sort of lesson. He had his stroke, but he kept going. He was undaunted—as he has always been—in the work, and open about it. He never hid. He never went into a cave in any of these things. He processed openly, I think, because there were students around, and he understood innately that the life that he lived was an example. The rigor. "Swing through. No one thing is going to kill you." Jerry taught that just by the way he was living.

I think it's important for them to know I too am fallible. I'm still puzzled at times. I'm still searching. Which one of us doesn't feel that with each production we are again at zero, starting another learning project?

NORMAN COATES (Lighting Designer, Teacher):
This is the guy who learns everything he can, all the time—including the time he was here. I never saw him just sitting around doing nothing. The only time I ever saw him sitting around apparently doing nothing, he was sitting around and reading the *New York Times*.

I don't know everything. I'm an artist that needs challenges all the time. I look for challenges. I look for what I don't know. That's the adventure of it, but I feel that if I'm challenged, I'm equipped to look for the answers.

I know I repeat myself, because there are certain fundamentals that are constant.[105]

Not everything I say is right, truly. Every time I make a dogmatic statement, I think, "it's bullshit." And I always point that out: "It is a method. A possibility. A tool." A hammer isn't just to pound a nail. A hammer might also take out a nail. A hammer might also get this goddamn machine working. It's a tool that you use imaginatively and creatively on your own.

SAM WATERSTON (Actor):
Jerry gave the invitation to come out and play and to bring all of yourself. You're not a teacher if you're saying, "This is the way it is." Then you're

kind of a gatekeeper. If you're saying, "What have you got? What's in you? Tell me what you have," that's teaching.

The students keep me fresh. They give me a young attitude.[106] What is most exciting about teaching is that, in trying to communicate with the students, it makes me continually examine what I am saying to them. Every time a sentence comes out of my mouth, I ask myself, "Do I really believe that? Is that what I really do?" Quite honestly, it has been a wonderful affirmation for me of rediscovering what I do, and then examining the truth of it. It not only keeps me on my toes, it challenges me to be clearer, more specific, and more dedicated to my art.[107]

BILL RUDMAN (Artistic Director, Educator):
What he knows, he wants to pass on. That's much of the joy for him, I think, in being an artist. Not simply directing productions or conceiving productions, but the effect that he can have on the younger people who are working with him.

What we do is teach craft, but there's another component that has to do with some responsibility to the art and the artist: cultivating the art and the artist.

We use the word *artist*, but perhaps a more appropriate word would be *artisan*. It's not that we're elevated. We're workers. That's our work. Artists carry more responsibilities than artisans. When you use the term *artist*, I don't want you to think that it separates you in any way from other people, or that you can patronize people's attitude. It means the tools you're discovering are gonna help you work.

I tend, as you may already have noticed, to speak passionately about what I believe in, and that is sometimes mistaken for anger. I am not an angry person. I do listen. I love listening, and that's the truth. But I am passionate about what I believe and what my experience is. I don't always know how to be objective about espousing my point of view.

JOHN TOIA (Stage Manager, Teacher):
I felt that he cared enough about me to yell at me. He cared enough. When he thought the stakes were high, and he thought somebody was talented enough to accomplish those tasks, it was *push, push, push,* and sometimes, *yell, yell, yell.*

I try to get some of them upset a bit so they will investigate themselves more. I want to broaden their point of view about the world. My expectations might be unrealistic or too high, but that's what we're doing here. It's not a question of being soft on them. It is a question of being persistent and making them work, but they synthesize at different levels, at different times.

I feel so impassioned about giving them everything I know, and I can't, of course. But I feel frustrated; sometimes I feel sad, I feel anxious, I have all the feelings, I think, of a parent wanting their children to be successful, wanting to spare them heartache—and of course I can't do any of those things. In every way, I want to prepare them for leaving.

JEREMY SKIDMORE (Director, Former Student):
Three or four days after his stroke, I went down to visit him in the hospital. He was going in and out of lucidity and still sleeping a lot, and he fell asleep very quickly after I got there. I was just sitting there with him and talking to his nurse, and she said, "I've been a nurse for fifteen years, and I've never had a patient who had this many visitors. It's nonstop, all day, every hour, from all parts of the world. People have just been coming." Then she asked, "Did he ever get married?" And I said, "No." And then she asked, "Did he ever have any kids?" And I was like, "Yeah. Thousands."

I have generations of children and grandchildren of my training already.[108]

I'm trying to prepare the students for a life in the theater. My students are my hope for the future. Our hope lies in transferring the energy, passing the torch. The theater ain't ever gonna run itself.

BARBARA KESSLER (Costume Designer, Teacher):
He needs this for life. He needs this going to the students, teaching. That's his life. That's the fire for him. The fire for his life. To keep him going on.

It allows me to pass on principles that I believe very strongly in: live theater, ethics, relationships. That's very important to me, for however long I'm going to be in this job. I'm making an impress of some sort. That means it will go on.[109]

GAYE TAYLOR UPCHURCH (Director, Former Student):
I remember Gerald would say to us, quite often actually, that he would sometimes have this image of himself in his coffin, and he would enact the

image, which was him with his arms folded across his chest, and his fists closed, and his body leaning back with his eyes closed. And he said that image would startle him awake and get him to sit up and say, "That is not the position that I want to go in! I want to see my last image like this—" and he would hold his hands out, open, and say, "I have learned all these things throughout my life, and I want to give them away. I don't want to die with my knowledge enclosed in my hands, and my heart crossed, and take all that to the grave with me. I want to give it to the next generation."

When you suddenly see an idea click in a young mind, or see that a student will take something that came out conceptually, and rather academically, and turn it into a viable reality in the theater—a *doing*— it's very gratifying. You feel you've had an impact in the cosmos, truly. Because I feel that kind of energy never diminishes; it gets passed on. It moves on to the next and the next and the next. It resonates. That's become very important to me.[110]

The Faculty

Gerald did not advance the School of Drama at the University of North Carolina School of the Arts singlehandedly. He had an exceptional team of teachers, and through inspired leadership, he united them in a shared philosophy. While Gerald had strong beliefs, he was always willing to listen. It was his open-mindedness, paired with his passion, that helped him forge a faculty of such consistent strength. Gerald viewed teaching as a sacred responsibility, and he demanded that his faculty lead not only with words but with action, demonstrating commitment and discipline on all fronts.

Love what you do, with passion and commitment. Don't teach because it's a job. Don't just do it because it's a job. Love it. Love what you're doing. Then convey that love to your students.[111]

We are nothing less than the high priests of our art. We are responsible for handing on the torch, the Promethean fire.

Nothing is more firmly planted and immortal than an idea in the heart of another human being. This is permanent and irrevocable and is passed on from one human being to another, and it's passed on through THE WORD.

In our manner and behavior, we are setting the strongest example. Our comments and observations should be phrased in a constructive manner. Language—the careful and considered choice of words—is of major importance. The art of theater lives in ritual and text. That is what we are all about, all the time. Our behavior is ritual, and our observations and teachings become the text. We live with this responsibility *every day* as we enter class or rehearsal.

This requires first from us, as faculty, a deep commitment to the careful nurturing of and responsibility to the student's talent and psyche. I cannot emphasize this enough. The task is awesome. We can all remember the profound influence certain teachers had on our development that has affected us for the rest of our lives—artistic and otherwise. We must never cease to be aware of this primary responsibility. Both in our actions and our teachings, we must set an example of professional discipline and self-examination.

BARNEY HAMMOND (Teacher, Colleague):
He created and demanded and nourished unity of a training team that was totally focused on the acting student in training—not on the individual egos of the people that were training the acting students.

The demand must be great from them. Every class, every hour must carry a lot of weight. This means starting classes and rehearsals on time, every time. It means not cancelling a rehearsal or class unless there are extreme circumstances.

It's hard to separate being authoritarian from being principled and professional. I don't want to set up a situation where we are only disciplinarians, or where we impose a false sense of ritual on them, but I don't think talent is the only card to acceptance in a place like this. Discipline has to do with professionalism. It is part of being an actor.

They will respond to us like we treat them. I feel we have to be as close and as intimate and as nurturing as possible, but we also have to maintain standards. It's very important. There are always exceptions, but we have to be sure we're not just opening up doors of lenient behavior.

How we conduct ourselves in the studio has everything to do with the end result. Unless we reinforce that in the studio, it doesn't matter how many times we say it.

We have to bring all the enthusiasm, all the passion, and all the industry that we can to it. But they've got to do it, or they're not gonna make it.

MARY IRWIN (Teacher, Colleague):
Gerald was able to make everyone on the faculty feel special—to make everyone feel like he was really invested in them. It was genuine. For everybody to feel like there's a very special thing between them, that is leadership. He was an exceptional leader. He was not afraid to be critical with their work, and he was also effusive with praise. He was very hard but very fair.

We have to work together toward a common goal: a skilled, flexible, and thinking creative artist. High standards must be set and made clear to the students as the expected goal.

LOGAN FAHEY (Actor, Former Student):
He was one of the first ones there every day, and often the last to leave. Having the dean of the school have that work mentality and that dedication—the trickle down of that to the teachers and the students was really powerful. It unified the entire school.

To the Faculty: I am asking for your patience, as well as your advice and wisdom, in achieving a professional training program of integrity and vision, and a faculty of dedicated professionals who are committed to carrying forward this vision so we may attract the most talented and worthy young people to our school.

CIGDEM ONAT (Teacher, Colleague):
In the faculty meetings, I would watch him. "How is he doing this? What is he doing?" And I noticed that he would listen. He would really listen. Usually you feel that when somebody's listening, they are also preparing to say something—to participate. I would find none of that energy. He was in deep listening. And then, after everybody had their say, he would summarize the points that were made. He had marked every one of them. Then he would articulate his vision and position on the issues. He led by allowing everyone to be heard and participate. But he was very clear on his choices. That was a great lesson in leadership for me.

I want your input, just as I want the students' input. I don't think that I know it all. I'm not looking for resistance, but I am looking for informed opinion and experience. If you have a different point of view, speak up. Don't be timid; you're not going to incur my anger or my wrath. I look forward to challenging you, and learning from you.

It Is All Acting

Gerald worked tirelessly to build a unified approach across every discipline. It all fed into one common purpose: the training of professional actors.

For me, it is all acting. Movement, speech, special techniques—it is all acting work. That's what we're doing; we're preparing people for acting, and I feel we have to make that clearer to them. Everybody has to reinforce that all the time.

BARNEY HAMMOND (Teacher, Colleague):
The first day when the new students came in and we were all sitting up on the stage, he said, "This is your acting faculty." And there was Bob in Movement, and there was Mollie in Dance, and there was Cigdem in Acting, and there I was; but he swept around and said, "All of these people are your acting teachers. And all of their classes are acting classes." It was so freeing because, right off the bat, nothing was compartmentalized. He immediately kicked it off holistically.

We have to get to some place in each class where it is clear that what we are all doing is acting. It's not separate. And it's not just that you tell them that; it is demonstrative. No matter how much we say it or want to encourage them, they've got to experience it. We have to get our language closer together, and reinforce in each class what we are doing.

JACKLYN MADDUX (Teacher, Colleague):
It wasn't just a voice or a speech class or an Alexander Technique class; it was always about the acting, always about bringing all the elements together, always taking it back to that. There was a huge emphasis placed on integrating the whole training.

It's one thing to learn waltz steps, but if you and your partner have an antagonistic relationship, say, you execute the steps in a different way than if you're young and in love, or meeting for the first time. It's adding given circumstances so that it all becomes acting.

We must keep reinforcing. What I feel happens too often is that the students tend to compartmentalize the different areas, and not understand that it demands a constant putting together, melding the things together. It can only happen if we all understand what we all do.

BOB FRANCESCONI (Teacher, Colleague):
He took an existing program and gave it a language. One of the lasting legacies of Gerald here was that he got people to understand the language of acting. Up to that point, it was all over the place. It was eclectic. And it moved from being eclectic to having a strong point of view. Through patience, he evolved it.

There is *nothing* in this program that is not focused toward the end of working professionally. Every exercise in every class in four years is necessary to train your instrument, or it wouldn't be part of the program. We call this the *process*: a sequence of exercises that keep building your tools. These exercises are all important at each stage of development, and for the rest of your life. You do not finish with one and go on. You keep adding, and each skill begins to grow with the next one. It is not movement and singing and voice work and Alexander—it is all acting.

Casting the Class

Students at Gerald Freedman's School of Drama were given time to orient and ground themselves in the training before beginning public perfor-mance in their second or third year. Gerald did not cast actors in roles to get the best performances; he assigned students challenges to teach the greatest lessons.

You are evaluated in each term as the faculty share their observa-tions of your growth. I begin thinking of plays at the end of your second year by what I have observed of your particular class as a whole. What are the class's strengths? What are your strengths? What do you need in order to be challenged, both as an ensemble and as an individual within the ensemble?

I spend months reading plays and try to balance the season, not in terms of play selection but in terms of opportunities for each member of the class. [112]

An attempt is made to give each student challenges for growth, and casting that addresses specific problems. It is not done in a vacuum, and an effort is made to give every member some interesting challenges in the year. Your progress is monitored and evaluated as the year unfolds. Casting is not open for discussion. It is my judgment and overview of individual progress—in consultation with the full faculty—that sets the goals. Every class and project contributes to my impressions of you. Professional discipline, attendance at classes, and taking the training are all factors in my decisions. I think of casting over a two year period. I observe how you handle each assignment, which then affects the choice for further assignments.

Do not look at casting as a small role or a big role. That's high school thinking. That's ego-negative. *Every* role needs commitment and full energy. Every role is an opportunity to exercise your craft.

I'm not interested so much in what the audience will see as the opportunity it gives me to help the student understand my point of view, which goes from the academic and exercise part of acting into the actual *doing* of it.[113]

Those of you who are audience must learn how to observe. Enjoy the actors' achievements, but are you helping when you bring your sense of their classroom personas into the playing area? Learn to objectify.

You must be careful not to indulge in critical nit-picking that passes for knowledgeable criticism. You must take time to celebrate the achievements of your peers as well.

Standards and Evaluations

Entrance into the School of Drama at the University of North Carolina School of the Arts was—and still is—highly competitive. But acceptance was only the first of many hurdles on the track to graduation. Continuance in the program demanded successful integration of the training. Engaging in ongoing dialogue with his faculty, Gerald strove to refine and specify the standards for the program while considering the personal needs and challenges of each student.

You have to set standards and evaluations, but they can't be rigidly applied. They're applied with sensitivity, with compassion, with awareness, with knowledge, with care, to whatever extent you can.

BARNEY HAMMOND (Teacher, Colleague):
Jerry was about constant evaluation. He looked at individual students in terms of the talent they possessed, and what they needed more of in particular areas. He could see what the blocks were that stood in their way.

An evaluation is subjective by nature. It does not preclude a student's chances of success in their chosen art. It does sometimes mean, however, that in the combined judgment of the faculty, this student will not benefit from the next two years of intensive and focused training in professional aspects of theater, television, and film. The student could be very diligent, pursuing the work with success, yet still not possess the qualities deemed necessary to enter at a professional level.

JANET FOSTER (Casting Director, Guest Teacher):
He's lived such a long time that I don't think he would ever discount anyone, no matter how they behaved or how disappointing their classwork was, because with some people, it doesn't kick in until after they leave. What Jerry understands is that each individual is going to absorb the information differently. People will always surprise you. So you can never discount anyone. The big picture is that there's no formula.

I myself have a problem: where does my compassion and generosity leave off, and where does my professional expertise take over? I don't think it's necessarily a perfect line, and it's not a line that we would all draw exactly the same. But we have to get closer to understanding where that line should be drawn, and when. If we see a pattern of behavior that indicates a lack of professionalism, it could result in probation and dismissal from school.

Our expectations have to be realistic in terms of the first two years. They come to us—most of them, not all of them—basically unprepared in every way: mentally, culturally, and spiritually. They have a dream, a vision, a possibility—and it takes us certainly the first year and probably the second year to transform that toward craft. That's why I can be patient—exceedingly patient, I think—in the first two years, and it is why I feel that we can be more demanding in the third and the fourth, if we have prepared them properly.

I think it ought to take us two years to see where a student is going, to open up their potential, to give them a chance to mature. Starting at the end of the second year, we have to be clear about who can really advance in this program. It may take two years for them to get it together. It may take at least two years for us to see that it is possible for someone to get it together. Even into the third year, breakthroughs are just beginning to happen to many people.

QUIN GORDON (Teacher, Former Student):
In training the young actor, so many of them are also going through the process of transitioning into adulthood while trying to become professional actors, and it's just a lot to put on a young artist, so you never know when it's all gonna click. You can see the talent, and you can see the possibility, but you never really know when it's all gonna come together.

Everyone does not have to equally measure up in order to become an actor. That's another criterion that mustn't get confused. Everyone isn't capable of being a great actor, but that does not mean that they are not capable of being a working actor, or someone who will do wonderful things. That's part of the equation that we have to recognize. It's very hard for me to sit in judgment about who will work and who won't work.

In my opinion, any rule that we've made needs to be stretched to accommodate someone who comes from such a disadvantaged background that it takes time to catch up. What I don't want to get into is setting up rules where if somebody doesn't do something, they're automatically kicked out. That is no way of handling a problem, and it just backs you up into a corner. Because a lot of these people, I don't want to kick them out; I want to teach them things. How do we do it? Somehow, we all have to be responsible for them.

Gerald's Teachers

Gerald studied with various teachers, assimilating the knowledge and methods that resonated with him, and blending them with his own thinking, resulting in his distinct approach.

Alvina Krause was my first acting teacher and mentor at Northwestern University. She created her own set of exercises from reading Stanislavski and observing professional actors.[114] Others, like Lee Mitchell, provided me with production skills I use to this day. Another teacher, Robert Breen, gave a group of us students a challenge in presenting non-dramatic texts in a theatrical way. My production of *The Robber Bridegroom* was a direct product of that training.

I had the opportunity to work with George Cukor, who worked on Judy Holliday's films. George Cukor was one of the great Hollywood film directors, who had come from the theater. We had a great rapport. I learned a great deal about working with actors in film from Cukor. [115]

In New York, I then studied briefly with Bobby Lewis and Harold Clurman, and I also consider Jerome Robbins an important mentor. I was an early member of the Actors Studio, and became most active in the '60s when I was an observer and moderator of the Directors/Writers Unit at the Studio. It was there that I encountered Strasberg, as well as Elia Kazan and Cheryl Crawford. So, my bias is heavily weighted on the side of The Group Theatre experience, as those artists interpreted Stanislavski's system in their individually diverse ways. [116]

It's not as if there was no acting before Stanislavski. Stanislavski didn't invent anything. He observed great actors and he asked actors questions. How did they get to where they ended up? Especially those who professed to have no technique. The [Stanislavski] System is not about inventing; it's about codifying, helping the actors to understand the task. That's all that Strasberg is, that's all that Stella Adler is, that's all that David Mamet is, that's all that whoever you want to mention is. It's observation taken from life. When Franchot Tone, who was a member of The Group Theatre, was asked if you need to study the [Stanislavski] System, he said: "No, not if you know how to act."

What I teach is basically Stanislavski, as filtered through a series of great American actors and teachers who've taken the Stanislavski method and discovered more things about it, filtered through their actual experience.

I was with Bobby Lewis for about a year, and his way of breaking down a script just made such sense. And his perspective to acting, I keep renewing those points of view. Bobby Lewis was part of The Group Theatre; he was one of the seminal acting teachers, the American branch. Bobby Lewis codified it for me. He was full of good sense and good humor, and he wrote a couple good acting books, which I have in my office.

I attended Harold Clurman's late night classes. He was my mentor. I admired his wonderful choices and his humor.

Harold Clurman was very influential, as was Uta Hagen, Stella Adler, and Lee Strasberg. Having been at the Actors Studio influenced what I do. They all represented different facets of the Stanislavski System. It's the same thing, except with different emphasis. At the same time, I was doing Broadway musicals and working at the New York Shakespeare Festival. It all influenced the way I teach acting.[117]

BONNIE BARTLETT (Actor, College Classmate):
Jerry picked up the best of wherever he went. Throughout his life he has learned from everywhere, and then developed his own way of projecting it and communicating it. He was always investigating ways of doing things. He was not rigid. He just kept developing and developing and developing, which is wonderful, rather than just staying in one narrow little place.

I never failed to respond to a teacher who demanded things from me, made me think I could do more, or do better. That's what made me go on. I'm talking about in a lot of different disciplines. The very fact that they expected more was a positive experience for me that I felt I had to rise to.

Spotlight: Alvina Krause

Gerald's star teacher was Alvina Krause, with whom he studied as an undergraduate at Northwestern University. He often spoke of her prime influence on his method of teaching and directing. Other Krause alumni include Joe Bova, Warren Beatty, Richard Benjamin, William Daniels, Penny Fuller, Carol Lawrence, Charlton Heston, Walter Kerr, Jerry Orbach, and Paula Prentiss. Gerald and Alvina remained friends for the rest of her life, maintaining a warm correspondence in which they discussed their shared passion: the work.

I went to Northwestern University and fell under the guidance of Alvina Krause, an acting coach, and she awakened me to the world of being an artist in the broader sense.[118] I arrived at Northwestern loaded with potential, a hunger to learn about everything, and boundless curiosity and energy. Alvina Krause guided me through a maze of possibilities to a clearer vision of who I was meant to be.

Alvina just opened up my whole life in art. I was an artist and musician when I came under her tutelage, but I didn't know how to relate them. I didn't know that art and music were related areas. I never saw the interaction of theater, music, art, and literature. She made all that apparent to me. I didn't know how my personal emotions found outlets in artistic creativity. She made that clear to me. She showed me all the connections in my behavior with my work.

I came from a middle-class, Midwestern upbringing that put great store in the acquiring of knowledge, but had no understanding of art as legitimate expression of one's lifework. So, I needed help. And I think we all need help, frankly, in America. Even though she led me in those directions, it took me many years to come to be at peace with that—that my pursuit of art did not need justification.

RICHARD BENJAMIN (Actor, Director):
You can see the line from Krause to Jerry to all of us because her sense of theater was passed along to certain people, and Jerry was one of the major people who understood her and used what she taught to continue that line, so he is a direct line to her.

Miss Krause equates theater and all art, and in turn equates art and life. It is finally a way of looking, seeing, and reacting in total. Her method is to make you aware, to make you begin to investigate and question, to ask *why* of this total yet ever-changing vision.

I remember that Krause had specific observation training. For instance, go to a museum and observe a painting and translate it into character. Put the painting into action. Observe people at a bus stop and bring in your observations.

She is a great teacher in the Socratic tradition, aware of the terrifying responsibilities and yet compelled by love and mind to go on.

Ms. Krause was a former girls' gym teacher and eurhythmics instructor. She was really self-taught. She didn't teach acting; she taught oral interpretation, and she observed actors—in much the same way as did Stanislavski—and tried to figure out what they were doing. When she heard about Stanislavski, she said, "Oh, there's someone else who's doing what I've been doing." She had the ability to observe the actor and put her finger on what their exact problem was. I'm still using much of what she taught.

It was less about theater, per se, and more about: wake up, look around, absorb everything, do your best, push yourself to the limit. Ask questions, questions, questions, questions, why, why, why, why. That's still the basis of a lot of my work.[119]

Her creed is *do* according to your fullest capabilities. The way to her heart is through action. The only thing that defeats her is apathy. She is shocked by its presence, disgusted at its recurrence and her failure at times to dispel it.

RICHARD BENJAMIN (Actor, Director):
In each quarter of her classes, she only lectured one day, and that was the first day, and after that you were just on your feet. Jerry was the same: you learn more by doing it than you do by talking about it. He followed all of that, turning it into action.

She is a catalytic agent; something has to happen when you come in contact with her. You cannot ignore her. You suddenly realize you have collided with someone that demands you take the full measure of yourself. Anything short of the full measure, cognizant of individual limitations, is to acknowledge failure.

Her intense regard for discipline made me aware that the theater had to be a craft, and that the pursuit of art was a dignified one that didn't need to be explained or justified.[120]

She sometimes bruises when she only means to nudge, she cannot cope with stupidity, and she is sometimes blinded by a dedication to the world as she experiences it that makes her intolerant of those less willing to give and experience. But it is a blindness resulting from the dazzling richness of art in life and not a shutting out of experience.

Five and ten and fifteen years after one has met and come in contact with her, she is still discussed when her students get together. She is argued with passion. She is still an immediate experience.

Great teachers in any subject of any time in history are rare, and thus Miss Krause is surely one of them. Her insights and imagination carry on through the seeds she has planted, long after one has left Northwestern or even the theater itself. She is still a source of inspiration and a reference point of glowing integrity.

Alvina Krause reinforced in art what I had learned from my Jewish parents in Lorain, Ohio: an unalloyed, irreducible, inflexible respect for integrity of execution in all things.

Gerald in discussion with his design team for their 1992 production of *Cyrano de Bergerac* at Great Lakes Theater. From left: Lighting Designer Thomas Skelton, Set Designer John Ezell, Gerald, and Costume Designer James Scott.

CHAPTER EIGHT

DESIGN

This chapter is primarily composed of quotes from Gerald's colleagues. Through discussion of their work with Gerald and other experiences, they provide advice for theater design that is consistent with Gerald's philosophy.

Included here are mainly thoughts on working with set, lighting, and costume designers, but there are many other important collaborators in the theater, including sound designers, projection designers, props masters, and technical directors, just to name a few. The fundamentals in this chapter can be applied to these fields and more.

The Director / Designer Collaboration

For Gerald, the partnership between director and designer required that both parties remain open, engaged, and patient in order to allow ideas time to develop. Gerald taught his directors to guide the process while offering their designers freedom and trust, knowing that it would elicit their best work. He also knew it was the director's job to bring all of the different design elements together to form a unified whole.

I am eternally grateful to Gerald for making design courses a part of our directing curriculum at the University of North Carolina School of the Arts. My work has been invaluably informed by the hours I spent agonizing over the selection of fabric swatches, the calculation of lighting angles, and the construction of my first and only set model. Gerald knew that considering things from a designer's perspective is a cornerstone of successful collaboration.

I depend absolutely on a good relationship with my designers in my professional work. I look forward to that collaboration with joy and anticipation. Although sometimes it is arduous and challenging, it has never been anything but creative and supportive.

MING CHO LEE (Set Designer, Teacher):
Collaboration between directors and designers, which is the most exciting part of the work, is very very, very difficult.

JOHN EZELL (Set Designer, Teacher):
I think collaboration is difficult to learn how to do. I had to learn it. What I didn't know when I graduated was how to collaborate. I knew how to draw. I knew how to paint. I had ideas about plays when I read them. I didn't really know how to get into a director's head, in thinking about the play, and then to collaborate.

MING CHO LEE (Set Designer, Teacher):
The collaboration between director and designer is a very precarious one, and you don't really have that many lasting relationships, because it is so precarious. You're talking about words, and through the conversation, the life, the architecture, the ground plan, the whole way of behavior is somehow all put together.

HOWARD JONES (Set Designer, Teacher):
Never feel threatened when you're having a conversation as designer and director. And frequently, don't have anybody else there, because other people can cloud the ideas that are really stupid. But you need to talk about the stupid ideas, or the outrageous ideas, to figure out the good ideas. And you just keep talking and talking and talking.

We never really talk about design. We talk about the play.

AMY SALTZ (Director, Former Assistant):
He didn't talk about what it should look like; he talked about the play, and he talked about what the play meant and how he felt about it. And there was a dialogue, but it always started with the play.

MOLLYE MAXNER (Director, Former Student):
In the conversation, you learn more about the play, and create a relationship with that designer that makes them want to engage, because they're not just being told, "Here, make this." They're getting to engage their own artistic ideas. Through this kind of conversation, what can emerge is something that no one person could have thought of alone. And those are often the most exciting collaborations and products at the end.

AL KOHOUT (Costume Designer):
Jerry gave you a lot of freedom. There are other people who are not going to give you freedom, and those are the people who I think are scared of the process, whether they know it or not.

TONY FORMAN (Production Manager, Colleague):
He gives a designer or an actor what they need to springboard, and then lets them fly with it and try things. That's where the exciting things happen.

JOHN BOWHERS (Set Designer, Former Student):
I remember feeling like he had entrusted me with my job, and unless I was really off point, he let me design the thing. We've all had the directors that prescribe the design, and that wasn't Gerald. He was very trusting and very open-ears about where I wanted to go.

DESMOND HEELEY (Set and Costume Designer):
He was gracious enough to let me alone to do my things.

MOLLYE MAXNER (Director, Former Student):
I remember Gerald saying, "I have my version of what will work that I can pull out if I need to. But there's a chance for something far superior, beyond what I could think of in our collaboration, and so I make space for that."

You have to give them time for their process. And sometimes they need to be urged on. Sometimes you have to make demands. But they need time for their process, which a lot of directors don't allot.

I've done it all [as a designer] and was good at it, but I'm in touch with people who are better at it. They can take my sense of a piece and carry it to a higher sense of fulfillment. I am the energizer, the central spirit, the one who provides the aesthetic framework.[121]

JOHN CONKLIN (Set Designer, Teacher):
There always has to be a leader of a production. That is inevitably, I guess, and correctly so, the director, but he or she should be open to real input from the designer—input that might go beyond just the visual, that might be involved in staging. On the other hand, directors should feel that they can become directly involved in design ideas. Ultimately, it has to be a real slow back and forth, and in a good production, one doesn't end up knowing who did what. Certainly, my memories of Jerry were very much that sort of feeling.

JOHN EZELL (Set Designer, Teacher):
The director is the filter. The director is the connection between everybody. He or she is the pivotal conduit that facilitates collaboration between designers.

JOHN CONKLIN (Set Designer, Teacher):
There are often, of course, set, costume, and lighting designers—three separate people—and they all want to be involved all the time with the director, so that it becomes an organic discussion, rather than just something divided up into its roles.

GENE FRIEDMAN (Set Designer, Teacher):
Jerry wanted a full, complete collaboration: "I'm going to take your ideas, you're going to take my ideas. We're going to mix those and elevate the entire artistic expression of the event," as opposed to, "You go do sets, you go do costumes." There was always room in collaboration with Jerry for the interface and cross pollination of ideas.

Breaking Down the Script for Design

As always for Gerald, it all comes back to the text. Great acting, great direction, and great design can happen when the richness of imagination and personal experience rise through the filter of the script. Just like in the director/actor collaboration Gerald espoused, it's not about forcing ideas; it's about allowing the text work to inform and enrich the conversation.

It's your first reaction to the text that influences you so much, and that's why I always encourage you to write down in the margins whatever comes into your mind during the first reading of a play.

Although I say "Write it down," I don't mean write it down with any sense or trying to get anywhere. Eventually there's a process, but not the first time. The first part is the intuition and the imagination.

You think of colors. You think, "I remember once when Grandpa smoked his pipe." You write it down. You don't know what it means at that moment, but later on, you can figure it out, or you figure out the layers that may have come to you from that first reading of the play, which I think is almost the most valuable—when you're just reacting.

MING CHO LEE (Set Designer, Teacher): I tend to read the play through without analyzing it; just read it through. What do you get in terms of a response? This is pretty much how I prefer to work, and that is to read the play to get an immediate visual response and emotional response. It's usually once I have done the first meeting with the director that I'm beginning to re-read the play in a more analytical way. But that doesn't happen until about the third time around. At some point, you have to do it, but the trick is, you need to do it at a point where this very methodical analytical way of approaching the work doesn't diminish your emotional connection with the play. I strongly believe that no matter what you do, you want to keep that emotional connection.

When I read, I will sometimes see—I get images; the characters start to move around in my head, at the same time that I'm wondering, "What is the subtext? What is really going on here?" Both things really happen all the time, but I have disciplined myself to not preset those images. So even though those images come, I'm open to receive other possibilities.

I can't help thinking in terms of theater. I write down whatever is in my mind. And then I go back and do all the breakdown that you're learning how to do, and then I try to fold those thoughts in. Some of them I can never figure out, and some of them come to me a week or two later, and it's an association that I would never have made, but is incredibly valuable in terms of my understanding the play. Through that, I come to the spine of the play, and I come to the intuitive things that translate into design.

That's why to me the spine of the play is so important. Now, what's important is not the statement of the spine, but the thought process that gets me to the statement of the spine. So just to say to a designer, "This is the spine of the play," can be meaningless.

JOHN LANGS (Director, Former Student):
I'm not trying to teach anybody spine in a design meeting; I'm just trying to get them to where I think it needs to be through evocative images, and give them enough room to work.

Your thinking about the play shouldn't be vague. And that's where the spine work comes into play. You've examined the play from a lot of different angles that get you to the point, so that you have a lot of reference in your head to make a judgment, and still be open. I mean totally open. That's why the spine is a bit abstract. But in getting to the spine, you've examined so many possibilities within the text—and discarded some—and made some big, universal gulps that encompass the play.

All that thought that got you to distilling the spine will also help you know when it *won't* work: "This is very attractive, but it has nothing to do with my thinking about the play." "This would not work for the play, the production that I'm doing." "I can imagine a play in this, but it would be very refined and elegant, and the people would walk around in period costume. It isn't the production that I was talking about, and that my spine work led me to," so that you know that it isn't right. "I'm not sure where I want you to go, but this isn't right." I try not to dictate the design, I just say, "This one isn't right." That is why preparation is so important: the thought process.

JOHN BOWHERS (Set Designer, Former Student):
That process [with Gerald] was really an exercise in specificity, and in constant attention to the choices that I am making—whether or not they are in line with the core of the story—and knowing that every single choice I make is affecting the audience's perception of the story before the actors even set foot onstage. "Is this choice furthering the storytelling?" I would ask that with every line I drew, every color I picked.

HOWARD JONES (Set Designer, Teacher):
It's not about drawing pretty stuff. Who cares about that? Anybody can draw pretty. It's, "What are you thinking?" I like approaching a design thinking like Gerald likes to think of the spine, asking, "What is the through line? What's the thread?" Those kinds of questions are how you get out a good design. You have to find it in the text. It's in there; you've just got to find it.

JOHN BOWHERS (Set Designer, Former Student):
There would be so many moments where I would have a question about whether or not a choice that I was making was appropriate onstage, and he would immediately point out to me in the script where that answer could be found.

NORMAN COATES (Lighting Designer, Teacher):
The director's going to know the play better than anybody else in the room. So when you have your first meeting with the director, I tell my students, you need to really know the play. You really need to know the story that's being told. You need to know why each scene is in the play. How does this scene work in the arc of the storytelling? When you talk to the director, then you have something to talk to them about. Get to the story. Get to the ideas of the story. You can contribute to the director's vision because, let's face it, all of us don't know everything.

JULES FISHER (Lighting Designer, Teacher):
I read the play twice and then meet with the director, because if I read it any more than that, I'm going to lock in my own ideas, which may not be relevant after I talk to the director.

The First Meeting

Gerald and his collaborators consistently advised: Let the first meeting be relaxed. If it's a new collaboration, the conversation might be more about getting to know each other than the project at hand. Feel free to talk about anything, explore together, and see what you happen to find.

In the first meeting, talk about the play, sure, but not about the design. Talk about impressions, and ideas, and whatever comes up between the two of you from those ideas. Build relationship and conversation. Trust time. Don't rush into the specifics of the design. If you jump the gun, you will miss so many opportunities for the play to work on you both, and you will likely get a far less useful design—and a far less effective collaboration.

MING CHO LEE (Set Designer, Teacher):
First of all, my feeling is the meeting between the director and the designer should never be formal. It should be among friends. If I drink, I will have

a little drink. If you realize, after drink, the director gets out of hand, then don't encourage him, until when you're ready. Give a sense that everything is still open to possibilities, so you're not locked in. If you can provide alternatives, by all means do so; that shows that you have many ways of looking at the work.

JOHN EZELL (Set Designer, Teacher):
Gerald and I usually begin at a table over food, over dinner, so we draw on a lot of napkins, and on the backs of envelopes, just to get things started. There was a restaurant we went to quite often for our first meetings, and they had paper table cloths and cups of crayons. And so we would draw on the table cloth, and then we'd have to take the table cloth with us when we left.

TRAVIS McHALE (Lighting Designer, Former Student):
Jerry bought me a really nice dinner, and we just sat there and we spent the whole time talking about the play. We didn't have a design meeting per se. Eventually we got there, and it was brief. We weren't talking cue to cue. We were talking about the play, and the history of the work, and the approach to how and why and what it means today, so that we were approaching it as a piece of literature, not as a honed, pre-thought-out piece of design.

JOHN CONKLIN (Set Designer, Teacher):
Designers shouldn't go into a meeting, particularly with a new director, and expect the director to tell them what they want from the visual world. And in the same way, the director doesn't need to know the answers to everything. These answers, answers to any production, are going to be difficult to arrive at. They will take work to get them. So it's good to have a kind of ease and relaxation between the roles of designer and director.

DOUGLAS W. SCHMIDT (Set Designer):
I would encourage a young director to explore all the alternatives, rather than latch onto something early in the process. Because often you find that what you thought after you first read the play is an awful lot different from what you think about it after you've lived with it for a couple of months, and have wrestled through what you're actually going to do onstage.

JOHN EZELL (Set Designer, Teacher):
The first question is, why do this play? Why bother figuring this out? Directors usually have a reason they want to do a play at a given time, and so it's important to try to figure that out.

HOWARD JONES (Set Designer, Teacher):
What's the story we want to tell? You're going to listen and respond, just like any other communication. If you walk in with preconceived notions, you're going to be in trouble.

JULES FISHER (Lighting Designer, Teacher):
I've always thought that my job as a lighting designer was to inhabit the mind of the director, to find out what the director wants out of it. I can see what the playwright has said; I'm reading the words, but what does the director bring to it that I'm not getting from the page? What is his vision? How does he see this production? Now, some directors may hold back to see what I have to offer before they tell me everything. But I would like the director to guide me so I don't waste time going totally in the wrong direction.

JOHN EZELL (Set Designer, Teacher):
Listen. First of all, listen. Don't worry about bringing ideas to the table in the initial encounter with a director. Take a piece of paper and a pencil and listen. Carefully take notes. It somehow opens a valve up in the director's head, if the designer is actually sitting there writing things down. I think that designers need to learn how to listen to what directors are saying and just stay cool initially, before trying to come up with ideas that will please the director. Listen to what he's saying—and what he's saying between the lines—and then you can respond.

MING CHO LEE (Set Designer, Teacher):
For directors, at the first meeting, I would suggest that you haven't written a PhD dissertation that you are trying to read to the designer. To read a paper at a designer is bad news. I think there is nothing like having a session that is just having a conversation. That is fun. That is enjoyable. That is exciting, because you are talking about a play that you care about. When you finish the first meeting, the designer is ready to pick up a pencil, or go into the library and look at pictures, and start drawing.

Research

Inspiration is lurking everywhere: at home, on the street, in theaters, in libraries, in museums, and in concert halls. Gerald and his collaborators never knew where the most stimulating research would come from, so they kept listening and looking.

MARY JANE DEGNAN (Administrator, Colleague):
Jerry did tons of research for his own shows. Tons. He never sat back and waited for a designer to bring him something. He had always done all kinds of preparation before any design meetings.

DESMOND HEELEY (Set and Costume Designer):
There used to be a time, which I'm sad has stopped, when people would go to galleries and see painters' work and say, "Gosh, this kind of style would be wonderful."

LAWRENCE CASEY (Costume and Set Designer):
Having a good visual sense is essential for a director. Look at paintings. Look at how great classical paintings are composed.

JOHN EZELL (Set Designer, Teacher):
See as much art as you can. I myself would sometimes, when starting a production, I would go to a museum, without looking for specific solutions or images that could be applied, but just to wander in a kind of aimless way through a museum, because it just somehow opens some pores, some vents. Somebody said, "A mediocre designer copies, and a brilliant designer steals." I think that is true, because we're always being fed by what's already there, what's hanging on the walls at the museum.

JULES FISHER (Lighting Designer, Teacher):
I like communication. As a designer, the more time you can spend with a director, the better. Can you go and look at a sunset together? Can you go to the Museum of Modern Art, or the Metropolitan Museum, or the Frick Collection, and look at paintings, and talk about them, all the while talking about the show?

BARBARA KESSLER (Costume Designer, Teacher):
When I start working, I live with pictures. When I have a story, I go with the story, I go through the streets, and suddenly I see something [and think], "Oh, that might fit. That is something within my play." I need these things. I build a kind of archive. I feed myself with pictures as well. And then out of this comes ideas.

MARGARET LYNCH (Dramaturg, Colleague):
Both [Gerald and John Ezell] were looking for visual and environmental elements that resonated with what they perceived to be the world of the play. Both liked to travel to soak in the sights, the sounds, the textures of that place—to Russia for *The Dybbuk* and Chekhov [*The Seagull, The Cherry Orchard, Uncle Vanya*], to Spain for *Blood Wedding*, to Texas for Horton Foote [*Dividing the Estate*]. They also both collected visual images that resonated with the look and feelings they were after. So I would say Jerry's research was less scholarly and more sensory.

JOHN EZELL (Set Designer, Teacher):
It's so much more vivid, so much more electrifying, to actually be in the location. There is something that gives you goose bumps to see the reality and the power of it. It's exciting to be able to connect to some elements that are that relevant, but might seem on the periphery of actually staging the play.

HOWARD JONES (Set Designer, Teacher):
The danger is that today, people frequently do research online and say, "That's what it looked like in research," but they don't know what the hell they're looking at. So verifying the online research is the hard part, I think. Who put up the site? Who said that was really that kind of tree? Are you sure? It could be a third grader, you know. You've got to know enough to know that you're looking at the right thing.

Process

Gerald valued process above result. As ideas take shape, as shapes are sketched, keep it rough. Keep it loose. Remain flexible. Entertain ideas with an open mind, even those which might at first seem impossible. The least likely roads can sometimes lead to the most rewarding places.

JOHN BOWHERS (Set Designer, Former Student):
He always loved seeing drawings. I just remember him being delighted every time a sketch came in, and he just would get filled up with energy to talk about it, and to talk about how things could move and change. So that taught me how essential that form of communication is to creating the world of a play.

MING CHO LEE (Set Designer, Teacher):
When in doubt, you just pick up a pencil and cheap piece of paper and just do a drawing. I feel that as the designer you must make sure that your work doesn't get precious, because the minute it gets precious, you become rigid and your ego gets hurt.

DESMOND HEELEY (Set and Costume Designer):
It would begin with a bunch of little sketches, first of all. There's always a list of what do you actually need—the cooking list, you know. It's a little list to begin with, and then building on that.

MING CHO LEE (Set Designer, Teacher):
You know, some of the great architecture, the great sets, start out with a doodle on a napkin. And that is process. And when you go too much further in sketch form for presentation, you may get sucked into the glamour of a well-painted rendering, but quite often it is useless. I dislike the word *rendering*. I think rendering is deadly. Rendering suggests a finished product. The designer's work is not finished until it is onstage and open.

JOHN BOWHERS (Set Designer, Former Student):
I think one of the most valuable things about being able to sketch with a director is that you can be talking, and you can pull out a piece of paper and visualize the thing that you're talking about right there, and then push that paper aside and do a better version of it. And you can keep doing that, and that's going to help you get somewhere that you couldn't get on your own.

JOHN EZELL (Set Designer, Teacher):
First of all, it's a process. It's an evolutionary process, and you're not going to be able to embrace the very first idea that you see. You never consciously think about what you are trying to achieve, what the goal is, but rather, what is the process that we are going to establish in order to have a kind of a journey? And we don't know where the process is going

to lead us. The Egyptian *Book of the Dead* says, "Process is all." So, we consciously think about constructing a process, and we think less about what the end result is going to be, because that'll take care of itself.

NORMAN COATES (Lighting Designer, Teacher):
In the long run, it's about the process. You're done. It's in the actors' hands. It's in the stage manager's hands. Everything you've done is in other people's hands. But if you get the process down, the product's going to be better. If you don't enjoy the process, you'd better not be doing it. If you're there for opening night and the party, I think you're in the wrong business.

Creating a Set

For each production, Gerald and his set designer's imagination of the staging determined the nature of the set. The realized set, in turn, determined the nature of the staging.

In creating a set, I first ask myself, "What are the physical requirements of the play?" These are usually dictated by the most demanding scene, in terms of physical action, or the intricacies of simultaneous scenes. I can usually select this scene after a few readings of the play, viewing the play through my imaginative resources.[122]

JOHN TOIA (Stage Manager, Teacher):
Gerald considered the design in terms of what he needed the movement to be onstage. He considered the design in terms of whether or not it was supporting the story, and whether or not it was going to allow the performers on the stage to quickly and easily tell that story.

JOHN EZELL (Set Designer, Teacher):
He would talk about a play, and talk about a set, and he'd make gestures. I was mesmerized. It was like he was drawing in the air with his hands. I used to think, if I could just capture what he was drawing in space, if I could just print out copies of the air drawings, we'd have the set.

I'm totally unaware of it. It isn't my gestures; it's John's ability to interpret them, I'm sure.

JOHN EZELL (Set Designer, Teacher):
In Chekhov, it is said that if you get the furniture in the right place, the play will direct itself.

I think that's pretty much what happened for us. Now, getting it in the right place is not about moving it during rehearsals, necessarily. It is about imagining the movement and the demands of the play in the preparation process. It's not that you don't move things, but it is about the ground plan. The play is almost done when you get the ground plan.

HOWARD JONES (Set Designer, Teacher):
In a way, the designer is the first person to stage the play. I set out a floor plan, and I tell you whether they're going to appear stage right or stage left. It depends on where I put the door, if I really *need* a door.

GENE FRIEDMAN (Set Designer, Teacher):
The solution is not in us; it's in the collaboration with the director, the nature of the current audience, who the target audience is, and what the piece means to this audience in this place at this time.

JOHN EZELL (Set Designer, Teacher):
You have a phalanx of craft people that are going to realize it—make it come to life on the stage. The designer can't singlehandedly do that.

DESMOND HEELEY (Set and Costume Designer):
You're not the designer; you're part of a team.

Designed by the Character

The world of the play is defined by the characters within it. To construct that world truthfully requires an intimate knowledge of those characters, which comes back again to breaking down the script.

HOWARD JONES (Set Designer, Teacher):
Find out who the people are, and that will tell you what the design looks like. Find the design for the people. You can't design *Bus Stop* until you know who Grace is. Anybody can design a diner, but just because you designed a diner doesn't mean you found *Bus Stop*. It's knowing who Grace is, and then knowing what happens inside Grace's world.

JOHN EZELL (Set Designer, Teacher):
Usually we try to make a set that is designed by the character who is the muscle in the play, as a matter of fact. What one has to do is dramatize the situation and try to imagine a set that is controlled by that character.

MING CHO LEE (Set Designer, Teacher):
The people who are living the life onstage are paramount. The design is to create a world in which that event can take place.[123]

HOWARD JONES (Set Designer, Teacher):
I think a lot of people start with the place as opposed to the person. Stories take place in a place, but stories don't happen because there's a place; stories happen because there's a person *in* a place. So it's the person that you've got to figure out, and then the rest of it will fall into place pretty easily.

I worked a lot with [theater director] Jim Assad when I was younger. I remember, it was probably the second show that I worked with him on, and we had to find a coffee cup. And we went through what seemed like a hundred coffee cups for this play. He had to have the coffee cup that that character would have. At the time, I didn't understand what we were looking for. And I think if I'd understood that he wanted the coffee cup for the character, as opposed to a stylish, nice, beautiful coffee cup, that I probably could have found it faster. Only in retrospect did I finally understand that it was about the character, not the coffee cup. And I think that's where you have to start.

Nothing's Written in Stone

Gerald and his designers left room for things to change. Naturally, as opening night approached, there would be increased limitations on what was possible, but it was never too late to entertain a new idea.

Sometimes as I read the play, I'll get an image of a moment in the play, like, *the* moment in the play, and it'll help me with the designers. And then, as it turns out, it never ends up like that onstage. So you use all that stuff, but nothing's written in stone.

Elements will fall away from a set, but they are as essential as the doodles and ideas on the way toward.

JOHN CONKLIN (Set Designer, Teacher):
You want to keep it fluid. You want to keep options open so that the piece can have a kind of organic growth as it moves into rehearsal, and then into techs, and then into previews. You need to start somewhere, but you might end up at the end someplace quite different than you started.

HOWARD JONES (Set Designer, Teacher):
You have to adjust, and you can't get upset about it. For god's sake, it's a creative process. If a designer gets upset every time a director changes a moment or a prop, then they should know that they've got to draw their whole design perfectly the first time, and never get to change a line, and never get to change a size, and never get to change a color. That's not how we do this. Everybody is changing throughout the process. Bring it on. Even during previews, we get to change.

DESMOND HEELEY (Set and Costume Designer):
You can do things economically; you can use less so you have things left in your larder, should they change. And they do. You have to be in supply, at the ready.

JOHN CONKLIN (Set Designer, Teacher):
If the scenery is conceived in sort of separate units, then they can be put together in a different way. You can build in a kind of flexibility. You usually do not have the time or the money to rebuild things—that is perfectly true—but even with that restriction, you can keep it so that it can be put together in different ways.

Limitations

Gerald and his collaborators viewed limitations as positives. Limitations create obstacles, and obstacles inspire creative thinking.

I feel that limitations are a help to experimentation and to growth. There are always limitations, even when you have an incredible budget and facilities. If you learn to cope with limitations early in your training, you can use those limitations as a tool, no matter what level you're working on. The training to do a million dollar production with only half a million dollars is best received when you're doing a five hundred dollar production and you only have ten dollars to do it with. Many of my most creative ideas have been pushed upon me by economic necessity. I look forward to it. I hate it when someone says that I can do anything. To me as an artist that is nowhere; it's marshmallow land.[124]

MING CHO LEE (Set Designer, Teacher):
I think if you are doing a play, you are always dealing with limitation, whether it's financial or whatever, because that is the nature of the work. It's the limitations that give theater a certain excitement, rather than the endless possibilities. Some limitation is good. Some limitation of money, it's very good, so that it gives you a sense of scale.

DESMOND HEELEY (Set and Costume Designer):
The fact that the purse strings were very tight added to the fun of doing it. Time and time again, that was the mother of invention.

JULES FISHER (Lighting Designer, Teacher):
I have to figure out, how am I going to accomplish this? I only have ten dollars, or I only have five days, or I only have this many helpers in the way of crew. I have to consider all those as limitations. It's like a canvas is to the painter. The limitations of a canvas stretch your imagination. Time is also a limitation, and it can spur your creativity.

DOUGLAS W. SCHMIDT (Set Designer):
Often, great art is born out of deprivation and paucity of means. Very often, too much wherewithal stifles creativity.

JULES FISHER (Lighting Designer, Teacher):
I was lucky that I started Off Off Broadway. I did tiny shows. I did dozens of them. I had no money for the equipment. I had no money, period. I worked in these little theaters where I built a lot of lights myself, as simple as tomato juice cans with light bulbs in them; things like that were effective in a small theater. Now I'm in a position where when I work on a show, I can order almost anything I want, so that allows the scope of what I'm doing to be larger, but not the aesthetics. I still think that a scene that would look beautiful with one light should be lit with one light, even if I have five hundred lights available.

Scenic Advice for the Director

DESMOND HEELEY (Set and Costume Designer):
Think carefully of who you ask to be your designers. Find out about them before you ask them. Find out what they can do.

MING CHO LEE (Set Designer, Teacher):
You should realize that the designer is a nervous wreck when they first show their design. And that never goes away. So you have to be fairly gentle. First you say, "Did the design really reflect what we talked about?" If it didn't, don't struggle to try to make it work. Say, "Well, it's fascinating, but I'm dying to see what we talked about, just to see whether we are right or wrong—just to take a look." And the designer owes you that look. A lot of designers have trouble accepting that the director may have some very good ideas.

DESMOND HEELEY (Set and Costume Designer):
The more information you can give a designer, the better. Things that you feel strongly about. If it's wishy-washy, what do you really want?

MING CHO LEE (Set Designer, Teacher):
For a director who actually knows what he or she really wants, why don't you just say it? Don't play twenty questions with a designer until they finally guess it. That's called *sadistic*. If you really want something, say it. When you say it, you actually make yourself a bit more vulnerable. I think to actually face being vulnerable without collapsing is at the very foundation of how to work with each other.

HOWARD JONES (Set Designer, Teacher):
You shouldn't be afraid of drawing with a designer. Okay, you're probably not going to draw as well as a designer, but you should have enough skill to go, "I want it to kind of be like that," and jump that fence every once in a while. It may not be a perfect drawing, but it's still a form of communication.

DESMOND HEELEY (Set and Costume Designer):
It's very important to convey to your designer your support. Big number, in my book.

Spotlight: *Uncle Vanya*

In 1991, Gerald Freedman teamed up with set designer John Ezell to create a very special production of Chekhov's Uncle Vanya, *starring Hal Holbrook and Robert Foxworth, at Great Lakes Theater in Cleveland, Ohio.*

In staging a work by Chekhov, one must be equipped to collaborate with actors in the deepest, most thoughtful way, because one is bringing out the subtlest, innermost aspects of human behavior.

In Chekhovian plays, objects carry history and emotion with them. If you have these objects from the beginning, the actors begin to relate to them like characters. If they don't get them before dress rehearsal, they're just props.

HAL HOLBROOK (Actor):
This is the remarkable thing that everybody will remember about what Jerry Freedman did when we began rehearsing *Uncle Vanya*. When we went to the rehearsal room on the first day, the whole set, that is to say, everything that would be on the stage when we eventually got on the stage—tables, chairs, books, lamps—was there on the first day of rehearsal. There was even stuff in the drawers, pictures on the tops of bureaus. Everything was there. He wanted us to live with those items from the very first day of rehearsal.

ROBERT FOXWORTH (Actor):
He wanted us all to be in the place and time as quickly and as thoroughly as possible. He wanted us to feel that when we walked into that space, the rest of the world didn't exist; this was another time and space.

GENE FRIEDMAN (Set Designer, Teacher):
It was a wonderful set on a turntable. The set simply revolved into the next room of the house, so the entire house was set up in situ on the turntable.

ROBERT FOXWORTH (Actor):
The entire set, including the turntable, was built in the rehearsal space. And lining the walls were long tables filled with possible hand props, I mean just hundreds of items that we could go through and find things that we wanted to use. You could see people being very thoughtful, and getting into this circumstance in this play through material and objects—pens,

knives, whatever writing instruments, all kinds of little items that were on these tables. That really brought us rapidly into that moment, that historical moment.

MARGARET LYNCH (Dramaturg, Colleague):
All these rooms were just filled with all this stuff that an old family that had lived in the same place for generations might have. It was an incredible amount of stuff, but it was all there early on in the rehearsal process, including the turntable. We rehearsed in the basement of an old YMCA—very old and somewhat decrepit. They built a turntable for the rehearsal room that had to be taken down, and this was not a place that had elevators. They had to build it in pieces and get it down there. They went through a lot of effort. It was very painstaking, but no pain was too great. Painstaking was nothing to them. They just committed to it and did it.

ROBERT FOXWORTH (Actor):
We sat at the table and read the script several times, and on about the third or fourth day, after a lot of conversation and analysis and cracking open the meaning and all of that, Jerry said, "I'm not pushing you, but any time anybody wants to get up and start moving around the set, you can do that." So very slowly, over the next few days, people started getting up from the table and moving into the space. It was just remarkable, because it was so organic. And slowly, once everyone was on their feet, then stage management began to turn the turntable as we would move from location to location.

HAL HOLBROOK (Actor):
For five weeks, from the very first rehearsal, I worked with exactly the same pen, exactly the same watch, exactly the same chair. It was all there. In the bureau on the set, every drawer was filled with period clothing and other items—an odd coin, a little box, a spare shaving razor, the old-fashioned kind. As you go along in the rehearsal process, you slowly invest these things with some kind of life. Maybe one of the pictures on the bureau is your sister who died, someone you felt very connected to. Suddenly, in performance, you see the picture and you react to it. It's a tiny thing. Probably nobody even notices. But that doesn't matter, because creating a role is like filling in the gaps. You get the basic things, but then you find all these little holes, little spaces—just moments—when there's something missing in your head. The longer you do a play, the more creative you become and the more you fill the empty places. So one advantage of having the set from the beginning is that it helps you fill up these spaces.[125]

JOHN EZELL (Set Designer, Teacher):

We had all the actual furniture that we finally used from the first day in the rehearsal room. But we had to have a temporary sideboard over on one side, a buffet. In the course of the rehearsal, Hal connected his performance to all of these various pieces of furniture. So we got onstage finally, and we had the actual piece, the actual sideboard, and Hal didn't recognize it. He said, "What is that? Where's my sideboard?" He had to detach his performance from that piece of furniture and attach it to this new sideboard.

ROBERT FOXWORTH (Actor):

Gerald said it took them a year to prepare to do that production, to get all of the technical elements and the visual elements together so that when we walked in, we were saturated [by] piles and piles of books and photographs, treatises, and all sorts of things like that. It was very rich.

JOHN EZELL (Set Designer, Teacher):

We were aiming for Stanislavski's ideal, a fusion of the naturalistic details with poetic atmosphere.[126]

HAL HOLBROOK (Actor):

That was an extraordinary experience as an actor. I had never run across that before, nor have I ever run across it since, and it gives what I think is a wonderful portrait of the kind of preparation and depth of thinking that Jerry Freedman puts into a production, even before he gets together with the actors on a stage.

Lighting the Story

Lighting designers need an intimate understanding of the story in order to know where that story needs to be focused. Gerald's work with lighting designers was about ensuring the clarity of the story, not micromanaging the execution.

TRAVIS McHALE (Lighting Designer, Former Student):
Besides basic illumination, lighting is primarily storytelling. In the [University of North Carolina School of the Arts] way, I was trained to serve the playwright first; that is the meat of our job. A play doesn't need design to exist, so what we do is a bonus to the storytelling. When a director has honored the playwright's intentions through his interpretation and staging, it makes the lighting choices obvious to me.

NORMAN COATES (Lighting Designer, Teacher):
The best directors I've worked with don't need lighting designers. Just by virtue of the relationship of people on the stage, I get it.

When you walk up to a painting in a gallery, you take in the whole painting, and then you follow through it, and you look where you're supposed to look—at the focal point of the painting. Well, Gerald's moments on the stage are paintings with live people. Gerald's staged it for me to look where I'm supposed to look, ninety percent of the time. And so if my eye's drawn away from there by the lighting, then I'm not telling the story right.

What we're all doing, all the time, is telling the story. And Gerald's pretty clear about what the story he's telling is. He's looking for story point moments, and he needs to see them.

I tell my students, the best insight you can get into the story a director's telling is to just go plant your ass in a rehearsal and listen to how he or she is talking to the actors. That'll tell you everything you need to know about how a director sees a story.

JULES FISHER (Lighting Designer, Teacher):
I go to as many rehearsals as I can. I'm looking to see if I understand the play. Am I still seeing what I thought I saw when I first read it, when the director first told me what it was about?

NORMAN COATES (Lighting Designer, Teacher):
[When Gerald worked with my students on a production], he often spoke in these really general terms which took them forever to grasp: "I didn't

see that. I didn't see that moment." Well, of course the student saw that moment, because they were staring at it. What Gerald might have been seeing is that the student had a light—maybe it was a hanging light, or a chandelier—that was actually brighter than the actor who was speaking. Well, Gerald didn't see the actor who was speaking because his focus was drawn away. He didn't necessarily tell the student, "Make the chandelier darker." He would simply say, "I'm not seeing what I'm supposed to see." Which is good in a way; it made them explore and think.

TRAVIS McHALE (Lighting Designer, Former Student):
Jerry responded immediately to what he was seeing and wouldn't let you go too far down an incorrect road. If he saw the writing on the wall of where this idea was going and he didn't like it, he'd speak up. There was a reason why Jerry responded or didn't respond to something. You knew exactly where to go after you got a note, which was wonderful. It was specific. He would be direct about what he didn't like, but he didn't give you the prescription on how to remedy it.

NORMAN COATES (Lighting Designer, Teacher):
Gerald relied upon you to do your job. There was never a time where I sat and got notes. There were moments of, "What do you think?" "I'm missing this." "Can we do this better?" But never this list of notes of what to do or how to do it.

JULES FISHER (Lighting Designer, Teacher):
Gerald was a nurturer, someone who's asking me how I see it, how I would do it. And then he would edit. He would guide me.

Lighting Advice for the Director

JULES FISHER (Lighting Designer, Teacher):
Include the lighting designer in all discussions. Very often, the director meets with the scenic designer alone. I say, meet with the director, the scenic designer, the costume designer, and the lighting designer all at the same time. Sometimes a scenic designer or even the director may not want me there, because the scenic designer wants to have free access to the director's mind, to concentrate and not be distracted by another voice. I understand and respect this. I say, "Let me just be a fly on the wall. Just let me listen. If I can learn a little bit of how you discover the play, it might

help me." I like to be included in every meeting about anything. There is always something I can learn.

As a director, you should encourage the lighting designer to be at every rehearsal he can. If I could be at every rehearsal, I would be. I want to learn the actors' motivations and the blocking. I want to know it so when I go to set the cues, I am filled with what happens at that moment, the subtleties that you have to light. I want to find them for myself, and that's not something the director can give me; I've got to find them, and that will only happen because I watched it over and over again.

TRAVIS McHALE (Lighting Designer, Former Student):
You don't really know what it's gonna look like until you start turning on the lights. You can map out certain broad stroke ideas that are specific to the scene, but light doesn't exist until it strikes something—so until you have an actor in costume in front of scenery, in three-dimensional space, it's hard to say.

NORMAN COATES (Lighting Designer, Teacher):
Lighting's tough. We don't have two or three weeks in rehearsal; we've got several hours.

"Make it darker" is not the direction I want. I want to know, why does it need to be darker? "Make it darker" is a very general thing to say. What's the story you're telling at this moment? Why is it dark? Where's the darkness come from? What's that darkness in relationship to the last moment of the play? How do you want dark? What's dark to you? Does dark mean shadowy? Or does dark mean evenly dark? It's about the storytelling. For me, a good director is the one who always gets back to talking about the story or the storyline, and we're back to Gerald.

It's the directors who would give line readings to actors, it's the directors who do the equivalent to me as a lighting designer who are the ones I don't want to work with. I want the ones who, just like they would work with an actor, get me to see what they're doing and allow me to find how to show it.

Don't tell me how to do it, because you're going to get more. You get more out of an actor by leading them to your idea than by telling them how to do your idea. And I think that's true with everybody who works in the theater.

Trust in Costume Design

Gerald found costume designers he could trust, offered his ideas, and then gave them the space to do their work, stepping in to edit only when necessary.

LAWRENCE CASEY (Costume and Set Designer):
He had ideas about specific characters, how he saw them, and he would give me metaphors like, "She's like a breath of eastern spring stepping into this dusty brown mining town in early California."

JEANNE BUTTON (Costume Designer):
He had this way of triggering your imagination, letting you go free, letting you be daring. He trusted me. And that was just a wonderful thing, to be trusted by a director to do what it is you believe, and take it as far as you can go.

AL KOHOUT (Costume Designer):
Until I did a couple of shows with Jerry, I didn't particularly like it, because I had come from a background where people told you what it was and you did it. If Jerry didn't like something, he didn't say, "You have to do it this way," he would just say, "It's not right." At which time, I would've liked to have throttled him. He would just say, "Go try it again. Go do something else." I think he learned to trust me, as much as I learned to figure out what it was he was looking for.

LAWRENCE CASEY (Costume and Set Designer):
I would show him sketches, and usually when I showed him the sketches he would make comments on certain things, maybe a few of the colors. But he really trusted me.

The Art of the Story

Gerald's first passion was visual art. He brought that talent and knowledge with him into the theater, and it served him in every project he worked on. In the end, the two are inseparable: visual art tells a story, and a well-told story is a work of art.

Artful, pictorial composition comes effortlessly to me, which I attribute to my early ambition to be a painter and to my studies in art school.

I came out of the womb drawing, and I always thought that's what I was going to do—just be a painter, for my first seventeen years. I used my spending money to buy art tools of one sort or another.[127] From my earliest memories, there was paper around me, and colored pencils; I was drawing from the time I was a little kid.[128]

JOHN EZELL (Set Designer, Teacher):
Jerry knows painters, and sculptors, not to mention the history of art. He was an art student himself, so he has, to say the least, an extremely refined and sophisticated knowledge of visual aspects, not only in the theater, but in the art world. Jerry loves art and understands art. That's what's really special about him.

HOWARD JONES (Set Designer, Teacher):
One thing that I've started doing in class when I talk about the elements of design is bring in classical paintings, and we break them down in terms of their geometry and their color and, "What's the flow? Where's the focus?" Well, we also talk about, "Hey, what's the story?" And even though there's still all of the elements of design, there's almost always a story. So I think it's hard to separate the two.

Gerald in his office at Great Lakes Theater in 1994.

1. Gerald flanked by his Assistant Deans Robert Beseda, left, and Bob Francesconi, outside the Gerald Freedman Theatre in 2012. **2.** Gerald directing Jon Hudson Odom as Chino in *West Side Story*, onstage at the Roger L. Stevens Center in Winston-Salem, North Carolina in 2007. **3.** Gerald giving notes for his 1968 production of *Henry IV Parts 1 & 2* at the Delacorte Theater, with actor Stephen McHattie looking on. **4.** Clockwise from left: Ruth Mitchell, Gerald, Mendy Wager, James Ray, and Leonard Bernstein at the piano in 1957. **5.** Gerald in class with students at the University of North Carolina School of the Arts in 1999. **6.** Gerald (right) with Jonathan Winters at the University of North Carolina School of the Arts in 1992.

CHAPTER NINE

THE BUSINESS
& THE LIFE

Starting Out

Like any of us, Gerald never could have guessed how his life would unfold. When he arrived in New York City after college, one opportunity led to another, and the path emerged as he walked it step by step.

I didn't start out in the business of theater knowing I wanted to be a director, but it's where I belong.[129]

I remember thinking, "Oh god, what will happen when I go to New York? I don't know anybody. I don't know how I will get started." But it all somehow happened. One foot went in front of the other, and one hour followed the next.

I first came to New York in the early '50s, fresh out of Northwestern University, looking for my place in the theater.

I got on a train in Lorain, Ohio, and ended up the next morning in Grand Central Station. I had some friends from school who had been there a couple of months, and I was going to stay with one of them until I could find my own apartment. They met me at the train and took me by subway to Times Square. I got out of the subway, and there it was,

New York! Oh my god. I had no idea how close Grand Central was to Times Square, or how I got there. I didn't know how to begin. I had no connections whatsoever. None. I had no idea how to deal with an agent or pictures or résumés. I just knew that that's where you had to go to get work if you wanted a life in the theater. So that's where I went.

For a while, I didn't know what I wanted to do. I knew I wanted to be an artist, either a painter or a singer or an actor. I knew that you went to producers' offices and tried to get an appointment and talk to them, and at that time I thought I would be an actor. So I was trying to get acting jobs.

My folks were willing to give me fifty dollars a week for a limited amount of time. I could sing, so I auditioned for church jobs because I heard that you could do that, and I met a guy who was singing in churches. I had a high tenor voice, which was in demand, I could sight read, and I could audition well. On Friday nights, I could do two Jewish services at different temples. On Saturday morning, I could do another Jewish service. On Sunday, I could do usually two churches. An early mass, Presbyterian or Episcopalian, and in late afternoon there would be another mass. And with five services, I could live off that for the next week.

Through the churches and synagogues, I met other singers, and then I got into a jingle group, so I was making money then.[130]

Before I left Northwestern, there was something on the board that said a theater was looking for a scenic designer. I filled out an application, and then I did an interview with those people, and that was the first theater job I got. I got to New York in February, and then I had a job at summer stock designing and painting scenery at an equity company in Massachusetts. Meanwhile, between February and June, I sang in churches.

When I got back, in my foolish optimism and naiveté, I directed a showcase production of Shakespeare's *As You Like It,* which, to my surprise, brought me to the attention of a Hollywood talent scout, and soon I was pursuing a film career under contract to Columbia Pictures in L.A., not in New York. It was a Midwestern boy's fantasy come true. I had spent Saturday afternoons at the movies—I think they cost a nickel then, and my allowance for the week was ten cents—watching the great names on the huge screen, and here I was fifteen years later directing Charlton Heston, Humphrey Bogart, Edward G. Robinson, Fred Mac-

Murray, Van Johnson, and eventually the great actress and comedienne of *Born Yesterday,* Judy Holliday. After her movie success, Judy was going back to Broadway in a musical written specially for her by Comden and Green called *Bells Are Ringing,* to be staged by Jerome Robbins.

Soon I was back in New York on Broadway, working with Judy Holliday and Jerome Robbins. Coming back to New York, I realized that I wanted to do theater, not film, because I just felt more at home.

Directing became a pragmatic choice for bringing all of my interests together. I kept my interest in music, visual arts, and dance alive, and I needed the kind of stimulation that would fulfill all of them.[131]

In retrospect, it's all clear. Directing theater was my destiny. At the time, I was just hustling to stay in the business, keep working, and follow up on great opportunities.

JOHN DILLON (Director, Guest Teacher):
He was driven when he arrived in New York. He was an improviser. I remember him telling the story of when he first started watching shows at the New York Shakespeare Festival and was distressed by the poor quality in the Shakespeare productions, so he wrote a letter to Joe Papp saying, "Your Shakespeare isn't very good." And Papp's reply was, "Well, come here and show me you can do better." And Gerald's response was, "Damn right." Well, that kind of bravado—how do you teach that? I don't think you teach it. You just have to see it. And Gerald had that kind of bravado, and I think the students saw it, recognized it, and realized that he was teaching them to be guerilla fighters. He wasn't teaching them how to direct at the Guthrie, should they receive an offer tomorrow, because they weren't going to receive an offer tomorrow. He was teaching them how to be in the trenches, how to improvise, how to create things on their own, how to beg, borrow, and steal the resources they needed to get their shows up.

Life in the Theater

Gerald Freedman devoted his life to the theater. It was a journey of many unexpected twists and turns. With persistence and vigor, he pursued his passion, ultimately defining himself through his actions—through the doing. He encouraged all of us to do the same.

Every man has his own journey, but every destination is a secret. I think of what a remarkable journey I've had: the great mentors I've encountered, and the choices I've made, mostly by accident or coincidence, that have shaped my life.

This is your life, this is your moment, and you've got to make what you can out of it.

You don't really have to worry about what will happen to you. Life just goes on. What's out there isn't really something you have to focus on, as strange as that may seem; it just happens, because one day follows the next. Tuesday follows Monday, and Wednesday follows Tuesday, and you do it.

BERNARD GERSTEN (Producer, Colleague):
You're not known for what you say; you're known for what you do. You don't create a new world by talking about it; you create a new world by doing something about creating a new world.

ALFRED UHRY (Playwright):
He made a whole rich life for himself. He never sat around brooding. He just *did*. That's his legacy now.

Days go by, and a lot of time goes by, and you start to take stock. Something's happening, or something isn't happening, and what do I do? If you can avoid it, you don't have to think that big. Set realistic goals. What I mean by realistic goals are ones you might be able to achieve in six months, or within a year, rather than, "I'm going to be a star, I want to be famous, I want to be rich." We all hope and fantasize, but super stardom is not likely to happen. I think it's a good idea to set some kind of goal so that the great-seeming void becomes opened up into terms of something that you can handle: "I need this much money to get to New York," or, "I can only afford this kind of rent."

God knows how many people are feeding into New York every day trying to be actors. Don't worry about it. You have to set a goal. You have to have tenacity. If you don't have it, don't waste your time. There's a whole additional set of values and needs in addition to your talent and your skill. Just sticking it out, being productive, getting seen, and getting talked to are big parts of it.

The biggest thing is tenacity. Without tenacity in your system, talent doesn't mean much. But if you have discipline and tenacity, coupled with talent, you're capable of doing anything.[132]

You need passion, tremendous passion.

I try to make it so clear to you how much you have to commit to it in order to get what you want. And if you're not prepared to make that commitment, don't waste your time. It's not a surface thing. It's not like, "Oh, I've got so much talent, or beauty, or whatever, that someone will see it, and they'll pick me out of the whole bunch, and I'm off!" It just isn't like that. You have to work, commit, reveal yourself. You have to be willing to put yourself on the line.

The important thing is to clearly understand what the choices are—what the alternatives are, instead of reacting just on the emotional level. And being professional. You have to look at the long term: *What am I after?*

Maybe the only thing you're thinking about is money. And there's nothing wrong with that, as far as I'm concerned. I'm not good at that, but if that's what you want, then you start making choices in that direction. It all becomes very clear. That's how we define ourselves, and gradually, if you're lucky, you'll have enough opportunities to begin to define yourself.

BOB FRANCESCONI (Teacher, Colleague):
Gerald did say this: "It's not necessarily that we're only creating actors; we're creating people who understand the arts. It's unimportant that they become actors. It's important that they're better for having come here, in understanding who they are and what the possibilities are."

JANET FOSTER (Casting Director, Guest Teacher):
Jerry always wanted his students to understand: Look at the opportunities where they present themselves. Don't ignore them. Explore them until you decide that they're not for you, but don't shut any doors, because you don't know where the opportunities are going to come from.

I found the theater to be a wonderful place to live in, but very difficult and arduous to maintain. You have to want that life and know that that's where your life belongs—or not. Many of the kids I went to school with are doing other things very productively and have wonderful lives, but not all as actors.

ASHLEY GATES JANSEN (Teacher, Former Student):
When an alumnus writes that they've made the decision to leave New York, Gerald is so thrilled that they've recognized that New York isn't the place for them, and they want to go do something else, or be someone else. He celebrates that as genuinely as he did any of the theatrical, artistic achievements that alumni have. That's what made him, and makes him, such a special teacher.

BOB FRANCESCONI (Teacher, Colleague):
There are wonderful stories out there of people who've graduated and slowly evolved into who they should be.

There's no embarrassment or shame or humiliation or anything in saying, "You know, I don't want to, now that I've done it." Or, "I want whatever else—the alternative." Please, make yourself happy. There's no reason to suffer, because it's a lifetime of this. Believe me. I've lived it. And as a matter of fact, I love it. But that's me.

JOHN CULLUM (Actor, Singer):
It all boils down to the idea of why you're in the theater in the first place. Why do you want to be an actor? Why do you want to work in the theater? I think that's the only reason you should stay in the theater, because you've got plenty of things that will discourage you. The only reason you stay in the theater is because you're doing what you love and expressing what you want to express as an artist. Why you're in the theater is to do something that moves you, and then, to move other people. That's the best way to do it: to move them by moving yourself.

I have had such a terrific life in the theater. I've met such interesting people. It's taken me to extraordinary places in the imagination and reality. I didn't always know where my next meal was coming from, but the adventure has all been worth it. It's like a lifetime of anxiety and wonder.

The Pursuit of Excellence

As a student, director, writer, leader, dean, teacher, and friend, Gerald's goal was always to do things as well as he possibly could. For him, the recognition and the money were always secondary to the quality and integrity of the work. He put everything he had into it. His work was his life, and his life was his work.

My history—maybe it's typical in not being typical.[133]

My background and my experience and my interests have all led me to this moment. I see that in retrospect.

I was raised in a Jewish home by wonderful parents in a small town. One of the things that meant to me is compassion. That has to do with everything from how I approach the theater to how I relate to people.[134]

My grandfather was a chazzan [cantor], as well as a shochet, and we sang songs, and music was always a part of our upbringing. And storytelling, the richness of ritual, was always a part of our lives. I'm wondering how much of that went into a love of theater.[135]

My father was a dentist. My mother was a former school teacher, and after my brother and I grew up, she went back to teaching school. Although they were not very versed in the arts, they were tremendously supportive of any talents that their children exhibited. They did everything they could to further my work in those areas.

Learning was very important in our home, of course. I was valedictorian in my class, and I was an honors student in high school.[136]

When I began, I didn't think I was going to be in theater at all. I mean, I had no real knowledge of the theater. I thought I was going to be a painter. From my earliest years I trained as a painter, a visual artist. I won national recognition while still in high school and was awarded scholarships to schools of art.

However, at the same time—from the time I was three or four, I was told—I would organize my cousins into plays. We'd dress up and I would tell them, "You do this and you do that," and we'd either imitate films or I'd make up plays. And then when I was about eight I started getting interested in puppetry, hand puppets. I made them, and I then painted the scenery for them and wrote the stories, and it got known, and so I did some at the public library. Then the schools asked, and my father built a little theater for me which we could cart to the schools. So I was doing all this theater. And I had some talent and I was in the school plays, and I loved all that. I was Santa Claus in the Christmas play, and by the time I got to high school I had a good singing voice, so I sang all the solos. It was just doing, doing, doing, but I never thought of it as a life or as a career.[137]

Now that I look back on some of my paintings and drawings, I see that they're all little stories; they're compositions. Very often there's a figure in the foreground that is watching the action that's happening in the picture. It's like an audience watching a happening. So when I look back and reflect, I think, well, maybe theater was what I wanted to do all the time.

The areas of color, composition, design, and non-verbal communication were already highly developed when I felt the need for a stronger grounding in liberal arts. At Northwestern University I was led into the exalted realms of literature and language and became a true believer. Shakespeare and Dickens and Dostoyevsky and Chekhov and Ibsen, Shaw and Arthur Miller, all opened doors to rooms I never knew existed. And I fell in love with the theater, where ideas and human relationships could be explored and examined. But in what manner! With the use of visual arts and music and movement, and with the added dimension of language. "In the two hours' traffic of our stage," as Shakespeare inelegantly but indelibly labeled it, theater and ideas and language could be fun, and thoughtful, and exhilarating to the spirit, could approach a religious experience, and reduce us to fits of laughter, sometimes all in the same evening. I was hooked, and have been ever since. My life in the theater has led me through Broadway musicals, through Shakespeare in the Park, through Hollywood filmmaking, through the early days of live television (as well as its current high-tech and often low-content form), through revolutionary Off Broadway musicals and award-winning new plays, and through residency at one of the nation's great regional theaters. I have been lucky to experience it all and bring that background and my still-burning passion to the training of young artists.

MING CHO LEE (Set Designer, Teacher):
If you're an artist, you are not a static entity, and that is the important thing about working in theater as an artist, because it's a kind of work that enriches one's life. You cannot do a lifetime's worth of it without becoming a different person. And then, the fact that you have lived your life affects the work you do.

When you live a life alone, you don't go into all these things. But because I'm forced to communicate with you [the students], it makes me examine these things so much more fully than I did my whole life. And then I come to these conclusions. I mean, this is the way I've lived my life. Everything I'm saying to you is what I've done, how I've lived my life. It has forced me to articulate it in a much clearer way. You have to be comfortable with confusion. Life isn't perfect. I didn't know that. It tortured me for a very long time. But because I needed to communicate, I realized how true it is.

WILL ROGERS (Actor, Former Student):
He talked about the sacrifices. He talked about being married to one's work, as opposed to being married to a person, and how that's a constant struggle, and something you can decide along the way which road you want to go down.

You can't have it all. Now, that doesn't mean you can't have some of all of it. *Some* of all of it. My observation is, you pay a price. Every artist pays a price, and it depends on what you're willing to pay, or what you want in your life. It doesn't mean that you can't; it means, what do you have to give up for it?

You can't solve those problems at a distance. You can't put it off. You have to ask those questions every day. You have to be in touch with it every day. Is this who I want to be? Is this what I want? And if not, what do I want, and how do I get it?

MARY JANE DEGNAN (Administrator, Colleague):
He was such a hard worker. His work was his life. It is what he enjoyed the most in life, and that was really the top of the list for him. I've never met anyone that worked as many hours in a day as he did.

JOHN WOODSON (Actor):
It kept him vibrant and young, and it was because of his passion for the craft and the passion for the people involved. I mean, every aspect of it. I think everybody's trying to find a passion of some sort. People who are lucky enough to find that have really wonderful lives.

I invited George Abbott, who is a great theater showman/director/writer, to Great Lakes to celebrate his one hundredth birthday, and he directed one of his early successes for me, at *one hundred*! That's now my fantasy—that I will, at one hundred, be as capable as George Abbott was, and still working somewhere. I'm curious about everything. I want to still paint, I want to write, I want to direct. What George Abbott did for me is suggest that it might be possible, it's within the realm of possibility, if you have good health, to continue doing those things.[138]

Friends ask me when I am going to retire. Retire to what? They wanted to retire because they didn't like what they were doing. Now they think they're pursuing what makes them happy, and maybe they are. But it wasn't what they made their lives out of. Why would I want to give up the theater when that is what brings me satisfaction? I love what I'm doing—passing on what I know. I've always loved what I do. I am still learning, every day. I love the theater with an undiminished passion.

BOB FRANCESCONI (Teacher, Colleague):
His entire focus was the theater. Someone in his job interview asked him what hobbies he had. He must have thought that person was crazy. His answer was, "I have no hobbies. I'm here to do theater. And that's it."

VICTORIA BUSSERT (Director, Former Student):
I remember someone said to him, "You need to get a life." And he said, "This is my life! This is what I love." As artists, we may not be following what people think is the typical "get-a-life" kind of life.

LOGAN FAHEY (Actor, Former Student):
His work is his life and his passion and his heart. The people that he works with are the people that he shares his passion and his heart and his life with. That is certainly what has made me a lifer for the theater. And I hope to God that I maintain that until I'm as old as Gerald is.

I never thought of it as a risk. I thought of it as wanting to do something I loved. All during my life, when I made the decision because it made really good sense, or I thought everybody would say I'm a jerk if I don't do it, those were always the bad decisions. They always turned into flops—unsatisfying, unfulfilling, and didn't get me anywhere. The best ones were what I wanted to do, I guess because you can't change the animal. That's how you find out who you are. I didn't think of it as a risk. I thought that was the fun part of what I was doing.

ROBERT BESEDA (Administrator, Former Student):
I've never heard him say "I hate doing this." I've never heard him say anything negative about what he does. I could tell the times when he was unhappy, and more often than not, those times had to do with not believing it was a project he should be doing; and more often than not, those were commercial projects, accepting a job because it was a career move, or accepting a job because the money was really good. He never had the bloodlust of being the top banana, of making it really big.

I look at achievement not in terms of human goals. I want to become a purer artist, more concerned with substance and relationship. That's what I aspire to.[139]

I want to be a little daring so that I will grow. I don't want to just repeat things that I've done before.

I'm not interested in reviews anymore; I'm interested in growth of myself as an artist, which also means growth as a human being. I notice that my feeling about North Carolina is, I have a lot to offer, I have a lot of experience, I have a lot of ideas, I have a lot of technique that I've accumulated, and I don't care to please anyone; I care to pass this on in the most creative and comfortable way I can. I try to make myself available to the students, to teachers, to my friends; but I no longer think about being the best or being first or being "the most." The best is the fullest realization of who I am. Who is that? I don't know unless I explore.[140]

I want to further define myself. As I say, I've given up the idea of being first in anything or the richest or the best. I just want to find out who I am. I'm as interested in and curious about what that'll turn out to be as anyone.[141]

In truth, you do it because you love it. There would be no other reason, because the monetary rewards are not great, but the spiritual rewards are tremendous.

Theater embodies the main hope of humanity today. For, if theater is free conversation—free dialogue among free people about the mysteries of the world—then it is precisely what will show humankind the way toward tolerance and mutual respect for the miracle of being.[142]

It's never "good" to an artist; it's on the way towards something. We're always in process. You never get it right, and that's the joy of it. You never get it right. The hope is that you get another chance at it. And that's the fun and the agony of it.

You get older, and better, and wiser, and you gain more experience—but you're always starting from zero, and you never feel really comfortable. You think you know how to do it, but you don't know how it's going to turn out.

The pursuit of excellence was always a part of my background. It wasn't being the best or getting A's; it was the pursuit of art. That was the task. Looking, and never to stop looking. You may grow tired looking. You may grow weak looking. You may get diverted. But looking is the task. And there is no end.

Gerald in rehearsal for the 1980 revival of *West Side Story*.

LOGAN FAHEY

Gerald at home in Winston-Salem, North Carolina in 2014.

ACKNOWLEDGMENTS

I must begin again with Robert Beseda, whose loving devotion to Gerald's life and work is a perpetual inspiration.

I was born to extraordinary parents, both of whom are extraordinary writers. Art Klein and Dava Sobel were there for me every step of the way with love, support, and keen advice—in this and all of my endeavors.

An army of advocates aided in this book's editing and advancement, namely Victoria Bussert, Michael Carlisle, Chance Carroll, Matt Cowart, Logan Fahey, Pat Feinman, Marilyn Flaig, Jerzy Gwiazdowski, Ethan Hova, Mitchell Ivers, Nathaniel Jacks, Ashley Gates Jansen, Zoë Klein, Jenny Leon, Mollye Maxner, Jesse Patch, Harry Poster, Amy Saltz, Jeremy Skidmore, Jordyn Rebecca Smith, Stephen Sobel, Brian Sutow, Gaye Taylor Upchurch, and Jeremy Webb.

Early and crucial support was given by Carroll Carpenter, Claire Christopher, Jack and Anne Curlett, Lynn and Barry Eisenberg, Carol Fine, Charlotte Hanes, Jane Harmon, David Kay, Lisa Keating, The Kenan Foundation, Lauren and Bradley Poster, Jane Johnston Shearing, Jim and Patricia Toole, Steve Vinovich, and William and Judy Watson.

This book would not be nearly as rich without its contributing interviewees, as well as the sage insights of Barbara Barrie, Barry Bostwick, Micky Callan, Alex Ewing, Alan Filderman, John Gates, Margot Harley, Rosemary Harris, Paulette Haupt, Adrienne Kennedy, Shirley Knight, Piper Laurie, Kate Lundsford, Galt MacDermot, David Manis, John Morris,

Larry Moss, Paula Prentiss, Hal Prince, Jim Rado, Harvey Schmidt, Matt Shea, David Shimotakahara, and Harris Yulin.

I was helped on the hunt for materials by Ian Belknap and Anna Schultz at The Acting Company, Dave Thomas Brown, Mary Jane Degnan, Gresdna A. Doty, Gene Friedman, Todd Krispinsky at Great Lakes Theater, Jeni Dahmus at the Juilliard Archives, Brandon Kahn, Mark Karafin, Daniel Kelly, Amanda Faehnel and Tess Hamilton at the Kent State University Library's Special Collections and Archives, Brent E. LaFever, Margaret Lynch, Roger Mastroianni, Rick Miller, Bridget Regan, Bill Rudman, Faye Sholiton, Nicolas Townsend, Jon J McNeil and Patrice Slattery at the University of North Carolina School of the Arts Archives, Kenton Van Boer, Wendy Barrie-Wilson, and Lee Grady and Mary K Huelsbeck at the Wisconsin Historical Society Archives.

Experts in their respective fields took time to counsel me along the way, including Crystal Arnette, Lindsay Bierman, Joseph K. Chung, Sam Corbin, William Elkington, Joshua Gelfand, Gil Hova, Paul Mullin, Kathy Riemer, Anna Rooney, Seth Shelden, John Sherer, Robin and Scott Sokoloff, Myles Thompson, James T. Tynion III, and the fine folks at Volunteer Lawyers for the Arts.

An extra two cents was always there when I needed it thanks to John Bowhers, Tim Donnelly, Ava Eisenson, Josh Gladstone, Sharone Halevy, Matthew Jellison, Andy Lefkowitz, Celia Michaels, Kate Mueth, Chiara Peacock, Honie Ann Peacock, Augie Praley, Thomas J. Rowell, Steven Royal, and Greg Vore.

Key connections were made for me by Leigha Barr, Rosie Bentnick, Jeff Burroughs, Tiffany Little Canfield, Joyce Cohen, Richard Costabile, Katharine Elkington, Devan Hibbard, Tom Kenan, Betsy Lee, Erik Liberman, Todd Loyd, John Mauceri, Laura Palese, Gail Papp, Lonny Price, Malini Singh McDonald, Emily Takoudes, and Jordan Thaler.

Pleasant places to write were provided by Mica DeAngelis, Barry Mansfield, Joy Parisi at Paragraph workspace, and Greg Walter.

Thanks last but not least to the many generous backers of this book's Kickstarter campaign.

WHO'S WHO IN THE CAST

(Contributors to this book)

DEBBIE ALLEN: Actor, dancer, choreographer, director, teacher, producer. Golden Globe, Drama Desk, three-time Emmy and ten-time Image Award winner. Tony Award nominee. Awarded honorary doctorates by the University of North Carolina School of the Arts and Howard University. Founder of Debbie Allen Dance Academy. Known for her Broadway performances in *West Side Story* and *Sweet Charity*, her performance and choreography in *Fame*, and her direction of *Cat on a Hot Tin Roof* on Broadway. Directed by Freedman in *West Side Story* (co-directed with Jerome Robbins), Broadway's Minskoff Theater, 1980.

CHRISTINE BARANSKI: Actor. Tony and Emmy Award winner. Known for her work on the television shows *Cybill*, *The Big Bang Theory*, *The Good Wife*, and the films *Mamma Mia!*, *Into the Woods*, *Chicago*, and *The Birdcage*. Trained by Freedman at the Juilliard School, 1970 to 1974. Directed by Freedman in *Hamlet*, New York Shakespeare Festival, 1972; *Room Service*, Juilliard School, 1973.

BONNIE BARTLETT: Actor. Two-time Emmy Award winner. Known for the television series *St. Elsewhere*. Classmates with Freedman at Northwestern University. Played Lady Macbeth to Freedman's Macduff in *Macbeth* at Northwestern, 1947. Played wife to Freedman's Androcles in Shaw's *Androcles and the Lion*, directed by Alvina Krause, 1948. Directed by Freedman in *A Midsummer Night's Dream*, Eaglesmeare, 1955.

RICHARD BENJAMIN: Actor, director. Known for acting in the films *Goodbye, Columbus* and *Catch-22*, and directing the films *My Favorite Year*, *The Money Pit*, *Made in America*, and *Mermaids*. Fellow student of Alvina Krause at Northwestern University. Assistant Directed for Freedman: *The Gay Life*, Broadway's Shubert Theater, 1961. Directed by Freedman in *The Taming of the Shrew*, New York Shakespeare Festival, 1960; *As You Like It*, New York Shakespeare Festival, 1963.

ROBERT BESEDA: Administrator, teacher, agent, actor. Assistant Dean, University of North Carolina School of the Arts, 1991 to 2013. Emeritus Faculty in the School of Drama at the University of North Carolina School of the Arts. Trained by Freedman at the Juilliard School, 1970 to 1974. Directed by Freedman in *Room Service*, Juilliard School, 1973; *Six Characters In*

Search of an Author, Juilliard School, 1973. Assistant directed for Freedman: *Hamlet*, New York Shakespeare Festival, 1972; *Coronation of Popea*, Caramoor Center, 1972; *The Adams Chronicles* (Pilot), PBS, 1973.

GLORIA BIEGLER: Actor, teacher. Voice and acting teacher at Geva Theatre Center's Summer Academy. Voice teacher at Hofstra University. Former voice teacher at National Theatre Conservatory at Denver Center Theatre. Directed by Freedman at Great Lakes Theater in *Romeo and Juliet*, 1987; *Love's Labor's Lost*, 1988; *King Lear* (also at Roundabout), 1990; *Cyrano de Bergerac*, 1992.

NEAL BLEDSOE: Actor, writer. Known for his roles on the television shows *Ugly Betty*, *Smash*, and *The Mysteries of Laura*. Trained by Freedman at the University of North Carolina School of the Arts, 2001 to 2005. Directed by Freedman at the University of North Carolina School of the Arts in *As You Like It*, 2002; *Engaged*, 2004; *Romeo and Juliet* (workshop), 2005; *Hogan's Goat*, 2005.

JOHN BOWHERS: Set designer, exhibit designer, theatrical fabricator. Producing Director of Peppercorn Theatre at Kaleideum, 2011 to present. Studied scenic design at the University of North Carolina School of the Arts, 2008 to 2012. Designed for Freedman at the University of North Carolina School of the Arts: *Light Up the Sky*, 2010; *Much Ado About Nothing*, 2012.

MATT BULLUCK: Actor, director, teacher. Acting and directing teacher at the University of North Carolina School of the Arts, 1993 to 2015. Trained by Freedman at the Juilliard School, 1970 to 1974. Directed by Freedman in *Ariadne auf Naxos*, Juilliard Opera Center, 1974. Assistant directed for Freedman: *The Creation of the World and Other Business*, Broadway's Shubert Theater, 1972; *The Robber Bridegroom*, Mark Taper Forum, 1976; *Angle of Repose*, San Francisco Opera, 1976; *Chapeau*, The Acting Company, 1977 to 1978; *Song of Norway*, New York City Opera, 1981.

VICTORIA BUSSERT: Director, teacher. Director of Music Theater for Baldwin Wallace University. At Great Lakes Theater: Assistant to the Artistic Director, 1986 to 1988; Associate Director, 1988 to 1995; co-Artistic Director (with John Ezell) 1995 to 1996; Resident Director, 1996 to present. Assistant directed for Freedman at Great Lakes Theater: *Take One Step!* 1985; *Ghosts*, 1986; *Macbeth*, 1986; *The Boys from Syracuse*, 1987; *Romeo and Juliet*, 1987; *Absent Forever*, 1987; *Love's Labor's Lost*, 1988; *Blood Wedding*, 1988. Associate directed for Freedman at Great Lakes Theater: *Hamlet*, 1989; *A Christmas Carol*, 1989; *King Lear*, 1990; *Dividing The Estate*, 1990; *Uncle Vanya*, 1991; *The Cherry Orchard*, 1993; *Death of a Salesman*, 1994; *A Midsummer Night's Dream*, 1994; *The Bakkhai*, 1995; *The Dybbuk*, 1996. Also assistant directed for Freedman: *America's Sweetheart*, Hartford Stage, 1984; *Brigadoon*, New York City Opera, 1986; *La Boheme*, San Francisco Opera, 1986.

JEANNE BUTTON: Costume designer. Designed for Freedman: *MacBird*, The Village Gate, 1967; *The Robber Bridegroom*, The Acting Company, 1975 to 1976; *The Robber Bridegroom*, Broadway's Biltmore Theater, 1976; *Twelfth Night*, American Shakespeare Theater, 1979; *Second Avenue Rag*, Phoenix Theater, 1980; *La Boehme*, San Francisco Opera, 1986; *Mother Courage*, Williamstown Theater Festival, 1989; *The Crucible*, Roundabout, 1990; *Mother Courage*, Great Lakes Theater, 1992; *Hedda Gabler*, Alley Theater, 1999.

ANNA CAMP: Actor. Drama Desk and Lucile Lortel Award nominee. Known for her roles in the television series *True Blood*; the films *Pitch Perfect*, *The Help*, and *Cafe Society*; and her New York stage performances in *Equus* and *The Scene*. Trained by Freedman at the University of North Carolina School of the Arts, 2000 to 2004. Directed by Freedman at the University of North Carolina School of the Arts in *Man and Superman*, 2003; *Twelfth Night* (workshop), 2004.

TIFFANY LITTLE CANFIELD: Casting director for Telsey + Company. Two-time Emmy Award nominee. Guest teacher at the University of North Carolina School of the Arts, 2003 to 2011. Trained by Freedman at the University of North Carolina School of the Arts, 1998 to 2000. Assistant directed for Freedman at the University of North Carolina School of the Arts: *Ring Round the Moon*, 1998; *Richard III*, 2000.

LAWRENCE CASEY: Costume and set designer. Designed costumes for Freedman at Great Lakes Theater: *Macbeth*, 1986; *The Seagull*, 1989; *Hamlet*, 1989; *Uncle Vanya*, 1991; *The Cherry Orchard*, 1993. Other costume design for Freedman: *Angle of Repose*, San Francisco Opera, 1976; *Lady Macbeth of the Mtsensk*, San Francisco Opera, 1981 and 1988; *Richard II*, Shakespeare Theater, 2000. Designed sets and costumes for Freedman: *Cry of Clytemnestra*, San Francisco Opera, 1981; *The Italian Lesson*, *La Divina*, and *The Stronger*, Baltimore Opera, 1985.

NORMAN COATES: Lighting designer, teacher. Teacher at the University of North Carolina School of the Arts, 1990 to present. Designed for Freedman at the University of North Carolina School of the Arts: *Brigadoon*, 1996; *West Side Story*, 2007. Other design for Freedman: *Hamlet*, concert staging with score by Shostakovich, North Carolina Symphony, 2008; *A Midsummer Night's Dream* (adaptation), Winston-Salem Symphony, 2010.

JOHN CONKLIN: Set designer, teacher at New York University. NEA Opera Honors Recipient. Winner of the TDF / Irene Sharaff Awards' special Robert L.B. Tobin Award for Lifetime Achievement in Theatrical Design. Designed for Freedman: *The Au Pair Man*, New York Shakespeare Festival at Lincoln Center, 1973; *Death in Venice*, San Francisco Opera, 1975.

MATT COWART: Director, producer, teacher. Guest director and guest teacher at the

University of North Carolina School of the Arts, 2008 to 2012. Trained by Freedman at the University of North Carolina School of the Arts, 2000 to 2004. Assistant directed for Freedman: *Enemy of the People*, Williamstown Theater Festival, 2003; *Floyd Collins*, University of North Carolina School of the Arts, 2004.

JOHN CULLUM: Actor, singer. Emmy, Tony, Drama Desk, and Outer Critics Circle Award winner. Known for the television series *Northern Exposure* and his stage performances in *On the Twentieth Century*, *Shenandoah*, and *Urinetown*. Directed by Freedman in *The Taming of the Shrew*, New York Shakespeare Festival, 1960; *The Dresser*, Clarence Brown Theater, 2004.

GRACIELA DANIELE: Dancer, choreographer, director. Tony and Drama Desk Award nominee. Fosse Award winner. Known for choreographing the films *Mighty Aphrodite*, *Bullets over Broadway*, and *Everyone Says I Love You*, and such Broadway musicals as *Chita Rivera: The Dancer's Life*, *Annie Get Your Gun*, and *Once on This Island*. Choreographed productions directed by Freedman: *Naughty Marietta*, New York City Opera, 1978; *Twelfth Night*, American Shakespeare Theater, 1979; *America's Sweetheart*, Hartford Stage, 1984. Co-directed with Freedman: *Blood Wedding*, Great Lakes Theater, 1988.

WILLIAM DANIELS: Actor. Obie and two-time Emmy Award winner. Known for the film *The Graduate*; the television series *St. Elsewhere*, *Knight Rider*, and *Boy Meets World*; and his stage performances in *1776*, *A Little Night Music*, *A Thousand Clowns*, and *The Zoo Story*. Author of the memoir *There I Go Again*. Classmates with Freedman at Northwestern University. Played Macbeth to Freedman's Macduff in *Macbeth* at Northwestern, 1947. Directed by Freedman in *A Midsummer Night's Dream*, Eaglesmeare, 1955; Molly Kazan's *Rosemary* and *The Alligators*, York Playhouse, 1960.

MARY JANE DEGNAN: Administrator. University Administrative Manager at the University of North Carolina School of the Arts, 1992 to 2016.

JOSIE DE GUZMAN: Actor, singer, dancer. Tony Award nominee. Directed by Freedman in *West Side Story* (co-directed with Jerome Robbins), Broadway's Minskoff Theater, 1980; *The Game of Love*, Great Lakes Theater, 1985; *Ghosts*, Great Lakes Theater, 1986; *Blood Wedding*, Great Lakes Theater, 1988.

DANE DEHAAN: Actor. Obie Award winner. Known for the television series *In Treatment*, Off Broadway's *The Aliens*, and the films *Chronicle*, *Kill Your Darlings*, *The Amazing Spiderman*, and *Valerian and the City of a Thousand Planets*. Trained by Freedman at the University of North Carolina School of the Arts, 2004 to 2008. Directed by Freedman at the University of North Carolina School of the Arts in *West Side Story*, 2007; *The Game of Love*, 2008; *Henry IV Parts 1 & 2*, 2008.

JOHN DILLON: Director, teacher, administrator. Former Artistic Director of Milwaukee Repertory Theater. Former Director of the theater program at Sarah Lawrence College. Guest director and guest teacher at the University of North Carolina School of the Arts, 1996 to 2004, and 2010 to 2013.

OLYMPIA DUKAKIS: Actor. Academy and Golden Globe Award winner. Known for her roles in the films *Moonstruck*, *Steel Magnolias*, and *Mr. Holland's Opus*. Directed by Freedman in *Electra*, New York Shakespeare Festival, 1964; *Titus Andronicus*, New York Shakespeare Festival, 1967; *Peer Gynt*, New York Shakespeare Festival, 1969; *Mother Courage*, Williamstown Theater Festival, 1989; *Mother Courage*, Great Lakes Theater, 1992.

JOHN EZELL: Set designer, teacher. Currently serves as the Hall Family Foundation Professor of Design at the University of Missouri-Kansas City, where he leads the UMKC Theater Scenic Design program. Designed

for Freedman at Great Lakes Theater: *Twelfth Night*, 1985; *Blood Wedding*, 1988; *The Seagull*, 1989; *A Christmas Carol*, 1989; *The Lady from Maxim's*, 1990; *Uncle Vanya*, 1991; *The Cherry Orchard*, 1993; *The Dybbuk*, 1996; *Antony and Cleopatra*, 1997. Other design for Freedman: *Richard II*, Shakespeare Theater, 2000; *Enemy of the People*, Williamstown Theater Festival, 2003; *The Dresser*, Clarence Brown Theater, 2004; Beckett's *Happy Days*, International Istanbul Theatre Festival, 2006; *The Diary of Anne Frank*, Westport Country Playhouse, 2010.

LOGAN FAHEY: Actor, photographer. Trained by Freedman at the University of North Carolina School of the Arts, 2004 to 2008. Directed by Freedman in *Henry IV Parts 1 & 2*, University of North Carolina School of the Arts, 2008.

JULES FISHER: Lighting designer, teacher. Tony Award winner. Known for the Broadway productions of *Angels in America*, *Pippin*, *Jesus Christ Superstar*, and *Hair*, and the film versions of *Chicago*, *The Producers*, and *Dreamgirls*. Concert work for such artists as The Rolling Stones, David Bowie, and Kiss. Designed for Freedman: *Soon*, Broadway's Ritz Theater, 1971.

TONY FORMAN: Production manager. Co-founder of Nextstage Design. Production Manager at Great Lakes Theater under Freedman's leadership, 1987 to 1997.

JANET FOSTER: Casting director, teacher. Director of Casting / Artistic Associate / teacher at American Conservatory Theater in San Francisco. Former Casting Director at Playwrights Horizons. Guest teacher at the University of North Carolina School of the Arts, 2004 to 2013. Cast for Freedman: *The Diary of Anne Frank*, Westport Country Playhouse, 2010.

ROBERT FOXWORTH: Actor. Known for the films *The Black Marble* and *Syriana*, and the television series *Falcon Crest* and *Six Feet Un-*

der. Member of the board of directors of the Old Globe. Directed by Freedman at Great Lakes Theater in *Uncle Vanya*, 1991; *Cyrano de Bergerac*, 1992.

BOB FRANCESCONI: Movement/mask teacher, acting teacher, director, administrator. Assistant Dean, University of North Carolina School of the Arts, 1978 to present.

ELIZABETH FRANZ: Actor. Tony, Obie, Joseph Jefferson, Elliot Norton, Ovation, and Lucille Lortel Award winner. Drama Desk, Outer Critics Circle, Emmy, and SAG Award nominee. 2003 recipient of the Dramatist Guild Fund's Lifetime Achievement in the Theater Award. Known for her Broadway performances in *Death of a Salesman*, *Morning's at Seven*, and *Brighton Beach Memoirs*. Directed by Freedman at Great Lakes Theater in *Dividing the Estate*, 1990; *Death of a Salesman*, (also the national tour), 1994 to 1995; *The Glass Menagerie*, 1997.

GENE FRIEDMAN: Set designer, sculptor, teacher. Winner of the Peggy Ezekiel Award for Outstanding Artistic Achievement. Associate Professor of Scenic Design, University of Missouri-Kansas City. Resident Scenic Designer at the Heart of America Shakespeare Festival. Created sculpture for productions directed by Freedman: *The Bakkhai*, Great Lakes Theater, 1995; *Love's Labor's Lost*, Public Theater, 1989. Associate-designed and design-drafted for productions designed by John Ezell and directed by Freedman at Great Lakes Theater: *Twelfth Night*, 1985; *Blood Wedding*, 1988; *The Seagull*, 1989; *A Christmas Carol*, 1989; *The Lady from Maxim's*, 1990; *Uncle Vanya*, 1991; *The Cherry Orchard*, 1993; *The Dybbuk*, 1996; *Antony and Cleopatra*, 1997. Other associate designing / drafting for Ezell/Freedman: *Richard II*, Shakespeare Theater, 2000; *Enemy of the People*, Williamstown Theater Festival, 2003; *The Dresser*, Clarence Brown Theater, 2004; Beckett's *Happy Days*, International Istanbul Theatre Festival, 2006; *The Diary of Anne Frank*, Westport Country Playhouse, 2010.

PENNY FULLER: Actor. Emmy Award winner. Drama Desk and two-time Tony Award nominee. Fellow student of Alvina Krause at Northwestern University. Directed by Freedman at the New York Shakespeare Festival in *As You Like It*, 1963; *Richard III*, 1966; *Henry IV Parts 1 & 2*, 1968.

NICHOLAS GALBRAITH: Director of Marketing and Communications at MCC Theater, former Director of Advocacy Media Strategy and Projects at Autism Speaks, former Communications Manager at Planet Forward, former Deputy Executive Director at I'm From Driftwood, and former Volunteer Coordinator at Empire State Pride Agenda. Trained by Freedman at University of North Carolina School of the Arts, 2003 to 2007. Directed by Freedman at the University of North Carolina School of the Arts in *Habeas Corpus*, 2006; *A Funny Thing Happened on the Way to the Forum*, 2007; *West Side Story*, 2007.

PAUL GEMIGNANI: Music director. Tony, Emmy, and Drama Desk Special Award winner. Known for the Broadway musicals *A Little Night Music*, *Pacific Overtures*, *Evita*, and *Sunday in the Park with George*, and the films *Sweeney Todd*, *Into the Woods*, and *Kramer vs. Kramer*. Music direction for Freedman at New York City Opera: *Brigadoon*, 1986; *South Pacific*, 1987. Music supervision for Freedman: *West Side Story* (co-directed with Jerome Robbins), Broadway's Minskoff Theater, 1980.

BERNARD GERSTEN: Producer, stage manager, teacher. Winner of sixteen Tony Awards, including the 2013 Special Award for Lifetime Achievement. Executive Producer at Lincoln Center Theater, 1985 to 2013. With Joseph Papp, founded the New York Shakespeare Festival, now known as the Public Theater and Shakespeare in the Park, serving as Associate Producer from 1960 to 1978.

ANITA GILLETTE: Actor, singer. Tony and Lucille Lortel Award nominee. Known for her role in television's *Quincy M.E.* and the film

Moonstruck. Directed by Freedman in *The Gay Life*, Broadway's Shubert Theater, 1961; *Skin of Our Teeth*, Great Lakes Theater, 1985; *The Seagull*, Great Lakes Theater, 1989.

QUIN GORDON: Teacher, director, administrator. Acting and directing teacher at the University of North Carolina School of the Arts, 2014 to present. Trained by Freedman at the University of North Carolina School of the Arts, 2004 to 2008. Assistant directed for Freedman: *Habeas Corpus*, University of North Carolina School of the Arts, 2006; *Henry IV Parts 1 & 2*, University of North Carolina School of the Arts, 2008; *Hamlet*, concert staging with score by Shostakovich, North Carolina Symphony, 2008.

LEE GRANT: Actor, director. Academy, Obie, and two-time Emmy Award winner. Known for the films *Shampoo*, *Detective Story*, and *Mulholland Drive*. Directed by Freedman in *Electra*, New York Shakespeare Festival, 1964; *The Little Foxes*, Westwood Playhouse, 1975.

JERZY GWIAZDOWSKI: Actor, writer, teacher. Visiting faculty at The Norwegian Actors' Institute (NSKI Høyskole). Faculty at The New School for Drama. Trained by Freedman at the University of North Carolina School of the Arts, 2000 to 2004. Directed by Freedman at the University of North Carolina School of the Arts in *Floyd Collins*, 2004; *Waiting for Godot*, 2004. Collaborated with Freedman as librettist: *Take One Step!* Peppercorn Theater, 2015.

BARNEY HAMMOND: International voice and acting coach and teacher. Coached for The Stratford Festival, Shaw Festival, Shakespeare Theatre Company, the Old Globe, Seattle Shakespeare, Alley Theatre, and Canadian Stage. Faculty member and Head of Voice Department, University of North Carolina School of the Arts, 1988 to 2001, under Freedman's leadership beginning in 1991. Faculty Emeritus, National Theatre School of Canada. Emeritus Faculty in the School

of Drama at the University of North Carolina School of the Arts.

SHELDON HARNICK: Lyricist. Pulitzer Prize, Grammy, Drama League, two-time Drama Desk, and three-time Tony Award winner. Known for the musicals *Fiddler on the Roof*, *She Loves Me*, and *The Apple Tree*. Classmates with Freedman at Northwestern University. Lyricist for *Man in the Moon*, a musical directed and developed by Freedman, Broadway's Biltmore Theater, 1963.

GEORGE HEARN: Actor, singer. Emmy, Drama Desk, and two-time Tony Award winner. Known for his Broadway performances in *Sweeney Todd, La Cage aux Folles,* and *Sunset Boulevard.* Directed by Freedman in *As You Like It*, New York Shakespeare Festival, 1963; *A Time for Singing*, Broadway's Broadway Theater, 1966; *Henry IV Parts 1 & 2*, New York Shakespeare Festival, 1968.

DESMOND HEELEY: Set and costume designer. Drama Desk and three-time Tony Award winner. Known for designing *Rosencrantz and Guildenstern Are Dead, The Importance of Being Ernest,* and Peter Brook's production of *Titus Andronicus* starring Laurence Olivier. Designed sets and costumes for Freedman at New York City Opera: *Brigadoon*, 1986; *South Pacific*, 1987.

HAL HOLBROOK: Actor. Emmy, Tony, and Drama Desk Award winner. Academy Award nominee. Known for his ongoing portrayal of Mark Twain in *Mark Twain Tonight*, numerous television roles, and recent roles in the films *Lincoln* and *Into the Wild*. Directed by Freedman at Great Lakes Theater in *King Lear* (also at Roundabout), 1990; *Uncle Vanya*, 1991; *Death of a Salesman* (also the national tour), 1994 to 1995.

JOHN HOUSEMAN: Producer, director, actor, teacher, administrator. Golden Globe and Academy Award winner. Founding Director of the Drama Division at the Juilliard School. Co-Founder and former Producing

Artistic Director of The Acting Company (Freedman served as co-Artistic Director). As an administrator, oversaw Freedman's Juilliard productions of *The School for Scandal*, 1972; *Room Service*, 1973; *Six Characters in Search of an Author*, 1973; *The Duchess of Malfi*, 1973; *Le Bourgeois Gentilhomme* (Avery Fisher Hall), 1974; *Ariadne auf Naxos* (Avery Fisher Hall), 1974; *Jenufa*, 1978. As a producer, oversaw Freedman's The Acting Company productions of *The School for Scandal*, 1972; *Love's Labor's Lost*, 1974; *The Robber Bridegroom*, 1975; *Camino Real*, 1976; *Chapeau*, 1977; *The Skin of Our Teeth*, 1984.

MARY IRWIN: Actor, voice and speech teacher, dialect coach. Teacher of Voice & Speech, Dialects, and Shakespeare from 1995 to 2016, and Head of Voice from 2001 to 2016 at the University of North Carolina School of the Arts. Directed by Freedman at the University of North Carolina School of the Arts in *Richard III*, 2000; *The Mandrake*, 2006.

ASHLEY GATES JANSEN: Director, writer, teacher, interfaith minister, life coach. Adjunct director / faculty member at the University of North Carolina School of the Arts, 1996 to 2004. Text/acting teacher and director at the University of North Carolina School of the Arts, 2004 to present. Trained by Freedman in the inaugural directing class at the University of North Carolina School of the Arts, 1992 to 1994. Directing intern for Freedman's production of *Cyrano de Bergerac*, Great Lakes Theater, 1992. Assistant directed Freedman's production of *The Bakkhai*, University of North Carolina School of the Arts, 1994.

ANNALEE JEFFRIES: Actor and director. Known for her appearance in Horton Foote's *The Orphans' Home Cycle*. Guest director/teacher at the University of North Carolina School of the Arts, 1997. Directed by Freedman at Great Lakes Theater in *Dividing the Estate*, 1990; *Uncle Vanya*, 1991; *Antony and Cleopatra*, 1997. Also directed by Freedman in *Hedda Gabler*, The Alley Theater, 1999; *Enemy of the People*, Williamstown Theater Festival, 2003.

HOWARD JONES: Set designer, teacher. University of North Carolina School of the Arts Design Faculty 1983 to 1989, 1997 to present. Designed for Freedman at the University of North Carolina School of the Arts: *Ring Round the Moon*, 1998; *West Side Story*, 2007.

REBECCA NAOMI JONES: Actor, singer. Known for her Broadway performances in *Passing Strange*, *American Idiot*, and *Hedwig and the Angry Inch*. Trained by Freedman at the University of North Carolina School of the Arts, 1999 to 2003. Directed by Freedman in *Love's Labor's Lost* (workshop), University of North Carolina School of the Arts, 2003.

STACY KEACH: Actor. Golden Globe, three-time Obie, three-time Helen Hayes, and four-time Drama Desk Award winner. Emmy and Tony Award nominee. Inducted into American Theater Hall of Fame in 2015. Known for his roles in the films *Nebraska*, *American History X*, *Up in Smoke*, and *That Championship Season*. Directed by Freedman at the New York Shakespeare Festival in *Henry IV Parts 1 & 2*, 1968; *Peer Gynt*, 1969; *Hamlet*, 1972. Also directed by Freedman in *MacBird*, The Village Gate, 1967; *King Lear*, Broadway's Vivian Beaumont Theater at Lincoln Center, 1968; *Antigone*, Lincoln Center, PBS Great Performances, 1972.

BARBARA KESSLER: Costume designer, teacher. Studied Japanese classical arts alongside Freedman at Oomoto Institute, Kameoka, Japan. Designed for Freedman: *The Bakkhai*, University of North Carolina School of the Arts, 1994; *The Bakkhai*, Great Lakes Theater, 1995; *The Dybbuk*, Great Lakes Theater, 1996.

KEVIN KLINE: Actor. Academy Award Winner. Multi-time Tony, Drama Desk, Lucile Lortel, Obie, Screen Actors Guild, and Outer Critic's Circle Award winner. Emmy Award nominee. Known for his roles in the films *A Fish Called Wanda, In & Out, Dave,* and *Sophie's Choice.* Trained by Freedman at the Juilliard School, 1968 to 1972. Directed by Freedman in *The School for Scandal,* Juilliard School, The Acting Company, 1972 to 1973; *The Robber Bridegroom,* The Acting Company, 1975 to 1976; *Much Ado About Nothing,* New York Shakespeare Festival, 1988.

AL KOHOUT: Costume designer. Managed costume shop at Great Lakes Theater for twelve years. Former student of John Ezell. Designed for Freedman at Great Lakes Theater: *Dividing the Estate,* 1990; *Death of a Salesman* (also the national tour), 1994 to 1995; *The Glass Menagerie,* 1997.

EDDIE KURTZ: Political Organizer. President & Executive Director of Courage Campaign. Trained by Freedman at the University of North Carolina School of the Arts, 2002 to 2004. Assistant directed for Freedman: *Man and Superman,* University of North Carolina School of the Arts, 2003; *Enemy of the People,* Williamstown Theater Festival, 2003; *Waiting for Godot,* University of North Carolina School of the Arts, 2004.

JAKE LACY: Actor. Known for his roles in the films *Carol* and *Obvious Child,* and the television shows *Girls, The Office,* and *I'm Dying Up Here.* Trained by Freedman at the University of North Carolina School of the Arts, 2004 to 2008. Directed by Freedman in *Henry IV Parts 1 & 2,* University of North Carolina School of the Arts, 2008.

MARK LAMOS: Director, actor. Artistic Director at Westport Country Playhouse. Former Artistic Director at Hartford Stage (1989 Tony Award for Outstanding Regional Theater). Tony Award nominee. Also known for his Broadway productions of *Our Country's Good, Cymbeline,* and *Seascape.* As Artistic Director of Westport Country Playhouse, oversaw Freedman's production of *The Diary of Anne Frank* in 2010. Directed by Freedman in *The Creation of the World and*

Other Business, Broadway's Shubert Theater, 1972; *Twelfth Night,* American Shakespeare Theater, 1978.

JOHN LANGS: Director. Artistic Director at A Contemporary Theater, Seattle. Resident Assistant Director to Freedman at Great Lakes Theater, 1995 to 1996. Guest director and adjunct faculty member at the University of North Carolina School of the Arts, 2004 to 2012. Co-directed University of North Carolina School of the Arts consortium, 2007 to 2012. Trained by Freedman at the University of North Carolina School of the Arts, 1991 to 1995. Assistant directed for Freedman at the University of North Carolina School of the Arts: *Troilus and Cressida,* 1995; *Brigadoon,* 1996. Assistant directed for Freedman at Great Lakes Theater: *A Midsummer Night's Dream,* 1994; *Antony and Cleopatra,* 1997.

CAROL LAWRENCE: Actor, singer, dancer. Los Angeles Drama Critics Award winner. Tony Award nominee. Known for her performances in the Broadway musicals *West Side Story, Kiss of the Spiderwoman,* and *I Do! I Do!* Fellow student of Alvina Krause at Northwestern University. Assistant directed by Freedman (for Jerome Robbins) in *West Side Story,* National Theater and Broadway's Winter Garden Theater, 1957.

MING CHO LEE: Set designer, teacher. Former Co-Chair of the Design Department at Yale University School of Drama. Winner of two Tony Awards, including the 2013 Special Award for Lifetime Achievement. Obie Award for Sustained Achievement. Drama Desk and Helen Hayes Award winner. Known for his design of *Mother Courage, The Glass Menagerie,* and *K2.* Designed for Freedman at the New York Shakespeare Festival: *The Tempest,* 1962; *As You Like It,* 1963; *Electra,* 1964; *Timon of Athens,* 1971. Other design for Freedman: *A Time for Singing,* Broadway's Broadway Theater, 1966; *Hair,* Public Theater, 1967; *Ergo,* Public Theater, 1968; *Bach's St. Matthew Passion,* San Francisco Opera, 1973; *Twelfth Night,* American Shakespeare Theater, 1978; *The Tempest*, American Shakespeare Theater, 1979; *The Grand Tour*, Broadway's Palace Theater, 1979.

PEGGY LOFT (A.K.A. MARGARET FREED): Actor, vocal coach, director, teacher. Member of the first faculty of the Juilliard School. Professor Emeritus of Southern Methodist University's professional theater training program. Fellow student of Alvina Krause at Northwestern University, and a member of her summer company in Eaglesmere, Pennsylvania. Guest teacher and director at the University of North Carolina School of the Arts, 1991 to 1995. Acted with Freedman in Susan Glaspell's one act play, *Woman's Honor*, Northwestern University, 1945. Served as Vocal Coach for Freedman at the American Shakespeare Theater (Stratford, CT): *Twelfth Night*, 1979; *Julius Caesar*, 1979; *The Tempest*, 1979.

PATTI LUPONE: Actor, singer. Olivier, Drama Desk, Outer Critics Circle, Drama League, and two-time Tony Award winner. Known for her performances in the Broadway musicals *Evita*, *Sweeney Todd*, *Gypsy*, and *War Paint*. Trained by Freedman at the Juilliard School, 1968 to 1972. Directed by Freedman in *The School for Scandal*, Juilliard School, The Acting Company, 1972 to 1973; *The Robber Bridegroom*, The Acting Company, 1975 to 1976; *Regina*, The Kennedy Center, 2005.

MARGARET LYNCH: Dramaturg, educator, administrator. Dramaturg at Great Lakes Theater, 1984 to 2003, under Freedman's leadership from 1985 to 1997.

JACKLYN MADDUX: Alexander Technique and voice teacher, actor, playwright. Taught Alexander Technique and voice under Freedman's leadership at the University of North Carolina School of the Arts, 1997 to 2003.

BILLY MAGNUSSEN: Actor. Tony Award nominee. Known for his stage appearances in *Vanya and Sonia and Masha and Spike*

and *Sex with Strangers*, the television series *The People v. O.J. Simpson*, and the films *Into the Woods*, *Bridge of Spies*, and *The Big Short*. Trained by Freedman at the University of North Carolina School of the Arts, 2003 to 2007. Directed by Freedman at the University of North Carolina School of the Arts in *A Funny Thing Happened on the Way to the Forum*, 2007; *West Side Story*, 2007.

JOHN MAUCERI: Conductor, writer, educator. Tony, Grammy, Olivier, Drama Desk, Billboard, and three-time Emmy Award winner. Led the Hollywood Bowl for sixteen years. Known for his work in opera, musical theater, and with orchestras and opera companies around the world. Served as Chancellor at the University of North Carolina School of the Arts, 2006 to 2013. Conducted for Freedman: *Death in Venice* (west coast premiere), San Francisco Opera, 1975; *Angle of Repose* (world premiere), San Francisco Opera, 1976; *Naughty Marietta*, New York City Opera, 1978; *West Side Story* (fiftieth anniversary production), University of North Carolina School of the Arts, 2007; *Hamlet*, world premiere concert staging with score by Shostakovich, North Carolina Symphony, 2008.

KELLY MAXNER: Director, choreographer, writer, teacher. Helen Hayes Award winner for Outstanding Choreography. Director of the University of North Carolina School of the Arts School of Drama High School Program and Artistic Director of the Drama Summer Session. Trained by Freedman at the University of North Carolina School of the Arts, 1990 to 1994, and 2000. Directed by Freedman in *The Bakkhai*, University of North Carolina School of the Arts, 1994; *The Bakkhai*, Great Lakes Theater, 1995; *Richard III*, University of North Carolina School of the Arts, 2000. Choreographed productions directed by Freedman: *Revenger's Tragedy*, University of North Carolina School of the Arts, 1993; *The Bakkhai*, Great Lakes Theater, 1995; *A Time For Singing*, University of North Carolina School of the Arts, 2000; *A Midsummer Night's Dream*, Stevens Center, 2011. Co-directed with Freedman: *Take One Step!* NCSA Summer Performance Festival, 2007.

MOLLYE MAXNER: Director, choreographer, writer, teacher. Guest artist, part-time visiting faculty at University of North Carolina School of the Arts, 2009 to present. Trained by Freedman at the University of North Carolina School of the Arts, 2007 to 2009. Assistant directed for Freedman: *Sunday in the Park with George*, University of North Carolina School of the Arts, 2009.

TRAVIS McHALE: Lighting designer. Studied lighting design at the University of North Carolina School of the Arts, 2001 to 2005. Designed for Freedman: *Hogan's Goat*, University of North Carolina School of the Arts, 2005; *The Diary of Anne Frank*, Westport Country Playhouse, 2010.

BRIAN MURRAY: Actor and director. Two-time Drama Desk Award winner. Tony Award nominee. Known for his Broadway performances in *Rosencrantz and Guildenstern Are Dead* and *Noises Off*, and directing numerous Noel Coward Broadway revivals. Directed *Arsenic and Old Lace* under Gerald's leadership at Great Lakes Theater, 1986. Directed by Freedman in *Much Ado About Nothing*, New York Shakespeare Festival, 1998.

JACK O'BRIEN: Director, producer, writer, actor, lyricist. Artistic Director at the Old Globe, 1981 to 2007. Three-time Tony and five-time Obie Award winner. Also known for his Broadway productions of *Hairspray*, *The Full Monty*, and *The Coast of Utopia*. As Artistic Director of the Old Globe, oversaw Freedman's productions of: *Measure for Measure*, 1981; *Blood Wedding*, 1989.

CIGDEM ONAT: Director, actor, teacher. Drama Desk Award nominee. Theatre World Award winner. Known for her performance in *The Time of the Cuckoo* at Lincoln Center. Director and teacher at the Graduate Acting

Program at NYU Tisch School of the Arts, 2004 to 2011. Acting teacher, text teacher, and director at the University of North Carolina School of the Arts, 1979 to 2004. Emeritus Faculty in the School of Drama at the University of North Carolina School of the Arts. Directed by Freedman in Beckett's *Happy Days*, International Istanbul Theatre Festival, 2006; *Hamlet*, concert staging with score by Shostakovich, North Carolina Symphony, 2008.

PJ PAPARELLI: Director, playwright. Known for his play *Columbinus* and his work in Chicago, notably with American Theater Company, where he served as Artistic Director from 2007 until his death in 2015. Guest director and guest teacher at the University of North Carolina School of the Arts, 2002 to 2003. Associate directed for Freedman: *Richard II*, Shakespeare Theater, 2000.

JOSEPH PAPP: Director, producer. Founder and former producer of the New York Shakespeare Festival, now known as the Public Theater and Shakespeare in the Park. Produced Freedman's 1960 production of *The Taming of the Shrew* in Central Park. Produced Freedman's Delacorte Theater productions of *The Tempest*, 1962; *As You Like It*, 1963; *Electra*, 1964; *Love's Labor's Lost*, 1965; *Richard III*, 1966; *Titus Andronicus*, 1967; *Comedy of Errors*, 1967; *Henry IV Parts I & II*, 1968; *Peer Gynt*, 1969; *Hamlet*, 1972; *Much Ado About Nothing*, 1988. Produced Freedman's New York Shakespeare Festival Mobile Theater productions of *Take One Step!* 1968; *Black Electra*, 1969. Produced Freedman's Public Theater productions of *Hair* (also at Cafe Cheetah), 1967; *Ergo*, 1968; *Cities in Bezique*, 1969; *An Invitation to a Beheading*, 1969; *SAMBO*, 1969; *The Wedding of Iphigenia*, 1971; *Love's Labor's Lost*, 1989.

MANDY PATINKIN: Actor, singer. Tony, Emmy, Golden Globe, and Screen Actors Guild Award winner. Known for his performances in the television series *Homeland*, the film *The Princess Bride*, and the Broadway musicals *Evita* and *Sunday in the Park*

with George. Also known for his work with the International Rescue Committee, in trying to bring aid and attention to the world's most vulnerable among us. Trained by Freedman at the Juilliard School, 1972 to 1974. Directed by Freedman in *The Duchess of Malfi*, Juilliard School, 1973; *Enemy of the People*, Williamstown Theater Festival, 2003.

AUSTIN PENDLETON: Actor, playwright, director, teacher. Drama Desk and Obie Award winner. Tony Award nominee. Steppenwolf ensemble member. Current acting and directing teacher at HB Studio. Former Artistic Director of Circle Rep. Known for his performances in the Broadway musical *Fiddler on the Roof*, the play *The Diary of Anne Frank*, and the films *A Beautiful Mind*, *My Cousin Vinny*, and *Short Circuit*. Assistant directed by Freedman (for Jerome Robbins) in *Oh, Dad, Poor Dad, Mamma's Hung You in the Closet and I'm Feelin' So Sad*, Off Broadway's Phoenix Theater, 1961. Directed by Freedman in *An American Millionaire*, Broadway's Circle in the Square, 1974; *Mother Courage*, Williamstown Theater Festival, 1989. Collaborated with Freedman as playwright: *Booth*, University of North Carolina School of the Arts, 2010.

HARRY POSTER: Director, writer. Manager of Kennedy Center Theatre for Young Audiences. Former Artistic Director of Peppercorn Theater at Kaleideum. Trained by Freedman at the University of North Carolina School of the Arts, 2007 to 2011. Assistant directed for Freedman: *Light Up the Sky*, University of North Carolina School of the Arts, 2010; *The Diary of Anne Frank*, Westport Country Playhouse, 2010; *A Midsummer Night's Dream*, concert staging with score by Mendelssohn, Winston-Salem Symphony Orchestra, 2011.

MISSI PYLE: Actor, singer. Known for her roles in the films *Gone Girl*, *Charlie and the Chocolate Factory*, *Big Fish*, and *The Artist*. Trained by Freedman at the University of North Carolina School of the Arts, 1991 to 1995. Directed by Freedman in *Troilus*

and Cressida, University of North Carolina School of the Arts, 1995.

CHARLOTTE RAE: Actor, singer, dancer. Tony and Emmy Award nominee. Known for her television roles in *The Facts of Life* and *Diff'rent Strokes*. Classmates with Freedman at Northwestern University. Directed by Freedman in *Henry IV Parts 1 & 2*, New York Shakespeare Festival, 1968.

CHITA RIVERA: Dancer, actor, singer. Two-time Tony and Drama Desk Award winner. Kennedy Center Honoree. 2009 recipient of the Presidential Medal of Freedom from President Barack Obama. Known for her roles in the Broadway musicals *West Side Story*, *Bye Bye Birdie*, *Chicago*, *The Rink*, *Kiss of the Spiderwoman*, and *The Visit*. Assistant directed by Freedman (for Jerome Robbins) in *West Side Story*, National Theater and Broadway's Winter Garden Theater, 1957.

WILL ROGERS: Actor. Drama Desk Award Nominee. Known for his role in the film *Bridge of Spies*, and his Off Broadway performances in *The Submission*, *Golden Age*, and *From Up Here*. Trained by Freedman at the University of North Carolina School of the Arts, 2000 to 2004. Directed by Freedman at the University of North Carolina School of the Arts in *Man and Superman*, 2003; *Floyd Collins*, 2004; *Waiting for Godot*, 2004.

STEVEN ROUTMAN: Actor, writer. Helen Hayes and Kevin Kline Award nominee. Recently appeared in the films *Inside Llewyn Davis* and *Wolf of Wall Street*, and the Off Broadway musical *The Shaggs*. Directed by Freedman at Great Lakes Theater in *Romeo and Juliet*, 1987; *The Boys from Syracuse*, 1987; *The Seagull*, 1989; *Hamlet*, 1989; *A Christmas Carol*, 1989 and 1990; *The Lady from Maxim's*, 1990; *The Cherry Orchard*, 1993. Also directed by Freedman in *America's Sweetheart*, Hartford Stage, 1985; *Much Ado About Nothing*, New York Shakespeare Festival, 1988; *Love's Labor's Lost*, Public Theater, 1989.

BILL RUDMAN: Educator, broadcaster. Artistic Director and Founder of The Musical Theater Project. Host of the national radio programs *Footlight Parade* and *On the Aisle*. Associate Director in Charge of Educational Programming at Great Lakes Theater, under Freedman's leadership, 1985 to 1997.

ROB RUGGIERO: Director. Producing Artistic Director at TheaterWorks (Hartford). He is a freelance professional director whose work has earned him national recognition on both plays and musicals. Known for his Broadway productions of *High* and *Looped*, and his Off Broadway production of *Make Me a Song: The Music of William Finn*. Assisted Freedman for three years at the Great Lakes Theater Festival, 1990 to 1992. Assistant directed for Freedman at Great Lakes Theater: *King Lear* (also at Roundabout), 1990; *The Lady from Maxim's*, 1990; *Dividing the Estate*, 1990; *A Christmas Carol*, 1990; *Uncle Vanya*, 1991; *Ohio State Murders*, 1992; *Mother Courage*, 1992; *Cyrano de Bergerac*, 1992. Also assistant directed for Freedman: *Ohio State Murders*, Yale Repertory Theater, 1991; *The Lady from Maxim's*, Missouri Repertory Theater, 1992.

AMY SALTZ: Director, teacher. Known for her direction at Second Stage, the Public, Playwrights' Horizons, the Eugene O'Neill Theater Center's National Playwright's Conference, and regional theaters throughout the United States. Connecticut Critics Circle, Outer Critics Circle, Joseph Jefferson, and Handy Award winner. Helen Hayes and Grammy Award nominee. Professor Emerita, Rutgers University, where she served as Head of the MFA Directing Program from 2001 to 2013. Co-directed with Freedman: *Black Electra*, New York Shakespeare Festival Mobile Theater, 1969. Assistant directed for Freedman at the New York Shakespeare Festival: *Titus Andronicus*, 1967; *Comedy of Errors*, 1967; *Henry IV Parts 1 & 2*, 1968; *Peer Gynt*, 1969. Also assistant directed for Freedman: *Hair*, Public Theater, 1967; *Hair*, Cafe Cheetah, 1967; *Ergo*, Public Theater, 1968;

King Lear, Broadway's Vivian Beaumont Theater at Lincoln Center, 1968; *Take One Step!* (New York Shakespeare Festival Mobile Theater), 1968; *Cities in Bezique*, Public Theater, 1969; *An Invitation to a Beheading*, Public Theater, 1969; *Beatrix Cenci*, Kennedy Center, 1971; *Bach's St. Matthew Passion*, San Francisco Opera, 1973.

DOUGLAS W. SCHMIDT: Set designer. Three-time Tony Award nominee. Three-time Drama Desk Award winner. Known for designing Broadway productions of *Grease*, *Into the Woods*, and *42nd Street*. Assisted Ming Cho Lee on several early shows directed by Freedman. Designed for Freedman: *The Wedding of Iphigenia*, Public Theater, 1971; *The School for Scandal*, The Acting Company, 1972; *An American Millionaire*, Broadway's Circle in the Square, 1974; *The Robber Bridegroom*, The Acting Company, 1975 to 1976; *Angle of Repose*, San Francisco Opera, 1976; *The Robber Bridegroom*, Broadway's Biltmore Theater, 1976; *The School for Scandal*, Great Lakes Theater, Broadway's Lyceum Theater, 1995.

GABE SCOGGIN: Senior Program Manager at Google. Trained by Freedman at the University of North Carolina School of the Arts, 2000 to 2004. Directed by Freedman at the University of North Carolina School of the Arts in *Man and Superman*, 2003; *Floyd Collins*, 2004.

JOHN SEIDMAN: Actor, director. Assistant Directed for Freedman: *Mrs. Warren's Profession*, New York Shakespeare Festival at Lincoln Center, 1976; *Bach's St. Matthew Passion*, San Francisco Opera, 1976. Directed by Freedman in *A Midsummer Night's Dream*, Great Lakes Theater, 1994.

JEREMY SKIDMORE: Director, teacher. Artistic Director, RhinoLeap Productions. Former Artistic Director at Malibu Playhouse and Theater Alliance. Guest director and guest teacher at University of North Carolina School of the Arts, 2005 to 2012. Trained by Freedman at University of North Carolina School of the Arts, 1995 to 2000. Assistant directed for Freedman at the University of North Carolina School of the Arts: *A Time for Singing*, 2000; *Richard III*, 2000. Also assistant directed for Freedman: *The Antipodes*, Shakespeare's Globe, 2000.

ROBERT STATTEL: Actor, painter. Known for his roles in the Broadway productions of *Here I Come, Philadelphia*, and *Sherlock Holmes*. Directed by Freedman at the New York Shakespeare Festival in *Titus Andronicus*, 1967; *Henry IV Parts 1 & 2*, 1968; *Peer Gynt*, 1969; *Hamlet*, 1972. Directed by Freedman at the American Shakespeare Theater in *Twelfth Night*, 1978 and 1979; *Julius Caesar*, 1979; *The Tempest*, 1979. Also directed by Freedman in *Ergo*, Public Theater, 1968; *King Lear*, Broadway's Vivian Beaumont Theater at Lincoln Center, 1968; *The Incomparable Max*, Broadway's Royale Theater, 1971.

BRIAN SUTOW: Writer, actor, director, administrator. Founder and former Artistic Director of No Rules Theater Company. Trained by Freedman at the University of North Carolina School of the Arts, 2005 to 2009. Directed by Freedman at the University of North Carolina School of the Arts in *Henry IV Parts 1 & 2*, 2008; *Sunday in the Park with George*, 2009.

JORDAN THALER: Casting Director at the Public Theater. Guest teacher at University of North Carolina School of the Arts, 1998 to 2010. Cast for Freedman: *Love's Labor's Lost*, Public Theater, 1989.

JOHN TOIA: Stage manager, production manager, teacher. Director of Production for the Dallas Opera. Teacher at the University of North Carolina School of the Arts, 1989 to 2009. Assistant Dean for the Department of Design & Production at the University of North Carolina School of the Arts, 1994 to 2009. Production managed for Freedman: *West Side Story*, University of North Carolina School of the Arts, 2007.

RICHARD TROUSDELL: Director, teacher, Jungian analyst. Professor Emeritus of Acting and Directing at the University of Massachusetts Department of Theater. Trained by Freedman at Yale School of Drama, 1966. Assistant directed for Freedman at the New York Shakespeare Festival: *Titus Andronicus*, 1967; *Comedy of Errors*, 1967. Assistant directed for Freedman at the Public Theater: *Hair*, 1967; *Ergo*, 1968.

ALFRED UHRY: Playwright, screenwriter, book writer and lyricist. Pulitzer Prize winner. Academy and Tony Award winner. Known for writing the plays/films *Driving Miss Daisy*, *The Last Night of Ballyhoo*, and the musicals *Parade* and *LoveMusik*. Book writer / lyricist for musicals developed and directed by Freedman: *The Robber Bridegroom*, Juilliard School, The Acting Company, Mark Taper Forum, Broadway's Biltmore Theater, 1973 to 1976; *Chapeau*, The Acting Company, 1977 to 1978; *America's Sweetheart*, Hartford Stage, Coconut Grove Playhouse, 1984.

GAYE TAYLOR UPCHURCH: Director. Known for her productions at the Atlantic, the Women's Project, Rattlestick Theater, and the Old Globe. Trained by Freedman at the University of North Carolina School of the Arts, 2003 to 2005. Assistant directed for Freedman: *The Dresser*, Clarence Brown Theater, 2004; *Regina*, The Kennedy Center, 2005. Directed Freedman in *Visiting Mr. Green*, University of North Carolina School of the Arts, 2005.

STEVE VINOVICH: Actor. Trained by Freedman at the Juilliard School, 1972 to 1974. Directed by Freedman in *Six Characters in Search of an Author*, Juilliard School, 1973; *Le Bourgeois Gentilhomme*, Avery Fisher Hall, 1974; *The Robber Bridegroom*, Broadway's Biltmore Theater, 1976; *Twelfth Night*, American Shakespeare Theater, 1978; *The Grand Tour*, Broadway's Palace Theater, 1979; *America's Sweetheart*, Hartford Stage, Coconut Grove Playhouse, 1984; *The Diary of Anne Frank*, Westport Country Playhouse, 2010.

RAY VIRTA: Actor, teacher. Professor at the American Musical and Dramatic Academy. Directed by Freedman at Great Lakes Theater in *Twelfth Night*, 1985; *Macbeth*, 1986; *Love's Labor's Lost*, 1988; *Cyrano de Bergerac*, 1992; *Mother Courage*, 1992; *The School for Scandal* (also at Broadway's Lyceum Theater), 1995; *The Glass Menagerie*, 1997. Also directed by Freedman in *Mother Courage*, Williamstown Theater Festival, 1989.

GREG VORE: Director, photographer. Co-directed University of North Carolina School of the Arts consortium, 1992 to 2006. Assistant to Artistic Director Freedman at Great Lakes Theater, 1994 to 1995. Trained by Freedman at the University of North Carolina School of the Arts, 1992 to 1994. Assistant directed for Freedman at Great Lakes Theater: *A Midsummer Night's Dream*, 1994; *A Christmas Carol*, 1994; *The Bakkhai*, 1995; *Death of a Salesman* (also the national tour), 1994 to 1995; *The Dybbuk*, 1996; *Antony and Cleopatra*, 1997.

ROBERT WALDMAN: Composer, orchestrator. Drama Desk Award nominee. Known for the musical *The Robber Bridegroom*, and for the music he wrote for the New York productions of *The Rivals, Dinner at Eight, The Last Night of Ballyhoo*, and the world premiere of *Driving Miss Daisy*. Composer of musicals developed and directed by Freedman: *The Robber Bridegroom*, Juilliard School, The Acting Company, Mark Taper Forum, Broadway's Biltmore Theater, 1973 to 1976; *Chapeau*, The Acting Company, 1977 to 1978; *America's Sweetheart*, Hartford Stage, Coconut Grove Playhouse, 1984. Composed incidental music for Freedman's productions of: *A Christmas Carol*, Great Lakes Theater, 1989; *The School for Scandal*, Great Lakes Theater, Broadway's Lyceum Theater, 1995; *The Glass Menagerie*, Great Lakes Theater, 1997; *Richard II*, Shakespeare Theater, 2000; *The Country Wife*, University of North Carolina School of the Arts, 2001.

SAM WATERSTON: Actor. Golden Globe, Emmy, and Academy Award nominee. Known for his television roles on *Grace and Frankie, Law & Order*, and *The Newsroom*. Assistant directed by Freedman (for Jerome Robbins) in *Oh, Dad, Poor Dad, Mamma's Hung You in the Closet and I'm Feelin' So Sad*, Off Broadway's Phoenix Theater, 1961. Directed by Freedman at the New York Shakespeare Festival in *Henry IV Parts 1 & 2*, 1968; *Hamlet*, 1972.

JEREMY WEBB: Actor. Drama Desk Award winner. Helen Hayes Award nominee. Trained by Freedman at the University of North Carolina School of the Arts, 1990 to 1994. Directed by Freedman at the University of North Carolina School of the Arts in *The Revenger's Tragedy*, 1993; *The Bakkhai*, 1994. Directed by Freedman at Great Lakes Theater in *The Bakkhai*, 1995; *Antony and Cleopatra*, 1997.

ANNA WOOD: Actor. Known for her role in the television series *Reckless*. Trained by Freedman at the University of North Carolina School of the Arts, 2004 to 2008. Directed by Freedman at the University of North Carolina School of the Arts in *West Side Story*, 2007; *The Game of Love*, 2008.

JOHN WOODSON: Actor, director, visual artist, teacher. Founding company member at Signature Theater Company. Faculty member at Coastal Carolina University. Trained at the University of North Carolina School of the Arts, 1969 to 1972. Directed by Freedman at Great Lakes Theater in *King Lear* (also at Roundabout), 1990; *The Cherry Orchard*, 1993; *A Midsummer Night's Dream*, 1994; *A Christmas Carol*, 1994 and 1995. Also directed by Freedman in *Hamlet*, concert staging with score by Shostakovich, North Carolina Symphony, 2008.

AMY SALTZ

Gerald at the Delacorte Theater in 1968.

GERALD FREEDMAN PRODUCTION HISTORY

(Credit is for direction, unless otherwise noted.)

BROADWAY

Bells Are Ringing (Assistant Director), Alvin Theater, 1956

West Side Story (Assistant Director), Winter Garden Theater, 1957

Gypsy (Assistant Director), Broadway Theater, 1959

The Gay Life, Shubert Theater, 1961

Man in the Moon, Biltmore Theater, 1963

A Time for Singing (Director, Book and Lyrics), Broadway Theater, 1966

King Lear, Vivian Beaumont Theater, 1968

Soon, Ritz Theater, 1971

The Incomparable Max, Royale Theater, 1971

The Creation of the World and Other Business, Broadway's Shubert Theater, 1972

The Au Pair Man, Vivian Beaumont Theater, 1973

An American Millionaire, Circle in the Square, 1974

The Robber Bridegroom, Harkness Theater, 1975, Biltmore Theater, 1976

Mrs. Warren's Profession, Vivian Beaumont Theater, 1976

The Grand Tour, Palace Theater, 1979

West Side Story (Co-Director), Minskoff Theater, 1980

The School for Scandal, Lyceum Theater, 1995

NEW YORK SHAKESPEARE FESTIVAL
(The Public Theater / Shakespeare in the Park)

Artistic Director, 1967 to 1970

The Taming of the Shrew, Central Park, 1960

The Tempest, Delacorte Theater, 1962

As You Like It, Delacorte Theater, 1963

Electra, Delacorte Theater, 1964

Love's Labor's Lost, Delacorte Theater, 1965

Richard III, Delacorte Theater, 1966

Titus Andronicus, Delacorte Theater, 1967

Comedy of Errors, Delacorte Theater, 1967

Hair, Public Theater, 1967, Cafe Cheetah, 1967

Ergo, Public Theater, 1968

Take One Step! New York Shakespeare Festival Mobile Theater, 1968

Henry IV Parts I & II, Delacorte Theater, 1968

Cities in Bezique, Public Theater, 1969

An Invitation to a Beheading, Public Theater, 1969

SAMBO, Public Theater, 1969

Peer Gynt (Director, Lyricist, Adaptation), Delacorte Theater, 1969

Black Electra, New York Shakespeare Festival Mobile Theater, 1969

Timon of Athens, Delacorte Theater, 1971

The Wedding of Iphigenia, Public Theater, 1971

Hamlet, Delacorte Theater, 1972

Much Ado About Nothing, Delacorte Theater, 1988

Love's Labor's Lost, Public Theater, 1989

OFF BROADWAY THEATER

On The Town, Carnegie Hall Playhouse, 1959

Rosemary and *The Alligators*, York Playhouse, 1960

Oh, Dad, Poor Dad, Mamma's Hung You in the Closet and I'm Feelin' So Sad (Assistant Director), Phoenix theater, 1961

West Side Story, City Center Theater, 1964

The Day the Whores Came to Play Tennis, Players Theater, 1965

MacBird, The Village Gate, 1967

Collette, LaMama, 1970

The School for Scandal, The Acting Company, 1972

Love's Labor's Lost, The Acting Company, 1974

Second Avenue Rag, Phoenix Theater, 1980

Brigadoon, New York City Opera, 1986, 1989

South Pacific, New York City Opera, 1987

The Crucible, Roundabout Theater, 1990

King Lear, Roundabout Theater, 1990

GREAT LAKES THEATER
Cleveland, Ohio

Artistic Director, 1985 to 1997

Take One Step! (Director, Book and Lyrics), 1985

The Game of Love, 1985

Twelfth Night, 1985

Ghosts, 1986

Macbeth, 1986

The Boys from Syracuse, 1987

Romeo and Juliet, 1987

Absent Forever, 1987

Love's Labor's Lost, 1988

Blood Wedding (Co-Director), 1988

Hamlet, 1989

The Seagull, 1989

A Christmas Carol, 1989

King Lear, 1990

The Lady from Maxim's, 1990
Dividing the Estate, 1990
Uncle Vanya, 1991
Ohio State Murders, 1992
Mother Courage, 1992
Cyrano de Bergerac, 1992
The Cherry Orchard, 1993
Death of a Salesman, 1994
A Midsummer Night's Dream, 1994
The Bakkhai, 1995
The School for Scandal, 1995
The Dybbuk, 1996
Antony and Cleopatra, 1997
The Glass Menagerie, 1997

AMERICAN SHAKESPEARE THEATER
Stratford, Connecticut

Artistic Director, 1978 to 1979
Twelfth Night, 1978
The Tempest, 1979
Julius Caesar, 1979
Twelfth Night, 1979

REGIONAL THEATER

Oh Dad, Poor Dad, Mamma's Hung You in the Closet and I'm Feelin' So Sad,
National Tour, 1963 to 1964
Souvenir, Shubert Theater, Los Angeles, 1975
The Little Foxes, Westwood Playhouse, Los Angeles, 1975
The Robber Bridegroom, Mark Taper Forum, Los Angeles, 1976
Camino Real, The Acting Company, national tour, 1976

Chapeau, The Acting Company, national tour, 1977

Measure for Measure, The Old Globe, San Diego, 1981

Mahalia, Huntington Theater, Boston, 1982

The Skin of Our Teeth, The Acting Company, national tour, 1984

America's Sweetheart, Hartford Stage Company, Coconut Grove Playhouse, 1985

Blood Wedding, the Old Globe, San Diego, 1989

Mother Courage, Williamstown Theater Festival, 1989

Ohio State Murders, Yale Repertory Theater, 1991

Dividing the Estate, Stevens Center, Winston-Salem, 1991

The Lady from Maxim's, Missouri Repertory Theater, 1992

Death of a Salesman, Coconut Grove Playhouse, 1995

Hedda Gabler, Alley Theater, Houston, 1999

Richard II, Shakespeare Theater, Washington, DC, 2000

Enemy of the People, Williamstown Theater Festival, 2003

The Dresser, Clarence Brown Theater, Knoxville, 2004

Ellis Island, concert staging, Winston-Salem Symphony, 2008

Hamlet, concert staging with score by Shostakovich, North Carolina Symphony, 2008

The Diary of Anne Frank, Westport Country Playhouse, 2010

A Midsummer Night's Dream, concert staging with score by Mendelssohn, Winston-Salem Symphony Orchestra, 2011

INTERNATIONAL THEATER

Bells Are Ringing, London Coliseum, London, 1956

West Side Story (Assistant Director), Her Majesty's Theater, London, 1958

West Side Story, Habima Theater, Tel Aviv, 1961

West Side Story, Théâtre du Châtelet, Paris, 1981

The Sound of Music, Adalaide, Australia, 1983

The Antipodes, Shakespeare's Globe, London, 2000

Beckett's *Happy Days*, International Istanbul Theatre Festival, 2006

THE JUILLIARD SCHOOL

Acting Teacher and Director, 1970 to 1975
The School for Scandal, 1972
Room Service, 1973
Six Characters in Search of an Author, 1973
The Duchess of Malfi, 1973
Le Bourgeois Gentilhomme, Avery Fisher Hall, 1974
Ariadne auf Naxos, Avery Fisher Hall, 1974
Jenufa, 1978

UNIVERSITY OF NORTH CAROLINA SCHOOL OF THE ARTS

Dean, 1991 to 2012. Dean Emeritus, 2012 to present
Love's Labor's Lost, 1992
Revenger's Tragedy, 1993
The Bakkhai, 1994
Room Service, 1995
Troilus and Cressida, 1995
The Trojan Women, 1996
Brigadoon, 1996
End Game, 1996
Coriolanus, 1997
Into the Woods, 1997
Romeo and Juliet, 1998
Ring Round the Moon, 1998
All's Well That Ends Well, 1999
A Time for Singing, 2000
Richard III, 2000
The Country Wife, 2001
Yerma, 2001

As You Like It, 2002

Man and Superman, 2003

Floyd Collins, 2004

Waiting For Godot, 2004

Engaged, 2004

Hogan's Goat, 2005

Three Sisters, 2005

The Mandrake, 2006

Habeas Corpus, 2006

A Funny Thing Happened on the Way to the Forum, 2007

West Side Story, 2007

The Game of Love, 2008

Henry IV Parts 1 & 2, 2008

L'Arlesienne, concert staging, UNCSA Orchestra, 2008

Sunday in the Park with George, 2009

The Importance of Being Earnest, 2009

Booth, 2010

Light Up the Sky, 2010

OPERA

The Barber of Seville, New York City Opera, 1966

Beatrix Cenci, Kennedy Center, 1971, New York City Opera, 1973

L'Orfeo, San Francisco Opera, 1972

Coronation of Popea, New York City Opera, Caramoor Center, 1972

Bach's St. Matthew Passion, San Francisco Opera, 1973 and 1976

Idomeneo, Kennedy Center, 1974

Adradne, American Opera Society, 1974

Die Fledermaus, New York City Opera, 1974

Death in Venice, San Francisco Opera, 1975

Angle of Repose, San Francisco Opera, 1976

Jenufa, American Opera Company, 1978

Othello, Arizona Opera, 1979

Bach's St. Matthew Passion, Minnesota Opera, 1979

Song of Norway, New York City Opera, 1981

Lady Macbeth of Mtsensk, San Francisco Opera, 1981 and 1988

Cry of Clytemnestra, San Francisco Opera, 1981, Pepsico Summerfare, 1982

Nabucco, San Francisco Opera, 1982 and 1987

Katya Kabanova, San Francisco Opera, 1983

Lucia, Greater Miami Opera, 1984

Italian Girl in Algiers, Greater Miami Opera, 1985

The Stronger, Baltimore Opera, 1985

La Divina, Baltimore Opera, 1985

The Italian Lesson, Baltimore Opera, 1985

La Boheme, San Francisco Opera, 1986

The Postman Always Rings Twice, Miami Opera, 1988

Regina, Kennedy Center, 2005

TELEVISION & FILM

Under contract with Columbia Pictures, 1953 to 1957.

Bad for Each Other, Dialogue Director (uncredited), starring Charlton Heston and Mildred Dunnock, directed by Irving Rapper, 1953

It Should Happen to You, Dialogue Director (uncredited), starring Judy Holliday and Jack Lemmon, directed by George Cukor, 1954

The Caine Mutiny, Dialogue Director (uncredited), starring Humphrey Bogart and Van Johnson, directed by Edward Dmytryk, 1954

Phffft, Dialogue Director (uncredited), starring Judy Holliday and Jack Lemmon, directed by Mark Robson, 1954

Queen Bee, Dialogue Director (uncredited), starring Joan Crawford and Barry Sullivan, directed by Ranald MacDougall, 1955

The Solid Gold Cadillac, Dialogue Director (uncredited), starring Judy Holliday and John Williams, directed by Richard Quine, 1956

Full of Life, Dialogue Director (uncredited), starring Judy Holliday and Richard Conte, directed by Richard Quine, 1956

The Ford Television Theatre; Season 3, Episode 29: "Sunday Mourn," NBC, 1955

The Ford Television Theatre; Season 3, Episode 32: "The Policy of Joe Aladdin," NBC, 1955

The Ford Television Theatre; Season 3, Episode 33: "Mimi," NBC, 1955

Celebrity Playhouse; Season 1, Episode 4: "Mink Does Something for You," NBC, 1955

Celebrity Playhouse; Season 1, Episode 8: "He Knew All About Women," NBC, 1955

Celebrity Playhouse; Season 1, Episode 12: "Diamonds in the Sky," NBC, 1955

Celebrity Playhouse; Season 1, Episode 13: "The Hoax," NBC, 1955

Celebrity Playhouse; Season 1, Episode 23: "More Than Kin," NBC, 1956

Celebrity Playhouse; Season 1, Episode 28: "Deborah," starring Angela Lansbury, NBC, 1956

Celebrity Playhouse; Season 1, Episode 31: "No Escape," NBC, 1956

Blondie; Season 1, Episode 17: "Puppy Love," NBC, 1957

Oldsmobile Music Theatre, episode(s) unknown, NBC, 1959

The Dupont Show of the Week; Season 2, Episode 13: "Diamond Fever," NBC, 1963

ABC Stage 67; Season 1, Episode 23: "I'm Getting Married," 1967

The Anne Bancroft Special, CBS, 1970

The Adams Chronicles (Pilot), PBS, 1973

Antigone, Great Performances, PBS, 1974

Hot L Baltimore, episode unknown, ABC, 1975

The Adventures of Rin Tin Tin, year and episodes unknown, ABC

Robert Montgomery Presents, year and episode(s) unknown, NBC

ENDNOTES

1. Excerpt from an interview with Gerald Freedman from *The Soul of the American Actor* newspaper, conducted by Ronald Rand, Publisher. Vol. 4, no. 3, 2001.

2. Gerald Freedman, "Directing Love's Labor's Lost," from *THE FESTIVAL SHAKESPEARE LOVE'S LABOR'S LOST* by Bernard Beckerman and Joseph Papp, editors. Copyright © 1968 by The Macmillan Company. Reprinted with the permission of Scribner, a division of Simon & Schuster, Inc. All rights reserved.

3. Gerald Freedman, interview by Gresdna A. Doty, "Interview: Gerald Freedman on Building a Character," *Literature in Performance* 1, no. 1 (November 1980). Reprinted with permission of Taylor & Francis Ltd.

4. Gerald Freedman, interview by Gresdna A. Doty, "Interview: Gerald Freedman on Building a Character," *Literature in Performance* 1, no. 1 (November 1980). Reprinted with permission of Taylor & Francis Ltd.

5. Gerald Freedman, "Directing Love's Labor's Lost," from *THE FESTIVAL SHAKESPEARE LOVE'S LABOR'S LOST* by Bernard Beckerman and Joseph Papp, editors. Copyright © 1968 by The Macmillan Company. Reprinted with the permission of Scribner, a division of Simon & Schuster, Inc. All rights reserved.

6. Gerald Freedman, interview by Gresdna A. Doty, "Interview: Gerald Freedman on Building a Character," *Literature in Performance* 1, no. 1 (November 1980). Reprinted with permission of Taylor & Francis Ltd.

7. Josie De Guzman and J. Bilowit, "Turning Points, Freeing Yourself as an Actress," *Backstage*, December 17-30, 1993.

8. Gerald Freedman, "Directing Love's Labor's Lost," from *THE FESTIVAL SHAKESPEARE LOVE'S LABOR'S LOST* by Bernard Beckerman and Joseph Papp, editors. Copyright © 1968 by The Macmillan Company. Reprinted with the permission of Scribner, a division of Simon & Schuster, Inc. All rights reserved.

9. Gerald Freedman, interview by Gresdna A. Doty, "Interview: Gerald Freedman on Building a Character," *Literature in Performance* 1, no. 1 (November 1980). Reprinted with permission of Taylor & Francis Ltd.

10. Gerald Freedman, interview by Gresdna A. Doty, "Interview: Gerald Freedman on Building a Character," *Literature in Performance* 1, no. 1 (November 1980). Reprinted with permission of Taylor & Francis Ltd.

11. Gerald Freedman, interview by Gresdna A. Doty, "Interview: Gerald Freedman on Building a Character," *Literature in Performance* 1, no. 1 (November 1980). Reprinted with permission of Taylor & Francis Ltd.

12. Gerald Freedman, interview by Gresdna A. Doty, "Interview: Gerald Freedman on Building a Character," *Literature in Performance* 1, no. 1 (November 1980). Reprinted with permission of Taylor & Francis Ltd.

13. Gerald Freedman, "Directing Love's Labor's Lost," from *THE FESTIVAL SHAKESPEARE LOVE'S LABOR'S LOST* by Bernard Beckerman and Joseph Papp, editors. Copyright © 1968 by The Macmillan Company. Reprinted with the permission of Scribner, a division of Simon & Schuster, Inc. All rights reserved.

14. Gerald Freedman, "How Freedman Inspires 'The Lady's' Laughter," *Great Lakes Theater Festival Newsletter*, 1990.

15. Gerald Freedman, interview by Suki Sandler, February 1993, transcript, American Jewish Committee, New York, NY.

16. Gerald Freedman, quoted in Donald Wolfe, "Freedman Embraces the 'Real' in Live Theatre," *Southern Theatre*, quarterly magazine of the Southeastern Theatre Conference, Vol. 39, no. 3 (1998).

17. "Gerald Freedman Named Artistic Director of Great Lakes Shakespeare Festival," Great Lakes Press Release, November 1984.

18. Gerald Freedman, interview by Suki Sandler, February 1993, transcript, American Jewish Committee, New York, NY.

19. Gerald Freedman, "Great Lakes Theater Festival: A Perspective on Gerald Freedman."

20. Gerald Freedman, "Great Lakes Theater Festival: A Perspective on Gerald Freedman."

21. Gerald Freedman, "Hitch-Kick to Highgate," *American Theatre*, May 1995.

22. Gerald Freedman, "Hitch-Kick to Highgate," *American Theatre*, May 1995.

23. Gerald Freedman, "Great Lakes Theater Festival: A Perspective on Gerald Freedman."

24. Gerald Freedman, "Hitch-Kick to Highgate," *American Theatre*, May 1995.

25. *Kurt Herbert Adler and the San Francisco Opera*, "Gerald Freedman: Opera as Theater, An interview conducted by Caroline Crawford in 1986," oral history, BANC MSS 97/120 c pp.153-170. Courtesy of the Oral History Center, © The Regents of the University of California, The Bancroft Library, University of California, Berkeley, CA.

26. Gerald Freedman, "Hitch-Kick to Highgate," *American Theatre*, May 1995.

27. *Kurt Herbert Adler and the San Francisco Opera*, "Gerald Freedman: Opera as Theater, An interview conducted by Caroline Crawford in 1986," oral history, BANC MSS 97/120 c pp.153-170. Courtesy of the Oral History Center, © The Regents of the University of California, The Bancroft Library, University of California, Berkeley, CA.

28. *Kurt Herbert Adler and the San Francisco Opera*, "Gerald Freedman: Opera as Theater, An interview conducted by Caroline Crawford in 1986," oral history, BANC MSS 97/120 c pp.153-170. Courtesy of the Oral History Center, © The Regents of the University of California, The Bancroft Library, University of California, Berkeley, CA.

29. *Kurt Herbert Adler and the San Francisco Opera*, "Gerald Freedman: Opera as Theater, An interview conducted by Caroline Crawford in 1986," oral history, BANC MSS 97/120 c pp.153-170. Courtesy of the Oral History Center, © The Regents of the University of California, The Bancroft Library, University of California, Berkeley, CA.

30. Gerald Freedman, "Great Lakes Theater Festival: A Perspective on Gerald Freedman."

31. Gerald Freedman, interview by Suki Sandler, February 1993, transcript, American Jewish Committee, New York, NY.

32. Gerald Freedman, quoted in Faye Sholiton, "A Portrait of the Artistic Director," *Avenues Magazine*, November 1994.

33. Gerald Freedman, "Great Lakes Theater Festival: A Perspective on Gerald Freedman."

34. Gerald Freedman, interview by Suki Sandler, February 1993, transcript, American Jewish Committee, New York, NY.

35. Gerald Freedman, "Great Lakes Theater Festival: A Perspective on Gerald Freedman."

36. Gerald Freedman, "Directing Love's Labor's Lost," from *THE FESTIVAL SHAKESPEARE LOVE'S LABOR'S LOST* by Bernard Beckerman and Joseph Papp, editors. Copyright © 1968 by The Macmillan Company. Reprinted with the permission of Scribner, a division of Simon & Schuster, Inc. All rights reserved.

37. Gerald Freedman, interview by Gresdna A. Doty, "Interview: Gerald Freedman on Building a Character," *Literature in Performance* 1, no. 1 (November 1980). Reprinted with permission of Taylor & Francis Ltd.

38. Gerald Freedman, "Directing Love's Labor's Lost," from *THE FESTIVAL SHAKESPEARE LOVE'S LABOR'S LOST* by Bernard Beckerman and Joseph Papp, editors. Copyright © 1968 by The Macmillan Company. Reprinted with the permission of Scribner, a division of Simon & Schuster, Inc. All rights reserved.

39. Gerald Freedman, "Hitch-Kick to Highgate," *American Theatre*, May 1995.

40. Gerald Freedman, "Hitch-Kick to Highgate," *American Theatre*, May 1995.

41. Gerald Freedman, "Directing Love's Labor's Lost," from *THE FESTIVAL SHAKESPEARE LOVE'S LABOR'S LOST* by Bernard Beckerman and Joseph Papp, editors. Copyright © 1968 by The Macmillan Company. Reprinted with the permission of Scribner, a division of Simon & Schuster, Inc. All rights reserved.

42. Gerald Freedman, "Directing Love's Labor's Lost," from *THE FESTIVAL SHAKESPEARE LOVE'S LABOR'S LOST* by Bernard Beckerman and Joseph Papp, editors. Copyright © 1968 by The Macmillan Company. Reprinted with the permission of Scribner, a division of Simon & Schuster, Inc. All rights reserved.

43. Gerald Freedman, "Directing Love's Labor's Lost," from *THE FESTIVAL SHAKESPEARE LOVE'S LABOR'S LOST* by Bernard Beckerman and Joseph Papp, editors. Copyright © 1968 by The Macmillan Company. Reprinted with the permission of Scribner, a division of Simon & Schuster, Inc. All rights reserved.

44. Gerald Freedman, "Directing Love's Labor's Lost," from *THE FESTIVAL SHAKESPEARE LOVE'S LABOR'S LOST* by Bernard Beckerman and Joseph Papp, editors. Copyright © 1968 by The Macmillan Company. Reprinted with the permission of Scribner, a division of Simon & Schuster, Inc. All rights reserved.

45. "Gerald Freedman Named Artistic Director of Great Lakes Shakespeare Festival," Great Lakes Press Release, November 1984.

46. Gerald Freedman, interview by Suki Sandler, February 1993, transcript, American Jewish Committee, New York, NY.

47. Gerald Freedman, "Great Lakes Theater Festival: A Perspective on Gerald Freedman."

48. Gerald Freedman, "Directing Love's Labor's Lost," from *THE FESTIVAL SHAKESPEARE LOVE'S LABOR'S LOST* by Bernard Beckerman and Joseph Papp, editors. Copyright © 1968 by The Macmillan Company. Reprinted with the permission of Scribner, a division of Simon & Schuster, Inc. All rights reserved.

49. Gerald Freedman, interview by Suki Sandler, February 1993, transcript, American Jewish Committee, New York, NY.

50. Gerald Freedman, interview by Suki Sandler, February 1993, transcript, American Jewish Committee, New York, NY.

51. Gerald Freedman, interview by Suki Sandler, February 1993, transcript, American Jewish Committee, New York, NY.

52. Gerald Freedman, interview by Suki Sandler, February 1993, transcript, American Jewish Committee, New York, NY.

53. *Kurt Herbert Adler and the San Francisco Opera*, "Gerald Freedman: Opera as Theater, An interview conducted by Caroline Crawford in 1986," oral history, BANC MSS 97/120 c pp.153-170. Courtesy of the Oral History Center, © The Regents of the University of California, The Bancroft Library, University of California, Berkeley, CA.

54. Gerald Freedman, "Great Lakes Theater Festival: A Perspective on Gerald Freedman."

55. Gerald Freedman, interview by Gresdna A. Doty, "Interview: Gerald Freedman on Building a Character," *Literature in Performance* 1, no. 1 (November 1980). Reprinted with permission of Taylor & Francis Ltd.

56. Gerald Freedman, "Directing Love's Labor's Lost," from *THE FESTIVAL SHAKESPEARE LOVE'S LABOR'S LOST* by Bernard Beckerman and Joseph Papp, editors. Copyright © 1968 by The Macmillan Company. Reprinted with the permission of Scribner, a division of Simon & Schuster, Inc. All rights reserved.

57. Gerald Freedman, "Gerald Freedman, A Man for All Seasons," *Behind the Scenes*, Spring 1996.

58. Gerald Freedman, "Great Lakes Theater Festival: A Perspective on Gerald Freedman."

59. Gerald Freedman, interview by Gresdna A. Doty, "Interview: Gerald Freedman on Building a Character," *Literature in Performance* 1, no. 1 (November 1980). Reprinted with permission of Taylor & Francis Ltd.

60. Gerald Freedman, "Gerald Freedman, A Man for All Seasons," *Behind the Scenes*, Spring 1996.

61. Gerald Freedman, interview by Gresdna A. Doty, "Interview: Gerald Freedman on Building a Character," *Literature in Performance* 1, no. 1 (November 1980). Reprinted with permission of Taylor & Francis Ltd.

62. Gerald Freedman, interview by Gresdna A. Doty, "Interview: Gerald Freedman on Building a Character," *Literature in Performance* 1, no. 1 (November 1980). Reprinted with permission of Taylor & Francis Ltd.

63. Gerald Freedman, interview by Gresdna A. Doty, "Interview: Gerald Freedman on Building a Character," *Literature in Performance* 1, no. 1 (November 1980). Reprinted with permission of Taylor & Francis Ltd.

64. Gerald Freedman, quoted in Julie York Coppens, "The Undirector: How Gerald Freedman gets actors out of their own way," *Dramatics*, April 2009.

65. Gerald Freedman, interview by Gresdna A. Doty, "Interview: Gerald Freedman on Building a Character," *Literature in Performance* 1, no. 1 (November 1980). Reprinted with permission of Taylor & Francis Ltd.

66. Gerald Freedman, quoted in Faye Sholiton, "A Portrait of the Artistic Director," *Avenues Magazine*, November 1994.

67. Gerald Freedman, interview by Gresdna A. Doty, "Interview: Gerald Freedman on Building a Character," *Literature in Performance* 1, no. 1 (November 1980). Reprinted with permission of Taylor & Francis Ltd.

68. Gerald Freedman, interview by Gresdna A. Doty, "Interview: Gerald Freedman on Building a Character," *Literature in Performance* 1, no. 1 (November 1980). Reprinted with permission of Taylor & Francis Ltd.

69. Gerald Freedman, quoted in Julie York Coppens, "The Undirector: How Gerald Freedman gets actors out of their own way," *Dramatics*, April 2009.

70. Gerald Freedman, quoted in Julie York Coppens, "The Undirector: How Gerald Freedman gets actors out of their own way," *Dramatics*, April 2009.

71. Gerald Freedman, interview by Gresdna A. Doty, "Interview: Gerald Freedman on Building a Character," *Literature in Performance* 1, no. 1 (November 1980). Reprinted with permission of Taylor & Francis Ltd.

72. Gerald Freedman, quoted in Donald Wolfe, "Freedman Embraces the 'Real' in Live Theatre," *Southern Theatre*, quarterly magazine of the Southeastern Theatre Conference, Vol. 39, no. 3 (1998).

73. Gerald Freedman, interview by Faye Sholiton, transcript provided by Faye Sholiton, July 1994.

74. Gerald Freedman, interview by Gresdna A. Doty, "Interview: Gerald Freedman on Building a Character," *Literature in Performance* 1, no. 1 (November 1980). Reprinted with permission of Taylor & Francis Ltd.

75. Gerald Freedman, "A Summer of Directing Dangerously," *American Theatre*, December 2001.

76. Gerald Freedman, quoted in Julie York Coppens, "The Undirector: How Gerald Freedman gets actors out of their own way," *Dramatics*, April 2009.

77. Gerald Freedman, interview by Suki Sandler, February 1993, transcript, American Jewish Committee, New York, NY.

78. Gerald Freedman, interview by Gresdna A. Doty, "Interview: Gerald Freedman on Building a Character," *Literature in Performance* 1, no. 1 (November 1980). Reprinted with permission of Taylor & Francis Ltd.

79. Gerald Freedman, interview by Gresdna A. Doty, "Interview: Gerald Freedman on Building a Character," *Literature in Performance* 1, no. 1 (November 1980). Reprinted with permission of Taylor & Francis Ltd.

80. Gerald Freedman, interview by Gresdna A. Doty, "Interview: Gerald Freedman on Building a Character," *Literature in Performance* 1, no. 1 (November 1980). Reprinted with permission of Taylor & Francis Ltd.

81. Gerald Freedman, "Great Lakes Theater Festival: A Perspective on Gerald Freedman."

82. Gerald Freedman, interview by Suki Sandler, February 1993, transcript, American Jewish Committee, New York, NY.

83. Gerald Freedman, quoted in Julie York Coppens, "The Undirector: How Gerald Freedman gets actors out of their own way," *Dramatics*, April 2009.

84. Gerald Freedman, interview by Gresdna A. Doty, "Interview: Gerald Freedman on Building a Character," *Literature in Performance* 1, no. 1 (November 1980). Reprinted with permission of Taylor & Francis Ltd.

85. Gerald Freedman, interview by Gresdna A. Doty, "Interview: Gerald Freedman on Building a Character," *Literature in Performance* 1, no. 1 (November 1980). Reprinted with permission of Taylor & Francis Ltd.

86. Gerald Freedman, interview by Suki Sandler, February 1993, transcript, American Jewish Committee, New York, NY.

87. *Kurt Herbert Adler and the San Francisco Opera*, "Gerald Freedman: Opera as Theater, An interview conducted by Caroline Crawford in 1986," oral history, BANC MSS 97/120 c pp.153-170. Courtesy of the Oral History Center, © The Regents of the University of California, The Bancroft Library, University of California, Berkeley, CA.

88. Gerald Freedman, "Jerry and 'The Other One,' From *Bells Are Ringing* to *The Poppa Piece*," *The Journal for Stage Directors & Choreographers Foundation Inc.* 11, no. 2 (Fall/Winter 1998).

89. Gerald Freedman, "Jerry and 'The Other One,' From *Bells Are Ringing* to *The Poppa Piece*," *The Journal for Stage Directors & Choreographers Foundation Inc.* 11, no. 2 (Fall/Winter 1998).

90. Gerald Freedman, "Jerry and 'The Other One,' From *Bells Are Ringing* to *The Poppa Piece*," *The Journal for Stage Directors & Choreographers Foundation Inc.* 11, no. 2 (Fall/Winter 1998).

91. Gerald Freedman, "Jerry and 'The Other One,' From *Bells Are Ringing* to *The Poppa Piece*," *The Journal for Stage Directors & Choreographers Foundation Inc.* 11, no. 2 (Fall/Winter 1998).

92. Gerald Freedman, "Jerry and 'The Other One,' From *Bells Are Ringing* to *The Poppa Piece*," *The Journal for Stage Directors & Choreographers Foundation Inc.* 11, no. 2 (Fall/Winter 1998).

93. Gerald Freedman, "Jerry and 'The Other One,' From *Bells Are Ringing* to *The Poppa Piece*," *The Journal for Stage Directors & Choreographers Foundation Inc.* 11, no. 2 (Fall/Winter 1998).

94. Gerald Freedman, "Jerry and 'The Other One,' From *Bells Are Ringing* to *The Poppa Piece*," *The Journal for Stage Directors & Choreographers Foundation Inc.* 11, no. 2 (Fall/Winter 1998).

95. Gerald Freedman, "Jerry and 'The Other One,' From *Bells Are Ringing* to *The Poppa Piece*," *The Journal for Stage Directors & Choreographers Foundation Inc.* 11, no. 2 (Fall/Winter 1998).

96. Gerald Freedman, "Jerry and 'The Other One,' From *Bells Are Ringing* to *The Poppa Piece*," *The Journal for Stage Directors & Choreographers Foundation Inc.* 11, no. 2 (Fall/Winter 1998).

97. Gerald Freedman, "Jerry and 'The Other One,' From *Bells Are Ringing* to *The Poppa Piece*," *The Journal for Stage Directors & Choreographers Foundation Inc.* 11, no. 2 (Fall/Winter 1998).

98. Gerald Freedman, "Jerry and 'The Other One,' From *Bells Are Ringing* to *The Poppa Piece*," *The Journal for Stage Directors & Choreographers Foundation Inc.* 11, no. 2 (Fall/Winter 1998).

99. Gerald Freedman, "Jerry and 'The Other One,' From *Bells Are Ringing* to *The Poppa Piece*," *The Journal for Stage Directors & Choreographers Foundation Inc.* 11, no. 2 (Fall/Winter 1998).

100. Gerald Freedman, quoted in Donald Wolfe, "Freedman Embraces the 'Real' in Live Theatre," *Southern Theatre*, quarterly magazine of the Southeastern Theatre Conference, Vol. 39, no. 3 (1998).

101. Gerald Freedman, interview by Suki Sandler, February 1993, transcript, American Jewish Committee, New York, NY.

102. Gerald Freedman, interview by Gresdna A. Doty, "Interview: Gerald Freedman on Building a Character," *Literature in Performance* 1, no. 1 (November 1980). Reprinted with permission of Taylor & Francis Ltd.

103. Gerald Freedman, "Strasberg versus Chekhov," *American Theatre*, October 2010.

104. Gerald Freedman, interview by Suki Sandler, February 1993, transcript, American Jewish Committee, New York, NY.

105. Gerald Freedman, quoted in Julie York Coppens, "The Undirector: How Gerald Freedman gets actors out of their own way," *Dramatics*, April 2009.

106. Gerald Freedman, quoted in Julie York Coppens, "The Undirector: How Gerald Freedman gets actors out of their own way," *Dramatics*, April 2009.

107. Gerald Freedman, "Freedman: The Director's Role," *The Daily Pennsylvanian*, December 5, 1973.

108. Gerald Freedman, interview by Suki Sandler, February 1993, transcript, American Jewish Committee, New York, NY.

109. Gerald Freedman, quoted in Donald Wolfe, "Freedman Embraces the 'Real' in Live Theatre," *Southern Theatre*, quarterly magazine of the Southeastern Theatre Conference, Vol. 39, no. 3 (1998).

110. Gerald Freedman, interview by Suki Sandler, February 1993, transcript, American Jewish Committee, New York, NY.

111. Gerald Freedman, quoted in Donald Wolfe, "Freedman Embraces the 'Real' in Live Theatre," *Southern Theatre*, quarterly magazine of the Southeastern Theatre Conference, Vol. 39, no. 3 (1998).

112. Gerald Freedman, quoted in Alan Tyson, "A Reason for the Season," *UNCSA Magazine*, 2007.

113. Gerald Freedman, interview by Suki Sandler, February 1993, transcript, American Jewish Committee, New York, NY.

114. Gerald Freedman, "Strasberg versus Chekhov," *American Theatre*, October 2010.

115. Gerald Freedman, interview by Suki Sandler, February 1993, transcript, American Jewish Committee, New York, NY.

116. Gerald Freedman, "Strasberg versus Chekhov," *American Theatre*, October 2010.

117. Excerpt from an interview with Gerald Freedman from *The Soul of the American Actor* newspaper, conducted by Ronald Rand, Publisher. Vol. 4, no. 3, 2001.

118. Gerald Freedman, "Freedman: The Director's Role," *The Daily Pennsylvanian*, December 5, 1973.

119. Gerald Freedman, interview by Suki Sandler, February 1993, transcript, American Jewish Committee, New York, NY.

120. Gerald Freedman, interview by Gresdna A. Doty, "Interview: Gerald Freedman on Building a Character," *Literature in Performance* 1, no. 1 (November 1980). Reprinted with permission of Taylor & Francis Ltd.

121. Gerald Freedman, quoted in Faye Sholiton, "A Portrait of the Artistic Director," *Avenues Magazine*, November 1994.

122. Gerald Freedman, "Directing Love's Labor's Lost," from *THE FESTIVAL SHAKESPEARE LOVE'S LABOR'S LOST* by Bernard Beckerman and Joseph Papp, editors. Copyright © 1968 by The Macmillan Company. Reprinted with the permission of Scribner, a division of Simon & Schuster, Inc. All rights reserved.

123. Ming Cho Lee, quoted in Mel Gussow, *Sets by Ming Cho Lee*, Vincent Astor Gallery, New York Public Library, 1995.

124. Gerald Freedman, "Freedman: The Director's Role," *The Daily Pennsylvanian*, December 5, 1973.

125. Gerald Freedman, quoted in Felicia Londré, "The Way They Were," *American Theatre*, December 1991.

126. Gerald Freedman, quoted in Felicia Londré, "The Way They Were," *American Theatre*, December 1991.

127. Gerald Freedman, interview by Suki Sandler, February 1993, transcript, American Jewish Committee, New York, NY.

128. Gerald Freedman, "Great Lakes Theater Festival: A Perspective on Gerald Freedman."

129. Gerald Freedman, quoted in Julie York Coppens, "The Undirector: How Gerald Freedman gets actors out of their own way," *Dramatics*, April 2009.

130. Gerald Freedman, interview by Suki Sandler, February 1993, transcript, American Jewish Committee, New York, NY.

131. Gerald Freedman, quoted in Faye Sholiton, "A Portrait of the Artistic Director," *Avenues Magazine*, November 1994.

132. Excerpt from an interview with Gerald Freedman from *The Soul of the American Actor* newspaper, conducted by Ronald Rand, Publisher. Vol. 4, no. 3, 2001.

133. Gerald Freedman, quoted in Julie York Coppens, "The Undirector: How Gerald Freedman gets actors out of their own way," *Dramatics*, April 2009.

134. Gerald Freedman, "Great Lakes Theater Festival: A Perspective on Gerald Freedman."

135. Gerald Freedman, interview by Suki Sandler, February 1993, transcript, American Jewish Committee, New York, NY.

136. Gerald Freedman, interview by Suki Sandler, February 1993, transcript, American Jewish Committee, New York, NY.

137. Gerald Freedman, interview by Suki Sandler, February 1993, transcript, American Jewish Committee, New York, NY.

138. Gerald Freedman, interview by Suki Sandler, February 1993, transcript, American Jewish Committee, New York, NY.

139. Gerald Freedman, "Gerald Freedman, A Man for All Seasons," *Behind the Scenes*, Spring 1996.

140. Gerald Freedman, interview by Suki Sandler, February 1993, transcript, American Jewish Committee, New York, NY.

141. Gerald Freedman, interview by Suki Sandler, February 1993, transcript, American Jewish Committee, New York, NY.

142. Gerald Freedman, quoted in Donald Wolfe, "Freedman Embraces the 'Real' in Live Theatre," *Southern Theatre*, quarterly magazine of the Southeastern Theatre Conference, Vol. 39, no. 3 (1998).

INDEX

Clurman, Harold, xx, 211
Coates, Norman, 200, 225, 231, 240–241, 242, 269
collaboration
    director/actor, 85–87, 157–165
    director/designer, 219–222, 236
    in musical theater, 158
    questioning in, 156–157
Comden, Betty, 189, 251
comedy, in Shakespearean plays, 142
Comedy of Errors, The (Shakespeare), 111, 142
comedy technique
    beanbag, 101–102, 160
    end of line, 101–102
    entrances and exits, 106–107
    farce, 110–112
    important word, lifting, 98–99, 108
    incorporating, 107–109
    interrupted action/thought, 104
    surprise as basis for, 97–98, 104
    timing a line, 102–103
    topping, 105–106
    turn-out to audience, 104–105
    underplaying, 106
commitment, 74
concentration, 76, 77
Conklin, John, 222, 226, 234, 269
control, giving up, 80–81
costume design, 174, 175, 243
    See also design
Cowart, Matt, 15, 104, 106, 107–108, 164, 269
craft, teaching, 67–69
Crawford, Cheryl, 211
Crawford, Joan, xix, 126–127
Cukor, George, 189, 210–211
Cullum, John, 5, 89, 132, 254, 269
cuts, making, 181–182
Cyrano de Bergerac, 216–217

Daniele, Graciela, 11, 186, 269
Daniels, William, 120–121, 213, 269
Danner, Blythe, 144
Death of a Salesman (Miller), 169
DeBerry, Misty, *195*
Decatur, Christy Pusz, *195*
Dee, Ruby, *15*
Degnan, Mary Jane, 228, 257, 270
De Guzman, Josie, 51, 80, 133, 270
DeHaan, Dane, 21, 53, 59, *63*, 66–67, 82, 116, 270
dependability, 6–7
design
    adjustments of, 233–234
    by character, 232–233
    Chekhovian plays, 229, 232, 237–239
    costume, 174, 175, 243
    director/designer collaboration, 219–222, 236
    financial limitations on, 234–235
    first meeting, 225–227
    lighting, 240–242
    as process, 229–231
    research for, 228–229
    and staging, 231–232
    text work for, 222–225
    visual art in, 243–244
Dewhurst, Colleen, 144
Dillon, John, 9, 152, 251, 270
director/directing
    actor collaboration, 85–87, 157–165
    adjustments in rehearsal, 178–179
    assistant directing, 186–192
    in auditions, 90
    and author's intent, 154, 155–156
    collaborative relationships in, 156–159, 161, 193
    cutting, 181–182

-designer collaboration, 219–222, 236

for film, 118, 119

in gimmicky productions, 153–155

making something happen, 177–178

for musicals, 136–137

resistant actors, 179–181

role of, 152

and staging, 167–169

table work, xv-xvi, 84–85, 166–167

training program for, 151–152, 153, 184–185

transitions (dissolve), 182–183

for truthful acting, xvi-xviii, 176–177

visual art as influence on, 184–185

dissolve (transitions), 134–135, 182–183

Dividing the Estate, 229

Dorsey, Nadiyah Quander, *195*

Drulie, Sylvia, *149*

Duchess of Malfi, The, xv–xvi

Dukakis, Olympia, *63*, 127, 154, 160, 270

Duran, Paul, *63*

Durning, Charles, 144

Dybbuk, The, 229

Elizabethan stage, 133, 134

End Game (Beckett), 55

end of line, in comedy, 100–101

Enemy of the People, xvii

entrances and exits, 106–107

Ezell, John, *216*, 217, 220, 222, 226, 227, 228, 229, 230–232, 233, 239, 244, 270

Fahey, Logan, 83, 140, 205, 258, 270

Fakhoury, Jenna, *62*

farce, 110–112

Feydeau farce, 104, 110–111

Fiddler on the Roof, 190

film acting. *See* camera technique

film/television productions, of GF, 290–291

Fisher, Jules, 225, 227, 228, 235, 240, 241–242, 270

Flies, The (Sartre), 182

Floyd Collins, 137

Forman, Tony, 182, 221, 270

Foster, Janet, 209, 253, 270

Foxworth, Robert, 117, 155, 237–238, 239, 270–271

Francesconi, Bob, 172, 207, *247*, 253, 254, 258, 271

Franz, Elizabeth, 177, 271

Frayling, Christopher, *The Art Pack*, 184–185

Freedman, Gerald, *263*, *282*

with Acting Company, xix, *128–129*

with American Shakespeare Theater, Stratford, Conn., xix, 286

Broadway productions of, 283

characterized, xv

collaboration with Papp, 146–147, *149*

collaboration with Robbins, *148*, 189–192, 251

dedication to work, 6, 9, 257–260

directing career of, xix–xx, 4, 131, 250–251

family background of, 213, 215, 255

film/television productions of, 290–291

with Great Lakes Theater, xix, *217*, 237–239, *246*, 285–286

health of, xx, 202

influences on, 160, 210–215

international productions of, 287

with Julliard School, xv, xx, 71–72, 111–112, 197, 288

with New York Shakespeare Festival (Public Theater / Shakespeare in the Park), xix, 143–145, *149, 247,* 251, *276, 282,* 284

at Northwestern University, xx, 160, 210, 213–215, 249, 256

Off Broadway productions of, 284–285

opera productions of, 289–290

production history of, 283–291

regional theater productions of, 286–287

starting out in New York, 249–251

teaching career of, xx–xxi, 197

teaching principles/style of, 197–203

with University of North Carolina School of the Arts. *See* University of North Carolina School of the Arts

and visual arts, 184, 243–244, 255, 256

vocation in theater, 255–256

Freeman, Morgan, 144

Friedman, Gene, 222, 232, 237, 271

Fuller, Penny, 66, 213, 271

Galbraith, Nicholas, 68, 271

Game of Love, The, 111

Garrett, Tre, *15*

Gemignani, Paul, 155, 271

Gersten, Bernard, 143, 146, 252, 271

Gielgud, John, 82

Gillette, Anita, 85, 175, 271–272

given circumstances, in text, 21, 23–25

Globe Theatre, London, xx, 144

goal setting, 252

gofer, 187

Gordon, Quin, 25, 28, 30, 84, 210, 272

Grant, Lee, 87, 125, 272

Great Lakes Theater, Cleveland, Ohio, xix, 26, 28, 110, 111, *216–217, 246,* 285–286

Uncle Vanya, 237–239

Green, Adolph, 189, 251

groundlings, 133

Group Theatre, 211

Gwiazdowski, Jerzy, 12, 71, 101, 103, 104, 107, 109, 199, 272

Gypsy, 188, 192

Hagen, Uta, 211

Hair, Public Theater production of, xix, 145–146

Hamlet (Shakespeare), 133

slogan/theme in, 28–29

spine of the character, 34–36

spine of the play, 31

story/plot in, 26–27

Hammond, Barney, 113–114, 138, 204, 206, 208, 272

Happy Days (Beckett), 49

Harnick, Sheldon, 189, 272

health requirements for actors, 7–8

Hearn, George, 169, 272

Heeley, Desmond, 221, 228, 230, 232, 234, 235, 236, 272

Henry IV Parts 1&2 (Shakespeare), 168–169, *247*

Heston, Charlton, 213, 250

hit your marks, in film acting, 125–126

Holbrook, Hal, 86, 163, 237, 238, 239, 272

Holliday, Judy, 189, 190, 210, 251

Houseman, John, xix, 71, 131, 272–273

Hurt, William, xv, xvi–xvii, 112, 144

Importance of Being Earnest, The (Wilde), 29, 108

important word, lifting, 98–99, 108

inflection and pitch, end of line, 100

initiative, actor's, 11–12, 74, 85
intentions/actions, 22–23, 49–51
interrupted action/thought, 104
Irwin, Mary, 54, 109, 113, 205, 273

Jansen, Ashley Gates, 79–80, 162, 183, 254, 273
Jeffries, Annalee, 78, 170, 171, 273
Johnson, Van, 251
Jones, Howard, 220, 224, 227, 229, 232, 233, 234, 236, 244, 273
Jones, James Earl, 144
Jones, Rebecca Naomi, 50, 57, 77, 79, 273
Julia, Raul, 144
Julliard School, xv, xx, 71–72, 111–112, 197, 288

Karafin, Mark, 63
Kayne, Carrie Specksgoor, 195
Kazan, Elia, 211
Keach, Stacy, 19, 144, 145, 160, 168, 273
Kerr, Walter, 213
Kessler, Barbara, 202, 229, 273
key light, 120
King Lear (Shakespeare), 111, 133
Kline, Franz, 185
Kline, Kevin, 70, 91, 121, 134, 144, 159, 161, 173, 273–274
Kohout, Al, 221, 243, 274
Krause, Alvina, xx, 97, 182
    beanbag technique of, 101, 160
    influence on GF, 213, 214–215
    teaching approach of, 210, 213–214
Kurtz, Eddie, 154, 193, 274

Lacy, Jake, 4, 71, 75, 76–77, 274
Lady from Maxim's, The (Feydeau), 110–111, 167
Lamos, Mark, 168, 274

Langs, John, 20, 32, 77–78, 135, 152, 178, 186, 188, 200, 224, 274
Laurel and Hardy, 111
Laurents, Arthur, 188
Lawrence, Carol, 17, 73, 76, 158, 213, 274
Lee, Ming Cho, 220, 223, 225–226, 230, 233, 235, 236, 256, 274–275
Lemmon, Jack, xix
letting go / allowing, 80–81
Lewis, Robert, xx, 211
lighting design, 240–242
listening/talking, 75–78, 122, 178
Loyd, Todd, 194, 195
Loft, Peggy, 106, 141, 275
long-shot, 119
Love's Labor's Lost (Shakespeare), 128–129, 142, 182
Lumet, Sidney, 118
LuPone, Patti, 20, 83, 112, 136, 144, 275
Lutfy, Robby, 149
Lynch, Margaret, 6, 229, 238, 275

Macbeth (Shakespeare), 133
MacDermot, Galt, 145
MacMurray, Fred, 250–251
Maddux, Jacklyn, 206, 275
Magnussen, Billy, 7, 23, 69, 275
Mamet, David, 211
Man and Superman (Shaw), 72, 75–76, 181
Mantello, Joe, 15
Marx Brothers, 111
Mauceri, John, 132, 275
Maxner, Kelly, 155, 199, 275–276
Maxner, Mollye, 26, 31, 54, 165, 197–198, 221, 276
McHale, Travis, 226, 240, 241, 242, 276
McHattie, Stephen, 247

Measure for Measure (Shakespeare),
14, 15
slogan/theme, 43
spine of the play, 44
spine of the character, 44–47
medium shot, 119–120
Merman, Ethel, 135, 192
Midsummer Night's Dream, A
(Shakespeare), 142
Mitchell, Lee, 210
Mitchell, Ruth, 247
Moses, Robert, 143
Mother Courage (Brecht), 112
movie acting. See camera technique
Murray, Brian, 19, 99, 102, 176, 276
muscle memory, 18, 96
musical theater
acting process in, 133–134, 136–137
assistant directing, 189–192
collaborative effort in, 158
Hair, 145–146
Robbins/GF collaboration, 189–192
Shakespeare's plays compared to,
132–135
See also West Side Story

New York Shakespeare Festival (Public
Theater / Shakespeare in the Park),
xix, 143–145, 149, 247, 251, 276, 282,
284
Northwestern University, xx, 160, 197,
210, 213, 249, 256

Obie Award, xx
objective of character, 22–23, 48
O'Brien, Jack, 146, 155, 198, 276
Odom, Jon Hudson, 247
Off Broadway productions, of GF,
284–285
Ohio State Murders, 15
Oklahoma!, 133

Onat, Cigdem, 37, 49, 70, 205, 276
On the Town, 189
opera
acting process, 136–137
productions of GF, 289–290
Orbach, Jerry, 213
Othello (Shakespeare), 133

Paparelli, PJ, 8–9, 157, 276
Papp, Joseph, 182
collaboration with GF, 146–147, 149
and Hair, 145–146
and New York Shakespeare Festival,
138, 143, 251, 276
and Public Theater, xix, 145, 276
Patinkin, Mandy, xv-xviii, 27, 35,
49–50, 63, 68, 78, 81, 112, 144, 177,
276–277
pauses, overuse of, 81–82
Pendleton, Austin, 180, 277
pitch and inflection, end of line, 100
playwright, intentions of, 58, 59, 154,
155–156
plot/story, 21, 25–27, 38
Poppa Piece, The, 191
Poster, Harry, 184–185, 277
Prentiss, Paula, 213
preparation/homework, 55–57
professional discipline, 5–10
projection, voice, 114, 115, 120
Public Theater / Shakespeare in
the Park (New York Shakespeare
Festival), xix, 143–145, 149, 247, 251,
276, 282, 284
punctuality, 6–7
Pyle, Missi, 48, 63, 66, 277

questions
actor training, 12–13
in collaborative relationships, 156–157
in table work, 166

Rado, James, 145
Rae, Charlotte, 109, 172, 277
Ragni, Gerome, 145
Ray, James, *247*
regional theater productions, of GF, 286–287
rehearsal
actors' initiative in, 85–87
adjustments, making, 178–179
assistant director at, 187
discovery process in, 168, 169–171
film work, 118, 125
lighting designer at, 240, 242
musical theater, 137
staging, 167–169, 185
table work, 76, 84–85, 166–167
text work, 57–59
research, design, 228–229
resistant actors, handling, 179–181
reviews, 184
Reznick, Alex, *195*
Rivals, The, 112
Rivera, Chita, 56, 68, 72–73, 87, 192, 277
Robber Bridegroom, The, 210
Robbins, Jerome, xix, 71, 131, *148*, 211
collaboration with GF, *148*, 189–192, 251
Robinson, Edward G., 250
Rogers, Will, 37, 88, 97–98, 121, 175, 257, 277
Romeo and Juliet (Shakespeare), 135, 141
Routman, Steven, 50, 157, 165, 166, 277
Rudman, Bill, 201, 278
Ruggiero, Rob, 159, 167, 188, 278
Ryan, Jim, *195*

Saltz, Amy, 157, 220, 278
Santana, Astrid, *194*, 195

scenery changes, 134
Schmidt, Douglas W., 189–190, 226, 235, 278
School of Drama. *See* University of North Carolina School of the Arts
Scoggin, Gabe, 9–10, 56, 278
Scott, George C., 143
Scott, James, *217*
script breakdown. *See* text work
Seidman, John, 154, 173, 278
self-discipline, 8–9
set design. *See* design
Shakespearean plays, 131–132
and American English, 139
As You Like It, 133, 142, 143, 183, 250
in Central Park (New York Shakespeare Festival), xix, 143–145, *149*, *247*, 251, 276, *282*, 284
The Comedy of Errors, 111, 142
cutting, 182
and Elizabethan stage, 133, 134
Henry IV Parts 1&2, 168–169, *247*
King Lear, 111, 133
longevity of, 137–139
Love's Labor's Lost, 128–129, 142, 182
Macbeth, 133
A Midsummer Night's Dream, 142
musical theater related to, 132–135
obscurity in, 141–142
Othello, 133
as popular art, 132
Romeo and Juliet, 135, 141
soliloquy in, 135
The Taming of the Shrew, 111, 138, 142, 143
The Tempest, 142
text work for, 140–141
Timon of Athens, *149*
Titus Andronicus, 135
Twelfth Night, 141

See also Hamlet; Measure for Measure
Shakespeare in the Park (New York Shakespeare Festival), xix, 143–145, 149, 247, 251, 276, 282, 284
Sheen, Martin, 144
Skelton, Thomas, 216, 217
Skidmore, Jeremy, 195, 202, 278–279
slogan/theme, in text, 21, 27–29, 38, 43
Smith, Maggie, 98
soliloquy, Shakespeare's, 135
sound design. See design
specificity in acting, 74–75
speech technique, 113–114
spine of the character, xvii, 22, 32–37, 41–42, 44–47
spine of the play, 21, 29–32, 39, 44, 223–224
stage directions, 55
stage manager, 187
staging, 167–169, 185, 231–232
Stanislavski System, 211
Stapleton, Jean, 190
Stattel, Robert, 87, 279
stock companies, 3
story/plot, 21, 25–27, 38
storytelling, acting as, 66
Strasberg, Lee, 74, 211
Streep, Meryl, 144
style of performance, 82–83, 111–112
surprise, as basis for comedy, 97–98, 104
Sutow, Brian, 98, 103, 105, 279

table work, xv–xvi, 76, 84–85, 166–167
talking/listening, and truthful acting, 75–78
Taming of the Shrew, The (Shakespeare), 111, 138, 142, 143

teaching. See actor training; University of North Carolina School of the Arts
technique
incorporating, 96–97
as skill, 95–96
teaching, 199
voice, 113–114
See also camera technique; comedy technique
television acting. See camera technique
television productions, of GF, 290–291
Tempest, The (Shakespeare), 142
text
cutting, 181–182
staying true to, 81–82, 183–184
and style, 82–83
and table work, 84–85, 166–167
text work
actions/intentions, 22–23, 49–51
backstory, 54
benefits of, 51–53, 59–60
for design, 222–225
film script, 123–124
given circumstances in, 21, 23–25
as head trip, 17–18
objective of character, 22–23, 48
as preparation/homework, 55–57
reading/note-taking in, 19–21
and rehearsal, 57–59
for Shakespeare's plays, 140–141
slogan/theme in, 21, 27–29, 38, 43
spine of the character, 22, 32–37, 41–42, 44–47
spine of the play, 21, 29–32, 39, 44, 223–224
stage directions, 55
story/plot in, 21, 25–27, 38
terminology for, 21–23
underlying meaning in, 53–54
Thaler, Jordan, 5, 279